THE FEVER

To all my friends at Baker College: best wishes always!

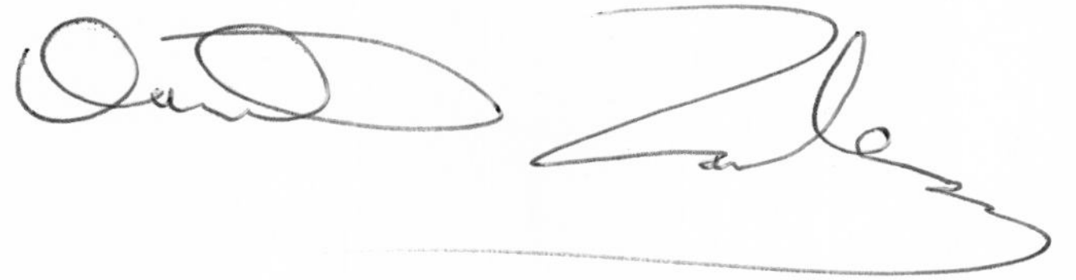

THE FEVER

✦

A complete account of how a team from Detroit rocked the basketball world in 2004—told by a fan

David Lawless

iUniverse, Inc.
New York Lincoln Shanghai

THE FEVER

A complete account of how a team from Detroit rocked the basketball world in 2004—told by a fan

iUniverse, Inc.

For information address:
iUniverse, Inc.
2021 Pine Lake Road, Suite 100
Lincoln, NE 68512
www.iuniverse.com

ISBN: 0-595-33474-1 (pbk)
ISBN: 0-595-66948-4 (cloth)

Printed in the United States of America

For Kirk Baldwin, Jay and Kristin Wise, Joe Conrad, and Erin Lawless

whose friendships are priceless and that without which this book would not have been possible.

And for my parents, Don and Mary Lawless

who always encouraged me to do the things in life that made me happy.

Contents

Foreword

Long before sports radio replaced the now P-Diddy and grunge as the non-Sirius rage, many a Detroit fan would down a few at the local pub and hold their own personal talk show amongst themselves.

I moved here from Baltimore as a toddler and from the minute my sister, Elsa, and I could initiate a neighborhood game of "pickle" (running bases) in February, I knew there was something more to sports in metro Detroit. The four major pro sports teams were an early staple in daily life.

My first Pistons' game was somewhere during the Ray Scott era and the Chicago Bulls were the victim (no one here really liked them or the Blackhawks) at Cobo Arena. I always did a game a year—even during the 16–66 year—and dad and I saw Dominique score in the 60's, but the locals prevailed at the Silverdome.

As the "Bad Boys" developed and won and won and won, so did my interest. I'd rate myself as a fair-weather fan with a passion chaser. Friends, workers, and yours truly split eight season tickets from 1987 to 1993, but when Dennis Rodman left, so did a lot of the spirit. We still would attend games throughout the '90's and certainly cheered Grant Hill, Otis Thorpe, and Doug Collins et. al., but it wasn't the same.

The last few years reflect the team and the author alike. No gimmicks or MC Hammer—just a great fan experience and something to be part of and treasure.

It was initially a pleasant surprise when Detroit earned its first NBA championship in 14 years in 2004. At first glance, Shaq was unstoppable and a trophy seemed to be about as attainable as a picture of Jack Nicholson without his sunglasses. However upon reflection, after Mr. Bryant and Mr. O'Neal, Detroit's 1-12 blew L.A.'s out of the lake (though last I checked there aren't many lakes in Los Angeles) and the ocean. The Pistons outplayed the favorite in every aspect of basketball skill, savvy, and street smarts and took out LA's pretty and their little dog too.

The same can be said of Dave Lawless. No gimmicks…just great storytelling and passion throughout. Dave is a man that could be an immediate cocky media star. He's got brains, looks, zeal, and a smile that could light up the North Pole in December; yet he remains as humble and loyal a fan as he's been since he could hold a basketball. He writes this for the loose-ball chasing, outrebounding, three-point prayer shooting love of sports in him and all of us. This book is really really real.

The tales that Dave shares with us weave inspiration, excitement, and 3-D personal visuals throughout. His heart and oomph starts at the rough draft and never ends. Hoist this book as the Pistons hoist the first of several championship banners this decade and be sure to toast your health, Detroit sports and the real team spirit amongst our teams, especially these Pistons.

—Josef A. Conrad
(my real name, that other famous one changed his)
—September 2004

Prologue

As a big Detroit Pistons fan for most of my life, there are several moments that stand out as memorable and exciting. The 2003–2004 season provided some of the best moments that anyone who follows a team on a regular basis could ever hope for—including that of winning a championship.

This book was written to capture the season for what it was: both factually and emotionally; from the business perspective of the building of a winning team, to the sights and sounds that a fan feels as he enters the arena before a big playoff game.

Most of this book was written during the season, though in a different format. I had begun doing "journal-like" entries featuring both basic and complex observations that I saw of the team during games, along with some news analysis about the team for a few friends who were on a weekly email newsletter list.

They had wanted a way to keep up on what was going on with the team, so I decided to chronicle the year from a big-picture standpoint. That big-picture being how what the Pistons were doing on a daily basis would impact their ability to challenge for a championship in the near future. We also made a web site, Pistonsfever.com, so fans could access back issues.

The term "Pistonsfever" itself accurately describes what a fan feels as his team becomes more and more successful and reaches the brink of greatness: an NBA championship.

I first felt "The Fever" in the late 1980's when the Pistons drove towards their first two championships: in 1989 and 1990. The funny thing is that while many fans felt the fever dissipate or disappear all together in the years since those fantastic seasons, it stayed with me throughout.

Even when the team went through the despair-filled years of 1994, 1995, 1998, and 2001, I followed the team as if they were still on the brink of a championship. There may have been more head-shaking and throwing of things at the TV during a Pistons broadcast. The games weren't always happy experiences. But I was hooked.

"The Fever" had gripped me and it wasn't going to let go. While each of those 16 seasons since the first championship has been fun, it's those three that resulted in championships that featured the most thrills and memories.

I must admit, before Rasheed Wallace joined the team, I didn't think that it would happen this year. Maybe it would be next year or the year after. But at least I wasn't like those misguided individuals in the national media who said that the team didn't stand a chance against the Lakers in the Finals!

Anyway, this book does feature the highlights of the season taken straight from those weekly emails, edited for length in the first 11 chapters. That is except for the two regular season Laker games and all the playoff games where the entire entries are included.

The game notes do not have perfect punctuation or grammar, but nor are they supposed to. These were thoughts, observations, and emotions that were written down as they happened—in the heat of the battle. They are preserved in their natural form here.

Each chapter covering the pre-season and regular season has a mini preview just prior to the game notes. Here, certain opponents are highlighted, marking games that included the most significant events that happened in that given month.

Think of this as sort of like the singles from a rock album that later make the *Greatest Hits* cd. If the reader chose to read just the journal entries, the highlighted games, and all the playoff entries and playoff game notes, then he or she would have a great grasp of the season and be able to relive its' best moments. However, just like the deeper cuts on an artist's rock album, the additional game notes have some good material as well, particularly for a die-hard fan.

Chapters 12–16 in the second part of the book, were written after the 2004 Finals ended. These chapters focus on all the excitement of, and include reflections on, certain key events that made up the magical season and all the things that happened after the Finals were over. These five chapters are all original to this book.

As I went back through those "Pistonsfever.com Newsletters" I was able to appreciate just how up and down and event-filled this season truly was. Sometimes in the afterglow of a team winning the championship, you forget all the little things that led to that moment. And what an exciting year it was!

There was the 13-game winning streak, concern because Darko Milicic wasn't playing while Carmelo Anthony was having a great rookie year, Chauncey Billups struggling to adjust to Larry Brown's system, Ben Wallace scoring off of solid offensive moves (for the first time in his career), Tayshaun Prince experiencing the ups and downs of being a young player in the NBA, Mehmet Okur getting good numbers but still not pleasing Larry Brown, everyone going crazy once

Rasheed Wallace came to the Pistons through a trade, a triple-overtime thriller in the second round of the playoffs vs. New Jersey, the greatest blocked shot in Pistons' history in the third round vs. Indiana, and the euphoria that was the NBA Finals.

There was also the octopus, the "Pistons Dork", Jimmy Kimmel, Isiah on a stick, a super-enlarged mug shot of Jason Kidd, and the "bladder buster."

There were many signs of things to come. Tayshaun had been blocking breakaway lay-ups all year long. The Pistons played very well against the Lakers in the two regular season meetings between the teams. Kid Rock was there all along as a fan supporting a team that is as real as he is.

There was also featured input by a "Dr. Fever" that allowed fans to pick his brain on what he saw happening: both the good and the bad with the team. Some "super fans" form emotional attachments to the players or certain aspects of the game, so Dr. Fever's extra college course work in psychology comes in handy.

PART I

1

October

09/20/03—Summer 2003

Welcome back, everyone! Though we have a new name, the focus remains the same. Training camp starts this week, so it's time to talk about the new faces on this team and how it has changed since last May when the playoffs ended.

The first big move that happened, obviously, was replacing Rick Carlisle with Larry Brown. We documented all the variables that factored into that decision last spring. But, it's important to also know a little bit about the Pistons new head coach.

Larry Brown has been in coaching forever. He has coached on every level: college; the NBA; even the ABA! He has 31 years experience and has won a lot of games. He won the NCAA National Championship in 1998 and got the Sixers to the Finals in 2001. He also got the Pacers to within one game of the Finals during the 1990's. But, he's never actually won the NBA Championship.

He also played in the ABA as a point guard, and was very good. As a result, he tends to be very demanding of the point guards that he coaches. His teams are known to be excellent defensive teams. He believes very strongly in getting a good shot on offense and is not a big fan of 3-pt shots. He is quite simply, a basketball genius.

Larry is considered to be a great teacher of the game. He loves basketball and coaching. Depending on who you listen to, he's either great with young players or terrible with them.

One thing's for sure: the Piston players will be exposed in playing for him. Their weaknesses will be pointed out, and he won't ignore them. It's been said in the past that he alienates certain players. Larry is a stubborn, veteran coach.

In other words, he's a lot like Scotty Bowman.

However, unlike Bowman, Larry is not coming to the Pistons with past championship experience. As mentioned before, he's been close. It's important to note, though, that virtually all the other NBA teams that he's been a part of had been poor teams when he first arrived there. He would then quickly turn them into at least a good team. After some success, he would then leave (sometimes after only about two years on the job).

Three promising things work in the Pistons' favor, regarding the length of his tenure, however. His last stint lasted an entire 6 years with the Sixers. Considering that he had to put up with Allen Iverson's antics for that long, he should be given some dog years added on to the total.

Plus, he did say that he wanted this to be his last stop on his coaching tour. He's said that before, but he's getting older now and maybe will settle in here in Detroit City.

Finally, the Pistons are $#&* good! Larry has never had a team this good when he started with it. Also, this bunch is a group of hard-working, focused, and dedicated guys. Coaches love that.

Whether or not the Pistons win a championship with Brown (or whether he sticks around for very long) remains to be seen. But, one thing is for sure: you will see some great basketball being played by the Pistons under this brilliant tactician, strategist, and teacher of the game.

The Players

There were some significant personnel changes that occurred this summer for the team. First up was the draft, which featured the selection of three talented young players.

I was at The Palace for the Pistons Draft Party, with subscribers Jay and Greg and I can tell you that there are some Serbian-Americans that live in Metro Detroit that are real fired up over the addition of **Darko Milicic**. As Joe Dumars was being interviewed immediately after the selection, a small contingent had gathered and was chanting, smiling, and waving the Serbian flag around.

At this point, the book on Darko is that he has extremely diverse and unique talents, especially for a man of his size. At the press conference announcing his signing, Coach Brown said that he plays like Toni Kukoc, but we want him to play more like Bill Russell. Problem is that he doesn't know who Bill Russell is.

That observation tells a lot. Right now Darko has a lot of finesse to his game and we need him to add force and a presence to the lane. He apparently can shoot it, pass it, take people off the dribble, and has a lot of quickness and some good moves down low.

But, if fans think he's just going to come in here and dominate right away, they're mistaken. It doesn't work that way. Not for an 18 year-old kid who not only has to adapt to the NBA game, but also to the American game.

And, not on a team as good and deep as this one is. The Denvers and the Clevelands of the league can play their high draft picks a lot of minutes, because what do they have to lose? In Detroit, we have more at stake. The types of mistakes he will make can cost games. Not only that, but his weaknesses won't have to be exposed right away. He can be brought along slowly and learn from the more-experienced and talented big men of Ben, Mehmet, Zjelko, and Elden Campbell.

If you see Carmelo Anthony averaging 18 pts or more per game and see Darko playing less than 18 mins. per game, don't panic. It does not mean that Anthony is the superior player. What it means is that he's got the mins. But, how many turnovers does he have? Is he shooting a low FG %? Does he make poor decisions with the ball? Does he get baked on defense?

More than likely many of those things will happen. The Nuggets won't really care and thus, they won't put much early pressure on him to improve. Whereas here, you have to earn your mins. out on the floor. This way Darko will surely get the point.

The other two draft picks: **Carlos Delfino and Andreas Glyniadakis** won't join the team till probably next season. Basically, Carlos is a multi-dimensional swing player with good size who D's it up and is tough as nails. Andreas is a bit of a house. At 21 years old, he's 7-1 and 280 lbs. The early indication is that he's not a project, but a bonafide solid player.

After the draft was over, several publications had given the Pistons extremely high marks. Many rated their draft as the best in the entire league. Obviously, international scout Tony Ronzone (who brought Dirk Nowitzki into the league) played a large role.

In the early moments after Larry Brown was hired, Joe told him how the draft would unfold. He pretty much knew who would go where and to which teams. He also said the Pistons would draft these three foreign kids. Coach Brown would say after the draft was over that he was "in awe" of what transpired on draft night. It went exactly as Joe had predicted. With all his experience, Brown said he had never been part of a draft that went that well and with a staff that was prepared the way that the Pistons were.

One last observation about Darko: The Pistons had to draft him. Even if he turns into a bust, you can't pass up on the opportunity for a 7-footer with skill. They're a rare commodity. Meanwhile 6'8" guys who can shoot and score like Anthony can are all over the NBA.

A force down low is one of the very last pieces to the Pistons championship puzzle.

Subtractions

The Pistons got rid of **Jon Barry, Cliff Robinson, and Mike Curry.**

Jon Barry is a great 3-pt shooter. In fact, he had the best long-range shot I've ever seen from a Pistons player. He's also fiery and exciting, and a real fan favorite. But for all the good, there were some underlying issues that would occasionally hurt the team.

Sometimes, he could be so wild with the ball and make turnovers when you least could afford them. On defense, his lack of quickness and size would cause periodic mismatches resulting in easy scores for the opposition. Plus, he's no spring chicken! He just turned 34 and little by little his shot is going to start to deteriorate and his lack of quickness will only grow worse.

Meanwhile, Mike Curry is an excellent defender and leader. As president of the players union and one of the few players with a Master's degree, his leadership and vision are unquestioned. However, there is a growing push to get Tayshaun and all of the younger guys integrated fully. This left no role for Mike. He wanted to play two more years to fulfill the length of his player's union contract. The Pistons did not envision him playing here that long.

At 35, his age is also starting to show. His offensive skills have left him in recent years and he's lost at least a half step on defense.

Then there's Uncle Cliffy. Cliff does everything well on the basketball court except rebound. Like Mike, his specialties are defense and leadership. He's a true winner. He's played in the league for 14 years, and he's made the playoffs all 14. That's amazing! He has 125 playoff games on his resume. That's shocking!

However, he has no championship rings. Cliff is a winner, but not a champion. He does so many things right, but doesn't quite do everything at the near-perfect level that NBA championships require. And, I don't just mean his performance in the playoffs this year (where he stunk and had 2 games with exactly 0 rebounds!).

A friend once told me that she has another friend who works for the Phoenix Suns. Talking to her after the trade that brought Cliff here from Phoenix, she quoted him as saying, "You guys got Cliffy? Shoot, here we call him Spliffy. That guy smokes more weed than anyone!"

Also, Terry Foster had said in the Detroit News this summer that Cliff is immature and that this had implications for our young roster and how these players could be influenced.

Plus, Cliff will turn 37 in December.

Do you see a trend here? Out with the old and in with the new (or young). The projected starting lineup this year is Chauncey, Rip, Ben, Mehmet, and Tayshaun. That's two second-year players up front and a very young backcourt. Then there's the teenager from Serbia!

Additions

The most significant veteran acquisition this summer was that of **Elden Campbell.** Make no mistake: this guy is a horse! At 7-feet and 280 lbs. he can control the paint for long stretches. Both offensively and defensively. While he helps out in blocking shots and rebounding (the Stones' most pressing need) he also will be extremely valuable as a post option.

Chuck Daly once said that the teams that win championships are the ones with the most toys. Toys meaning post options. Since Darko is probably going to be more perimeter-oriented at first, that leaves us with only one other post player: Corliss Williamson. This makes Elden very important.

Bob Sura shoots 3's well, though not at the same level of accuracy as Jon Barry. But he does many other things better. Defensively, he's much better. Bob is also a good draw & kick guy and can play the point position as well as the two. He has good size for a guard. Also, he's in the last year of his contract, so you know two things: one, he will play very hard; and two, we can get rid of him and clear cap space if necessary next summer.

Lindsey Hunter is back, though I'm not sure for how long. There are rumors that he may be traded soon and so might Chucky Atkins. The nice thing if they keep Lindsey is that he's a much better defender than Chucky, due mainly to his size. He's also in the last year of his contract, which means more cap space next summer as well.

Cap space is vital. It's vital to sign new free agents as well as keep your own. Look at how many teams right now can't make a move, simply because they are overloaded with bad contracts due to poor cap management. The Pistons are priming themselves to re-sign Mehmet, go after other free agents, or both.

Analysis

The Pistons are building towards the day when they can hoist the championship trophy over their heads and dump champagne on each other. Looking at this roster and the moves that helped create it, the team has obvious short-term and long-term goals.

In the short-term they want to become even better on the defensive end (a Coach Brown staple). They also want a dynamic offense that can attack from several different options and areas on the floor.

For the long run, they want players that perform as interchangeable parts. Guys who can play multiple positions and are multi-skilled, not specialists who can only do certain things well.

Cap flexibility is desired so that whatever tweaking needs to happen in the near future to make this a championship team, is possible. With the influx of youth now on the roster, Joe is positioning this group to be good for a long time. This is important because as a franchise, you need to give yourself at least a handful of chances to win the title. You need a good three to five year run going deep into the playoffs and knocking on the door to the championship, in order to actually win it once.

10/02/03—Franchise Growing Pains

Well training camp is finally underway. Darko is out of shape, which is disappointing, but not surprising for a young kid. The first pre-season game is next Tuesday and it will be Lebron James' first ever NBA game. It will be on UPN 50.

Yours truly will be out of town next week, attempting to establish a presence for Pistonsfever.com in Hawaii. (I'm joking, sort of.) So there will be no Pistonsfever Newsletters next week. But for now, enjoy the piece below talking about where the Pistons are really at in the grand scheme of things.

◆ ◆ ◆

Franchise Growing Pains

To truly understand where the Pistons are at as a franchise, you need to look no further than last year's playoff run. Their performance showed a team on the rise, but one that's not quite ready to sit atop the NBA's throne (or for that matter the Eastern Conference's throne).

In the first round, this young, inexperienced team got outplayed in three of the first four games. They weren't able to recognize and respond properly to a team gathering momentum on both offense and defense. Plus, they looked like a team fighting such a huge uphill battle on the road.

Once they figured Orlando out and started to play with the proper force, and to borrow a Rick Carlisle term, "defensive disposition," they beat them in a very convincing manner three straight times. This showed the Pistons' superiority, and allowed them to gain the sense of urgency and sense of purpose that is absolutely critical at the playoff level.

The second round featured a much better effort throughout the series. Fine basketball was played in four of the six games here, all Pistons victories. The middle two were horrid, once again on the road.

The series was fairly evenly matched, but the Pistons' performance in Game 6 in Philly showed a team that was clearly a notch or two above the Sixers, both in terms of playoff savvy, and long-term potential. While Allen Iverson was showing up late to the game, Chauncey was getting ready to put on one of the most spectacular performances of the entire 2003 NBA Playoffs, gunning down dagger after dagger on the Sixers.

Then there was the New Jersey series. You will recall that the first two games at The Palace were close (both 2-point losses), while the two in New Jersey were blow-out victories for the Nets. This clearly showed that the Pistons had maxed out for the season. Both home games were very winnable, but an inattention to key game initiatives, like rebounding, not allowing New Jersey to play exactly the way that they want to, and not matching the Nets' focus in winning on the big stage that is the Eastern Conference Finals, cost the Pistons.

New Jersey, to their credit, had the experience of making the Finals the year prior, and thus were very hungry to get back and had the experience to know how to get it done. They also had figured out how to exploit the Pistons' offensive weaknesses better than either Orlando or Philly. The Pistons offense last year was very good when everything was functioning properly within the system. But, there weren't enough dynamics in the overall attack to compensate when teams started to do things like double and triple Corliss on the block.

This is why Elden Campbell, Darko Milicic, and Bob Sura were brought here. Three guys that can play multiple positions and can attack opposing teams from a variety of ways and angles on the floor. The Pistons offense now has more options.

There are those in the mainstream media, both local and national, who have said that New Jersey is clearly a step or two above the Pistons at the top of the Eastern Conference this year. This is because the Nets re-signed Jason Kidd and added Alonzo Mourning. The Pistons' additions, many maintain, are more for the future than now. After all, Darko will have limited time and a limited role this year and Carlos Delfino, who is solid in so many ways and a part of the future, won't even be here till next year.

While it is true that the Nets have bolstered themselves and are the team to beat in the Eastern Conference, I think it's important not to over exaggerate the significance of their standing with respect to the Pistons. Yes Alonzo Mourning is a big catch. In the East, where there's hardly any dominant big men, it gives them a real advantage. On the flipside, had the Pistons signed Mourning, most journalists would say that they are now the odds-on favorite to win the conference.

But, what does that really mean? Put is this way: if the Pistons had Mourning would they win the East? Most Pistons fans would say yes. But, ask them if the Pistons would win the NBA Finals, and most people, media or fans, would say no.

The way the West is currently configured, it's going to be a tall order to win the championship this year. If the Kobe Bryant "circus" doesn't distract the Lakers too much, you're looking at a juggernaut. With Gary Payton and Karl Malone added to a group that already featured Bryant and Shaq O'Neal, this team will have four future Hall of Famers in the starting lineup!

What's more is that the Dallas's, the Sacramento's, and the San Antonio's will be tough to get through as well. Each of these teams, with the exception of Dallas, has far more playoff experience than the Pistons or Nets.

And that's the point. The Pistons aren't really developed enough as a group or as individuals to get it done just yet. They learned a lot last year, playing 17 playoff games. But consider this: other than Cliff Robinson's 100+ playoff games, only Jon Barry had more than 20 playoff games of experience entering this past post-season. The Pistons almost got that many this past year alone!

So while last year was great, it's really only the beginning of something, not the culmination of something. Another year or two going deep into the playoffs will help the Pistons figure out exactly what it's going to take to go from being a very good team to being a great team, and then a champion.

What's exciting is the fact that this team is constructed for the long haul. We talked about their relative youth in the first newsletter this week. Joe Dumars basically has assembled a group that is young enough and talented enough to make multiple runs at the title. The window of opportunity is so large!

On the other hand, Alonzo Mourning is no spring chicken, and really neither is Jason Kidd. They have to get it done in the short-term future or it's not going to happen for the Nets.

I said before last year's playoffs that the Pistons, no matter how well they were going to fare in the 2003 campaign, were going to be a much better team 2 years from then than they were at that point. Assuming everything continues to progress as planned, it is around this time that the Pistons should also be much better-equipped to go for the championship.

Not only will the experience be there, but young Darko won't be so young anymore. Rip will have added new moves and shots to his repertoire. Chauncey's role and leadership will have grown. Tayshaun and Mehmet will be true forces on the basketball floor. Ben will have scoring moves in his game.

That's exciting.

10/20/03—Training Camp and Exhibition Games

Sorry for the delay on this one, guys. Part of it was being out of town for a week.

In this edition we have a basic breakdown of each pre-season game thus far, highlights of the open-practice at U-D, a Chuck Daly sighting, an interesting analysis from an elementary basketball coach, and the vision of Rick Fox hula dancing.

Yes, that last one is true. Myself and a couple of Pistonsfever.com subscribers were in Hawaii 2 weeks ago and with the Lakers and Golden State Warriors having training camp out there, we caught some of the action.

We also ran into former player, Jack Haley, who now works for Fox Sports. He told us that he thought the Pistons lost an excellent coach in Rick Carlisle, but that Larry Brown will do a great job here. He also said that Darko will be an excellent player, just not right away. Maybe in two or three years. Of course, I've said that all along.

Now, the Lakers-Warriors game that we went to was a lot of fun. We got to talk to Jim Boylen, a Warriors Assistant who was almost hired at MSU for Tom Izzo's staff recently, and we got Brian Cardinal all fired up.

Hawaii loves the Lakers! They've trained there something like four out of the last 5 years and the people go nuts! Flashbulbs were popping all night long at the Stan Sheriff Center, University of Hawaii.

Now, the night before the game we encountered something we weren't planning on involving the Lakers. We were walking along the Waikiki strip of hotels, restaurants, and shops when we came across the restaurant, "Kobe" (no joke!). Kobe himself was not there, but apparently, several other Lakers were. People outside were all starry-eyed and said that we had just missed them.

Pistonsfever.com subscriber, Jay, who's been know to "Chevy Chase" his way into meeting many VIPs over the years, said, "Well, maybe we'll run into them on the way back to the hotel." Within 10 minutes we found them.

At a very upscale hotel, that was basically a village onto itself, was a bar with a local band playing Hawaiian music. As we walked in, we began to see some players. Gary Payton, Brian Shaw, Karl Malone, and Rick Fox, among others were there. Laker Girls were also in attendance, along with several women on the prowl. What you hear about professional athletes being in high demand by certain types of women is true.

Rick Fox was on stage dancing it up, while the band played some sweet island music. It was definitely different to see these guys outside the basketball floor.

◆ ◆ ◆

I met a guy this week who's a 4th grade basketball coach and used to play collegiately. He knows Lindsey Hunter and said he's a great guy. But, he also said something else that I found interesting.

He said that physically, Lindsey is far superior to Chucky Atkins. He has more tools to work with. But, Lindsey is such a nice guy, whereas Chucky has more of an edge. Chucky has this attitude like, "I belong!" and that is what allows him to shoot 3's with such confidence and is also why he hits so many clutch shots.

In a certain sense, at least on offense, Chucky has had a better career and I think he hit it on the head as to why.

◆ ◆ ◆

In last Monday's Detroit News, Chris McCosky made reference to the fact that Ben Wallace and Rick Carlisle saw their relationship deteriorate during the second part of the year. Ben would not elaborate on what happened or why, but it was revealed that he was carrying a heavy weight last year in dealing with both this and the death of his mother.

◆ ◆ ◆

Okay, now to the more current <u>basketball</u> happenings with our team. First off the players: Corliss is in better shape this year, as he's turned some fat into muscle; injuries have been prevalent right from the beginning of camp as Memo, Bob Sura, Lindsey, Rip, and Zeljko have all missed time.

Ben has been extremely aggressive on the offensive end throughout this preseason and he has been successful. Coach Brown is encouraging him to go at it, so Ben has the support he needs. He's making post moves, jump-shots, fade-aways, even FT's! Assistant Coach Mike Woodson has been working with him a lot on his shot, and it's paying off.

Speaking of the coaches, Larry Brown's style is becoming quite clear. Like Carlisle, he makes defense the #1 priority. However, he is willing to double-team, trap, and pressure full-court, sometimes quite extensively. These are things that Carlisle did not do.

Meanwhile on offense, he wants a lot of fast-break opptys and early offense opptys. The ball should go from side to side, inside first, then out. The weak-side should be explored and guys need to be patient and take good shots.

Coach Brown also requires all five guys to defensively rebound the ball and wants three to hit the offensive glass.

He wants Rip & Chauncey to be true aggressive scorers and is using Chauncey at the shooting guard spot more often.

10/27/03—Training Camp and Exhibition Games II

The Pistons finished the exhibition season with a split on a home & home with the Bucks. They finished 4-4 for the preseason and are now preparing solely for Wednesday's season opener at The Palace vs. Rick Carlisle's Pacers. The game is on UPN at 8:00, so you'll definitely want to check it out.

It's going to be a wild one with Carlisle returning to Motown and with the Pacers being our biggest rival last year for the Central Division crown. They'll also raise the Central Division Championship banner for last year that night. I'll be LIVE at The Palace and will have all the coverage for you in the next update.

An interesting item in this Saturday's Detroit News web page stories was written by Larry Lage of the Associated Press. It is a Chucky Atkins quote where he basically said that the players have much more confidence playing for Coach Brown than they did for Coach Carlisle.

It's fairly obvious that Chucky was not really a big Carlisle supporter anyway, but it cannot be denied that the confidence that Larry Brown has shown in Ben Wallace's offense has paid huge dividends. Ben looks like he's going to be a real offensive weapon this year. Now that's exciting!

Speaking of Darko, it looks like he won't be in the rotation at the beginning of the season. Now don't panic! It's actually great to know that the Pistons are so deep that they don't really need him right away. He's got time to develop.

Meanwhile, with Zeljko back, Ben playing out of his gourd on defense and offense, Memo continuing to get better and better, and Elden Campbell causing major match-up problems for opposing defenses every game during the preseason, the Pistons frontline is in good shape for now. Basically, it **rocks!**

And the last bit of info that I have for you guys other than the game notes from this week, is that the injury bug seems to finally have left the Pistons. They played Friday for the first time with their full complement of players. Now Coach Brown just needs to figure out what Coach Carlisle had to last year: who to play when in the rotation.

THE GAMES OF OCTOBER

Practice at Detroit Mercy: One of the first looks at the new coaching staff and Darko Milicic, the practice also had a surprise guest appearance.

Cavs: The first exhibition featured the NBA debut of Lebron James.

Nuggets: New uniforms were on display for Denver and Carmelo Anthony had something happen to him for the first time at the Carrier Dome.

Bucks (first game): Ben Wallace experienced a scary moment and then went on to do some incredible things on the basketball floor.

THE PRACTICE AT U-D

(October 4th, 2003)

This is always a fun event every year. The Pistons started doing this 3 years ago at Wayne State University. The last two years has been at University of Detroit. It's a way for the Pistons to reach the city of Detroit and to my knowledge it's the only practice of the year open to the public.

A free event, it does feature some entertaining by the Automotion Dance team and games and prizes. Basically, it rocks!

When I arrived at U-D a half-hour before start-time, the line to get in was already well past the first section of the parking lot. By the time the doors opened, it ran past that parking lot, along the end-line of the soccer field, then along the entire length of the field, all the way back to 6 Mile. Then, it kept going parallel to 6 Mile!

The Pistons have great fans!

Hooper was out early, playing with the kids. Some kids were tossing a football around, including a girl with a Pistons visor on who had a great arm, and some were racing each other up the soccer field and back. The kids had a blast.

There was also a group of what seemed to be Asian tourists (or maybe U-D students) that would pop up and take simultaneous pictures throughout the practice.

At the beginning of the practice, the players came out one by one to introductions and applause. Then the coaching staff came out, announced only as, "Larry Brown and his staff." Then I heard people in the crowd yelling, "Zeke! Zeke! Zeke!" and low and behold, Isiah Thomas came out.

Larry then addressed the crowd for a few moments and introduced his staff. At the end, he said, "And I believe you know who this next man is" and he pointed to Isiah. At this point, myself and several others in attendance got really fired up, because it seemed like Isiah was being introduced as an Assistant Coach.

Given the reported rocky relationship between Pistons owner, Bill Davidson, and Isiah it seemed unlikely, yet would be fantastic. Later, I found out that Isiah was actually just taking in practice as Larry's guest for a couple of days. He's going to tour the NBA this year and see how different coaches and organizations run their teams.

Rick Carlisle did the same thing the year before he joined the Pistons, and experience like that is invaluable. You can pick up on a lot of little things that can really help when running your team.

I tell you what.... the people still love Isiah! The place was buzzing after he came out and he was swarmed for autographs afterwards. Isiah is the man!

As for the practice itself:

—It looks like the Pistons will run some offensive stuff with Rip & Memo on one side of the floor in 2-man action. This is great, because inside or out Memo can score and he's a good passer. Rip is so quick that he can receive the ball off of cuts.

—Larry and his staff are constantly teaching. They would stop a drill or part of the scrimmage to show exactly how a screen should be set, where a pass should be thrown, etc.

—Larry especially got after Darko on multiple occasions

—Darko is good, but has a lot to learn

—Watching Elden Campbell, I can tell you that it sure will be nice to have his size on both offense and defense this year. The guy is built.

—It's quite clear there's going to be more running and early offense this year from the guys

—A lot of the drills were 2 on 1's and 3 on 2's

CAVS 100 PISTONS 96

(HOME)

It was Lebron James' NBA debut and over 100 media members were in attendance. ESPN, in its continuing attempt to put together a highlight package to tell a story, rather than the entire game story, showed at least 6 times as many James highlights as that of the Pistons on SportsCenter.

Pistons fans to their credit, are not easily impressed by national phenomenons. So, they booed Lebron in pre-game intros. and throughout. Welcome to the NBA, Lebron.

—I was shocked to learn that Lebron weighs 240 lbs., the majority of which is muscle. At, 18 he has a tremendous NBA body.

—Tommy "The Hit-Man" Hearns was in attendance

—In the 1st Q, Lebron shot an air-ball

—Darko (that other rookie) made his first ever NBA shot, a reverse spin to the baseline

—Chuck Daly was in the house

—Ben rejected Lebron on a breakaway

—You can definitely see the more up-tempo focus of the Pistons this year

—Lebron made some sweet passes and many jumpers

—Down 23 pts at one point in the 3rd Q, the Pistons were just giving up a lot of fast-break points and not converting on their own end

—Very little prep time for this game had Larry Brown upset. A new rule said that veterans could not participate in practice until Friday, when normally it would have been like Tuesday. Thus, there was only 4 days to get ready for this one.

PISTONS 104 CELTICS 89

(IN CONNECTICUT)

—With personnel and role changes, the Pistons are a big staring lineup now. Chauncey is a horse at the PG position, Rip is a good length at 6'7" for SG, Tayshaun has the 7'2" wingspan that is unheard of at SF, Ben is a monster no matter what position he plays, and either Elden or Memo are rock solid. Elden is a 7-footer who weighs 280!

—The Pistons pressure really affected the Celtics

—Ronald Dupree, a Pistons camp-invitee can flat-out sky

—There are a lot of weak-side shot opptys in a Larry Brown offense

—Larry, who I believe has a history with ref. Bennett Salvatore, got 2 techs. and an ejection at the 7:00-mark of the 2nd Q

—Assistant Jon Kuestner took over

—Lot of fouls both ways in the 1st H

—Lot of TOs both ways throughout

—With the Pistons looking to penetrate and probe inside so much now, it means that Ben's man is coming over to help out, leaving him easy opptys

—Rip shooting smooth throughout in front of his college coach, Jim Calhoun, and the Connecticut crowd

RAPTORS 88 PISTONS 81
(IN GRAND RAPIDS)

—Pistons are really running and pressing now

—It's weird to see Michael Curry playing against us and matched up with Tayshaun who he helped train and get ready to be the man that he now is and was in the playoffs last year

—Darko gets called for a lot of defensive 3-sec violations

—Very soft rims in Grand Rapids

—The Pistons still have only one offensive play installed. So far the focus has been entirely on defense, early offense and pass & cut, combined with a lot of side to side passing

—Ben was like a vacuum on the glass in the 3rd Q. He had 20 for the game.

—Fun finish, with good basketball. Vince Carter took over at the end.

—Ben blocked a soaring Carter dunk attempt

PISTONS 123 CELTICS 95
(HOME)

—Ben shot the smoothest, most natural looking 17-footer in the 2nd Q

—Chauncey had a 4-pt play in the 3rd Q

—Pistons were swatting everything

—Chauncey's the man!

—Triples were raining down all over the place

—The Stones were up 30 pts in the 4th Q

—Easy game for the Pistons

—Memo, showing his agility, made a hard and quick drive to the rack from the foul-line extended

HEAT 84 PISTONS 71
(HOME)

—I was LIVE at the Palace for this one, and unfortunately, it was a real stinker

—In fact, there's really not that much to say, other than that they were poor offensively, defensively, and throughout

—Larry Brown missed the game since Kansas was celebrating the 15-year anniversary of National Championship they won with him. He participated in the ceremonies.

PISTONS 93 NUGGETS 91
(AT SYRACUSE)

Since this game was at the Carrier Dome, it was a homecoming for Carmelo Anthony. There was a big crowd on hand. He was 17-0 on this floor until tonight.

The Nuggets have new uniforms that seem a little strange: they are light blue (almost like a powder puff blue) with a white strip going down the sides and a little yellow trim. They're also very shiny.

—Ronald Dupree had the best dunk I've seen since last year's All-Star break. He soared off the drive and jumped off 2 feet, throwing it right down on Francicso Elson! That was truly spectacular!

—Tayshaun had a sweet, Statue of Liberty style throw-down in the 1st H

—The Pistons were down 12 at the half, but had a good comeback. Then Denver surged ahead again. Then the Pistons game back and tied.

—Zeljko had an excellent game in his first one back, scoring 11 pts

—Carmelo had a good game in front of the home folks. But, he missed 2 key FTs with the score tied and a minute left. He atoned on the next possession when he scored on a strong drive.

—In case your wondering how our #1 pick fared, he had cut his hand on the rim prior to game time, so he didn't play much.

—Memo, showed a lot of aggression off the dribble in the game's final possessions. He drew a foul on one and scored another hanging, switching the ball from side to side, before scoring the game-winner.

—Rodney White finally settled down when playing against the Pistons and made 8 for 8 FGs

—Chucky was 8-9 on FGs

BUCKS 97 PISTONS 86
(HOME)

—Ben had 2 excellent post/slashing moves early in the game for scores

—This was Bob Sura's first game as a Piston

—Daniel Santiago of the Bucks committed 3 fouls in less than 30 secs during the 2nd Q

—I tell you what…the Bucks are small, especially after all the personnel changes they've had

—I tell you one more thing: the Pistons' offense looks really different this year: the pace is much quicker and the offense just happens sooner

—The 2nd Q is when things started to go wrong. The Bucks were attacking and our guys weren't getting back. The offense just stalled out.

—The Pistons still have a ways to go to sustain good offense and continuity and avoid things like TO's

—Scariest moment of the preseason: Ben fell awkwardly and laid on the floor for awhile. It looked like a knee. Larry Brown held his forehead. The Palace went silent. Then he got up and was fine.

—Then, he dominated. He was everywhere! Blocking, rebounding, shooting 3's!

—Then the Pistons fell apart again

PISTONS 96 BUCKS 86
(AWAY)

—The Pistons were hot out of the gate: getting whatever they wanted offensively

—They shot 92% through the 1st 8 mins. of the game

—Then with the reserves in, they went cold in the 2nd Q and Milwaukee took the lead

—Rip was on fire in the 3rd Q. This is good because a broken nose can make a player, especially a guard, tentative. But he was aggressive and got it done out there.

—The Pistons just took over and solidly put this one away in the 3rd & 4th Q's

2

November

11/04/03—The Regular Season Begins

The Pistons started off the first week of the regular season with two wins and one loss. Both wins came on the road in Florida. It's always good to beat Tracy McGrady!

Some interesting tidbits before we break down the games for you:

In Monday's Detroit News, Chris McCosky pointed out how Darko got an earful from Larry Brown at the Miami game after he seemed put off by being put in the game with less than 2 mins to go. His point was that <u>all time is important for rookies,</u> regardless of whether the game is in doubt or not.

The same day, Detroit Free Press writer Perry Farrell said that Darko is "800 percent" better than when camp first opened and Ben and Zeljko knocked the snot out of him everyday. He now understands the price you have to pay to get better in this league.

◆ ◆ ◆

On opening night at the Pacers game, I found myself sitting next to a very knowledgeable fan. Steve Benavides coached Detroit Holy Redeemer to the Class D state high school basketball championship in 1995. He also has coached for both Ferndale and Detroit Southwestern in Class A.

He said that this current Pistons team has many good qualities: "Unity, work ethic. Just like Joe Dumars." We also talked about an interesting scenario: if Kobe Bryant does opt out of his contract with the Lakers and looks to go elsewhere as he's suggested after his latest spat with Shaq, would Joe go after him?

Great question. As Coach Steve put it, this would allow the Pistons to get that superstar component that they're missing. He also wondered if the Pistons can win a championship without a superstar.

That, of course, is the $64,000 question.

11/11/03—A Great Home Stand

The Pistons did exactly what you want them to do going into a very difficult West Coast trip: win all 3 home games. Now at 5-1, they have the best record in the NBA in terms of percentage points except for Rick Carlisle's Pacers.

The West Coast trip begins Tuesday vs. Sacramento. Wednesday's game against Golden State is on ESPN, the first national broadcast of the year for the Stones. They then play the Lakers and Phoenix on Friday and Saturday. This is a tough trip.

The team still doesn't have its' offense flowing in a real consistent and powerful way. Last year, on a similar trip that occurred later in the season, the Pistons went 0-5, losing to Seattle by 7, Sacramento by 6, the Lakers by 10, Golden State by 2, and Portland by 17 when they ran completely out of gas.

The first West Coast trip last year happened around this time and the Pistons did better, going 3-2. They beat Phoenix, Utah, and Denver and lost to the Clippers and Dallas.

Remember, these trips are about more than just the Pistons vs. the Kings. They're about time changes that throw your body clock off, a lot of travel in a short period of time, playing a lot (in this case 4 games in 5 nights) in the space of just a few days, and weird, wild things. You can go out West and not make a jump shot for 8 straight mins. And this is after not missing for 6 straight mins! The momentum can swing faster than Wilt Chamberlain at a sorority house!

◆ ◆ ◆

In other news, Lindsey Hunter was activated and Chucky Atkins was put on the injured list with a leg problem. Some of you may have seen Tremaine Fowlkes play some spot duty this past week and wonder who the heck he is.

Well, at 6'6" and 212 lbs. he's the guy the Pistons might lean on to defend certain key offensive weapons for other teams. Without Cliff Robinson, there is some concern in the team's ability to defend tall and dangerous players out on the perimeter. You know the type: Kevin Garnett, Dirk Nowitzki, guys that bake you off the dribble just as fast as they can drop a jumper on you.

Larry Brown calls Fowlkes, "The best on the ball defender" the Pistons have. Though not overwhelming physically, he certainly *looks* like he could shut someone down defensively.

11/18/03—A Sobering Trip out West

Remember how last week we talked about how much the guys struggled last year when they went out West against some high-caliber teams? Well it happened again.

Just like last year, the Pistons were in every game. The largest margin of defeat was by 6. The Kings game was a throwaway performance; the Golden State game showed a lack of presence and will; the Laker game was just a dang good basketball game; and the Phoenix game saw the return of the Piston offense: flowing and scoring with dominate guard play.

Chauncey & Rip struggled mightily on the trip until the last game. Chauncey took some wild shots that were out of the context of good offensive decision-making on several occasions.

The two most disappointing things that happened were poor management of end-of-game situations (with the exception of the last one vs. Phoenix) and the lack of a presence, an attitude, or a force in the first 2 games. You cannot play in a reactionary mode (like let's try not to lose, instead of playing to win!) against a team like Golden State.

It's like Rick Mahorn used to say back in the Bad Boys days, regarding playing on the road, "We want your gym. We want everybody in your gym. We don't wanna hear any noise in your gym. Because it's our gym tonight."

The Pistons need to develop a greater killer instinct by the time the playoffs roll around in the spring.

◆ ◆ ◆

Ben tweaked his ankle, and like last year in the playoffs with his knee, he won't talk about it, but it's definitely affecting his play. So how can a guy who gets 16 rebs in his last outing be affected by an ankle problem?

Well, his explosiveness and lift aren't the same right now as they were during the first part of this season. But, being the warrior that he is, he can still perform at a high level game in and game out.

◆ ◆ ◆

The Pistons' offense sputtered mightily out West. At times, it looked like it was in disarray. Guys were confused on where they were supposed to be. Bizarre shot attempts and bizarre decision-making with the ball were going on.

It's like I keep telling everyone who has concern right now for certain things (sputtering offense, Darko not playing, poor road performances): all of these areas can work themselves out in the long run. And in the big picture, the entire team and its approach to winning an NBA championship in the near future, will be far better off than if the roster looked exactly the same as it did last year, with the same systems on offense and defense in place.

◆ ◆ ◆

The rematch with the Lakers is this Tuesday at The Palace. Tune in or miss out!

11/25/03—Four Victories & the Eastern Conference Player Of The Week

It was a great week in Pistons basketball, as they went 4-1 and beat the NBA's most powerful club: the L.A. Lakers. Chauncey was simply fabulous, averaging about 23 ppg, 8 assts, 5 rebs, and 1.5 stls. As a result of this magnificent performance, he has won Eastern Conference Player Of The Week honors.

Another Pistons player, who has a much different role, has broken through into the regular rotation and is contributing nightly in a meaningful way. Tremaine Fowlkes was brought in as a defensive stopper, especially out on the perimeter. But, he's also shown great energy to make other things happen out on the floor and doesn't make mistakes on the offensive end. He has successfully earned the coaches' trust.

◆ ◆ ◆

The Pistons have been beset by numerous injuries lately. Chucky's been out for a couple of weeks now and has had arthroscopic surgery to clean up his knee. This has helped relieve the pain he had throughout much of last year. He should be back soon.

Zeljko Rebraca has had mysterious problems that might be related to the heart medication he had been taking. He's had a lot of fatigue and nausea and has been unable to practice or play for awhile.

It doesn't appear that he's even still taking the medication (which was post-surgery medication), but the effects can apparently linger far after someone stops taking it.

Both Lindsey and Rip got hurt in games this week, though neither appear to be long-term injuries.

◆ ◆ ◆

Talking to a girl who couldn't have been more than 12 years old this week, I was struck by something she and her mother told me about Tayshaun. They're originally from Kentucky and said that the people down there are becoming big Pistons fans since Tayshaun is from U of K.

It has got to be exciting for the people of Kentucky, which is a true basketball hotbed, to have one of their players doing so well in the NBA.

◆ ◆ ◆

Alonzo Mourning retired from the NBA this week, requiring a kidney transplant. Losing a strong 7-footer, who is a force on offense & defense, will certainly make the Nets a weaker team this season. This is especially true of the stretch run (post All-Star game) and the playoffs.

The Pistons are certainly helped in their drive for the Eastern Conference Championship with this development. If Rebraca could ever get healthy, the Pistons will feature potentially the strongest frontline in the East and have tremendous advantages night in and night out.

◆ ◆ ◆

I get asked a lot about what kind of a player Bob Sura is. All I can tell you is that when he played with Cleveland, a division rival who we played all the time, he was <u>a pain in the neck</u> for opposing teams. He can D' you up, stick a triple on you, or drive & dish to open teammates (his specialty). He also plays both guard spots.

Quite simply, <u>he just makes plays.</u>

THE GAMES OF NOVEMBER

Pacers: Everything happened on opening night, including an emotional return for Rick Carlisle.

Nets: There was great theater in this first match-up with the team that eliminated the Pistons in the prior year's playoffs.

Lakers (both games): The two Laker games were a foreshadowing of things to come in June—the Piston defense was having a great effect on them, the Pistons' edge in depth shined through, and Gary Payton was out-played.

Knicks: This game featured multiple altercations between Ben Wallace and Kurt Thomas, as well as Chauncey Billups doing something he doesn't normally do.

Hornets: A very bizarre game.

76er's: Larry Brown's first game against his old team.

PACERS 89 PISTONS 87

(HOME, Wednesday, October 29th)

It was a festive atmosphere at The Palace for four reasons: it was opening night, Halloween was around the corner, last year's Central Division championship banner was being raised, and Kid Rock was in the house!

Lot's of kids were dressed in costumes and trick-or-treated on the concourse before the game. My personal favorite costume: "The Pistons Dork."

Before we could get started with the other festivities, it was time to hear "America the Beautiful" sung by the Motor City's own Kid Rock. Coming out in a black leather jacket, with his hair flowing you knew it would be a memorable performance.

He did it accapella with 2 others and at the end he yelled out, ***"You're my boy, blue!"***

The Pistons honored Rick Carlisle for his part in the Central Division championship (and #1 record in the East last year). As the spotlight shown on him, the crowd gave a loud and long ovation: showing the class of Pistons fans. Carlisle was really moved by it. You could see it in his face. He was shaken.

After the banner was raised, Ben took the microphone and addressed the crowd briefly, thanking us for our support.

At this point it was time to rock!

—Unfortunately, both teams played a very ragged brand of basketball in the 1st H. They both seemed tight, and for the Pistons part, they also seemed to be carrying the weight of expectations. Heck, they even dropped 2 easy passes early on.

—The Pistons players were trying to do too much and forcing the action early, especially off the fast-break

—Kid Rock was enjoying the game from the very first row at mid-court, talking frequently to the kids next to him. Like a real fan, he stayed to the very end of the game.

—Lot of blocks & steals for the Pistons tonight

—They had way too few assists, though

—Scot Pollard, who starts for them, wears number 62. What is that?

—Being a late start for a Wednesday night, and being a work day, quite a few fans had left before the end of the game. The ones that were left were a good crowd, because it was loud in The Palace!

—This was a bad basketball game (and it was rough around the edges), but it had a good finish.

—Chauncey & Rip missed a ton of shots

—When it was over, Carlisle was high-fiving and embracing his players. Between these actions and his response to the ovation he got at the beginning, it was more emotion than we ever saw from him in Detroit.

PISTONS 93 HEAT 81

(AWAY, Friday, October 31st)

The Heat are still rocked by Pat Riley's departure from coaching last week. He's only going to run the front-office as a GM now. I wonder how Lamar Odom feels knowing that he signed with the Heat this summer intending to play for Riley.

—Chauncey was hot early

—Udonis Haslem is a horse for them inside: he was rebounding, tearing it up, scoring

—Corliss hit 3 straight buckets in the 2nd Q and finished with 12 pts in only 14 mins

—Ben volleyball-spiked a shot by Haslem right out of the lane

—On another play, Ben doubled Lamar Odom on one side and rotated over to the other side of the floor and stole the ball: truly amazing! To cover that much ground that quickly is unreal, especially for a player his size.

—The Pistons showed a zone with less than a minute to go in the half: something that you would have never seen in the past two seasons under Rick Carlisle who vehemently opposed any such type of defense.

—Memo blocked a Haslem dunk in the 2nd H, but Haslem then got a 3-pt play out of it

—The Stones went to a big lineup in the 3rd Q: Chauncey, Tayshaun, Corliss, Ben and Zeljko

In the 4th Q, an interesting sequence of things happened. The Pistons had built a solid lead by patiently working the ball for a good shot. They were on the road and this is what you do.

But, as the Heat started to make a couple of shots, the Pistons suddenly went away from what had been successful and started shooting jumpers early in the shot-clock. Then immediately after receiving a pass from an off. rebound, Rip shot an ill-advised triple.

In the timeout, Larry Brown was livid. "Get the ball inside! We've gotta get to the foul line!" He was definitely not happy with Rip's 3-pt attempt and let him know about it.

Then, after the timeout Rip made another poor decision. Coach Brown pulled him out, sat right next to him on the bench, explained something to him, then put him back in the game 30 secs. later.

At that point, Rip went off! He scored 5 straight buckets and put away the Heat. Great moment for our team as Coach Brown explained to Rip what he wanted, then put him right back out there and went to him with the offense.

PISTONS 96 MAGIC 85

(AWAY, Saturday, November 1st)

The Magic have made a lot of personnel changes since last we saw them in the 7-game playoff last season. They have added Juwon Howard, Tyronn Lue, Britton Johnsen, and Shammond Williams. The first 3 are all in the starting lineup.

Funny thing is…they actually look worse than last year. They don't have the same guard play or guys gunning down 3-pt shots.

—Playing their 3rd game in 4 nights, the Pistons actually looked pretty fresh. This is a testament to their depth and Coach Brown willing to play at least 10 players these last 2 games

—Elden Campbell just tore up the Magic's paint with a lot of inside scores. He had 10 pts in the 1st Q and was blocking everything that came inside.

—The Stones had a lot of penetration on the left-side that created opptys on the right in the 1st H

—Something you don't see everyday: an out of bounds play was run for Ben in the 2nd Q for a jump-shot! He nailed it.

—In the Pistons' new fast paced attack, Rip runs like a gazelle and can beat a lot of defenders back

—They were trading baskets back & forth down the stretch of the 3rd Q, and T-Mac was on fire. He had 18 in the qtr.

—2 Ben alley-oops tonight!

—T-Mac had 0 pts in the 4th Q, baby!

—Rip had 10 pts in the 4th Q

—The Pistons out-scored them 29-13 in the 4th Q

PISTONS 96 CELTICS 88

(HOME, Wednesday, November 5th)

It was Ladies' Night at The Palace, meaning discounts on tickets and royal treatment for the ladies. For those that may have heard the rumors, no I did not in fact participate in the "Basketball 101" session where the ladies were taught the basics of the game beforehand.

—Chauncey threw **a perfect pass** to Rip on the break in the 1st Q that was like a QB threading the needle on a deep post route

—Vin Baker is **much better.** He's dropped weight and kicked alcoholism.

—The Stones were also giving up way too many drives for scores in the 1st H. This meant that virtually all of Boston's 1st H pts were scored in and around the paint.

—**Serious** energy by the Pistons in the 3rd Q

—Boston's offense was effectively shut down in the 2nd H, as the Pistons only allowed 34 total pts

—Rip had 10 pts in the 3rd Q

—Ben & Paul Pierce were talking smack as Ben hit his 2nd straight FT. Then they each got a technical.

—Ben **consumed** a Mike James shot in the 4th Q

—Great feeds by Chauncey much of the night. This went nicely with his 27 pts.

—He was simply amazing on the 3-pt bombs that he buried Boston with in the 4th Q

<u>PISTONS 105 BUCKS 99</u>

(HOME, Friday, November 7th)

As the sign said at The Palace, it's deer hunting season and it's time to get some Bucks!

—The Pistons led 26-8 at one point

—There was a Darko sighting: he got some good 2nd Q mins. and due to either a lack of game-shape or nerves, he became very winded

—Ben blocked a Desmond Mason dunk from behind in the 2nd Q

—The Stones had 14 1st H assts, baby!

—The Bucks were clicking in the 3rd Q on several levels

—At one point, Ben ping-ponged (with a hard smack) a Redd scoop-shot out of bounds in the 3rd Q

—At one point in the 4th Q, Chauncey made a shot after being hit in the eye. He had turned his head and didn't even see the basket when he let it go. It still brought nothing but **"sweet string music."**

—The Bucks were relentless and cut it to 1 at the 3:50-mark of the 4th Q

—Memo finished with a career-high 18 rebs and had 4 blks in only 26 mins. of play

—Up 4 pts with 25 secs left, Ben stole the inbounds pass to seal the victory. It was a **bad** Tim Thomas pass.

PISTONS 98 NETS 84

(HOME, Sunday, November 9th)

It's always good to beat the team that knocked you out of the playoffs the prior year. Especially when you were swept. This was also the "get-away game" because the Pistons are about to embark on the West Coast trip.

So this makes the win important even if Kenyon Martin, Lucious Harris, and Rodney Rogers sat out with injury and Jason Kidd was playing somewhat hobbled.

—The Nets led the NBA in fast break pts coming in. But not tonight, as the Pistons held them to 8 for the game.

—The Pistons early effort was **poor.** As a result, Coach Brown **lambasted** his team in a timeout near the end of the quarter.

—The Pistons responded, going on a 19-4 run to take the lead early in the 2nd Q

—The Nets had foul trouble all night long. Tamar Slay actually had 4 fouls by the 10:15—mark of the 2nd Q!

—Alonzo Mourning plays just like he used to: angry, with muscles flexing, and that vein in his head growing by the minute.

—When Z got in the game, he and Mourning went at it like 2 Brahma bulls. Pushing and holding each other in the post: neither willing to give up ground. You can say a lot of things about Z, but one thing's for sure: he's never backed down from a physical battle in the post ever since he first got here.

—Leading by 1 going into the half, the Pistons were involved in a 3rd Q battle that swung their way once the Nets started getting in major foul trouble. By the 2:30 mark of the 3rd Q, Mourning had 5 fouls and Aaron Williams picked up his 5th seconds later. This left the Nets with a weak and small frontline to battle the Pistons' 7-ft horses and Ben down low.

—Lindsey Hunter, showing the hustle that would make any Pistons fan anywhere pump his fist in the air, **threw his body** at the ball early in the 4th to go for a key possession.

—Lindsey was all over the place, pressuring, knocking away, and stealing. Even from Jason Kidd!

—Corliss had 20 pts in 26 mins to pace the Pistons

KINGS 97 PISTONS 91
(AWAY, Tuesday, November 11th)

The Kings have made some interesting personnel moves this year. They've added Brad Miller (giving them exactly 1 player that actually plays physical basketball) and lost Hidayet Turkoglu to San Antonio.

Chris Webber and Ben missed the game with injuries.

—Z started in Ben's place

—The Pistons gave up a bunch of buckets off of cuts and back-cuts. This is the influence of Sac's Assistant Coach Pete Carril, who ran back-door plays almost exclusively at Princeton.

—Speaking of assts., the Kings finished with 29 and the Pistons had 9 total for the game. That's sick and pathetic.

—Darko got in at the 4:37—mark of the 2nd Q. He did pretty well for himself, getting 2 blks (one on fellow big man Brad Miller) and enjoyed playing against his idol growing up: Vlade Divac.

—FTs helped the Pistons get back into it. They made 27 for the game to Sac's 17.

—It was a bad 3rd Q in just about every way imaginable. Then, the Pistons fought in the last couple of mins. of the quarter and cut the lead to 5.

—Bobby Jackson was killing us all night long: he had 16 pts. in 21 mins.

—Chauncey made virtually no jump-shots all night long

—The Pistons just fell apart in the last 1:30 of the game

—Too many rushed, ill-advised shots at the end when they could have gotten better ones

WARRIORS 87 PISTONS 85 (OT)

(AWAY, Wednesday, November 12th)

—Jason Richardson was out for the Warriors with injury

—Tayshaun hit for 10 quick pts, right out of the gate. Then he came out and the offense never really went back to him. Two things: he needs to be more aggressive, and the team needs to make a point of getting it back to him when he's hot like that!

—Cherokee Parks looks ridiculous with all those tattoos completely covering each arm

—What do you know, Cliff Robinson is playing major mins for Golden State this year

—Calbert Cheaney was a force early and often. He finished with 24 pts on 12-16 FGs.

—There were more off. fouls called on both teams in this game than any other that I can ever remember. It seemed like the refs. were ready to make that call tonight.

—Ben is not the same when playing with this ankle injury. It affected his aggression and explosiveness. His offensive game returned to last year's sub par level.

—The Pistons were just attacking Mike Dunleavy every chance they got. His defensive prowess (?) did nothing to stop them.

—I don't think I've ever seen Chauncey play this poorly: on the Pistons or on any of his other teams. He couldn't score in this game and took so many bad shots.

—On one key play towards the end, Rip passed it outside and Chauncey cut inside. What the $#%& was that?

LAKERS 94 PISTONS 89

(AWAY, Friday, November 14th)

This was just a good game throughout. Some solid Laker shot-making at the very end, combined with some poor decisions by the Pistons on some key possessions in the last minute, made for the difference.

—For those of you who might be wondering, Kobe Bryant did play in this game. I think his legal issues did take him away from the game briefly this week, but he was back in time for this one.

—He only had 16 pts

—Get this: The Pistons only gave up 21 pts to Gary Payton and Shaq O'Neal. Kobe and Karl Malone each had 16 pts. This is doing a pretty good job of keeping this star-studded team under control.

—By the way, the Laker bench is virtually non-existent

—Down 6 after the 1st Q, the Pistons then "***Went to Work***" in the 2nd Q on defense: Lindsey blocked a Derek Fisher lay-up, while Ben blocked lay-ups by both Malone and Kobe.

—Ben was just controlling the 2nd Q: he had 4 stls and 2 blks. The Lindsey block on Fisher was the best block by a small guard that you'll ever see: he just sized it up, met Fisher at the summit, and swatted it! He looked like Theo Ratliff just laying in the weeds, ready to reject it.

—Due to all this great defense by really the whole team, the Pistons had pulled even by the half

—Shaq only had 6 pts in the 1st H, and was virtually a non-factor

—The Pistons had 26 points-in-the paint in the 1st H, to go along with 8 fast-break pts: very good

—Chauncey had 14 pts at the half and 29 for the game

—The Piston bench was hammering LA's in the 1st H

—Elden was a force in the 3rd Q: scoring 8 pts and at one point, blocking Shaq at the rim

—With the score even after 3 Q's, this game was going down to the wire

—Ben drew a charge on Shaq late in the game

—Chauncey was the man down the stretch, getting it done on offense

—Karl Malone was behaving like an ass throughout the entire game

—Chauncey actually out-played Gary Payton. But, for some reason he also jacked up some ill-advised 3-pt shots with under a minute to go. Memo was guilty here too. We had plenty of time to get a good shot (and didn't really need a 3 at that point anyway). It seemed like our guys didn't know the clock. There was over 20 secs left and they were acting like there was about 5 secs to go.

—The Lakers got to the line twice as often as the Stones

PISTONS 100 SUNS 91

(AWAY, Saturday, November 15th)

*Playing their 4th game in 5 nights, things didn't look too good coming into this game. Luckily, the Suns were playing their 4th in 6 nights. With this win, the Pistons have now won **5 of their last 6 games in Phoenix.***

—Rip could not handle Joe Johnson in the 1st Q. He was scoring at will. Then Rip and the rest of the defense locked in on Johnson and got him under control.

—Elden keeps getting in early foul trouble

—The Pistons were giving up all sorts of dribble and drive penetration in the 1st H

—The Pistons had a bunch of steals early and often in this game. They had 12 total.

—The Stones got **a lot** of FT atts: 39 total for the game

—Chauncey played superbly all game long: he finished with 24 pts and only 1 turnover

—Rip had 16 1st H pts, finished with 27 and shot 10-20 from the field, bouncing back from some horrible shooting performances on this road trip

—By shooting 53% on FGs in the 1st H, the Pistons were controlling the game. Then, Phoenix put on a surge and led by 1 after 3 Q's.

—Then Chauncey and Rip, both of whom had struggled in different ways on this trip, came through. Chauncey **hit 2 back-to-back cold-blooded triples** toward the end of the game. Then Rip got a 3-pt play and school was out.

—The Pistons had 20 fast-break pts

PISTONS 106 LAKERS 96

(HOME, Tuesday, November 18th)

This was a fun one! Being part of this game was so much fun! It's always a different atmosphere when the Lakers come to town. There are more plastic people at the game. Of course, there were also a lot of true Detroiters in attendance and some of them booed Kobe Bryant every time he touched the ball.

After seeing the Lakers twice this year (not counting the party in Hawaii) I can say that they're going to have to find more scoring opptys in the paint if they're going to win the NBA title. I know the triangle offense is all about creating jumpshots, but come on. You've got Shaq posting up and then 4 other guys just spotting up all game long.

Kobe and Gary Payton will need to penetrate and break down opposing defenses if this team wants to taste champagne in June.

—Ben blocked Shaq at the summit of his attempt in the 1st Q

—Memo drew an off. foul on Shaq for his 2nd and then got him for his 3rd on the screen & roll

—Elden got 2 early fouls again. Fortunately Shaq also had foul trouble throughout. He got his 4th foul at the 4:45 mark of the 2nd Q.

—There was a Jack Nicholson impersonator in the house!

—Hooper looks different. He has a more pronounced flowing flame on his head, and his eyes have pupils swirling around constantly, with every move he makes. He looks a little more cartoonish.

—Memo had 3 straight buckets going right at Shaq in the 1st H. Shaq didn't have the foot-speed for him.

—The Pistons gave up 3 big off. rebs in the 2nd Q

—Just before the end of the half, Chauncey, unhappy at a no-call, rolled the ball ¾ the length of the court and got a tech. Not a good move. The officials are not going to give you the benefit of anything after that type of display.

—The Pistons led 54-49 at the half

—Pistons shot well in 1st H

—In the 3rd Q, Ben had a great spin move on Karl Malone, completely catching him off-guard and scoring on the other side of the bucket with his left-hand

—Then, Ben blocked a Malone jump-shot

—Robert Porcher & Tommy "Hit Man" Hearns were in the house

—Shaq drew his 5th foul at the 1:15-mark of the 3rd Q, giving the Pistons a big advantage going down the stretch

—Memo couldn't handle Shaq in the post

—Still a 1-pt game going into the 3rd Q, this game was close all the way. Neither team really was able to create or sustain a run until the very end.

—Bobby Sura was electric in the 4th Q! He sparked this team and it all started with a drive & dunk from the corner on the baseline all the way to the rack!

—Bobby was passing, creating, and was everywhere in the final quarter: making **big** plays.

—The Laker offense is all just Shaq post-ups or a pull-up or standstill jumper

—There was a small Pistons lineup in the 4th Q: Chauncey, Lindsey, Ben, Corliss, and Bobby

—This made for a weird situation when Corliss was guarding Shaq! He did so multiple times throughout the 4th Q.

—The Pistons shot 57% on FGs for the game and made 20 FTs

—Ben had 5 blk shots

—Chauncey outscored all Laker scorers with 24 pts

This was obviously a big victory for the Stones. It seemed to me that they didn't even blink when taking on this beast of a team that features 4 future Hall of Famers. They knew after playing them real close the week before on the road, that they can certainly beat this team. And they did.

<u>PISTONS 99 GRIZZLIES 92</u>

(AWAY, Wednesday, November 19th)

This game featured a contrast of rest and situations for these 2 teams. Memphis had played exactly 2 games in the last 8 days and had 3 straight days off coming in to this game. The Pistons were on the 2nd night of a back-to-back and were playing their 6th game in 9 days.

Memphis is no longer a pushover: they have already beaten the Spurs, Lakers, and Mavericks.

—New Grizzly, Mike Miller, lined up to take a triple, decided to pass it inside at the last second, <u>and hit Pao Gasol in the head!</u>

—The Pistons were either tired or not playing with enough intensity early and went down 27-20 after the 1st Q

—The Pistons shot <u>much better</u> in the 2nd Q

—Chauncey hit 2 **huge** triples on the break in the 3rd Q to give the Pistons the lead and <u>put a surge</u> on the Grizzlies.

—He was scoring everywhere

—The Pistons had a 19-3 run going

—The Pistons' D was leading to good O, especially on the break

—The Pistons were up 10 after 3 Q's and Chauncey had 14 pts in the 3rd Q alone

—Memphis has been a fantastic 4th Q team this year, but not this time!

—Chauncey had 33 pts for the game and the Pistons as a team shot 48% for the game: <u>a very good number for the road</u>

PISTONS 94 KNICKS 85

(HOME, Friday, November 21st)

Though not playing much, Darko has the fans excited about his potential as a force in this league. Friday nights are "Photo Fridays" at The Palace, meaning that fans can get free pictures taken with a Piston player before the game. The line of fans to have a photo shot with Darko was huge!

By the way, I recently got his autograph, and it's bizarre! The only thing I could make out on it was "#31". The rest was just scribbles and squiggles—Serbian style.

—The Knicks added Dikembe Mutombo and Keith Van Horn in the off-season. Van Horn was out with injury and so was Antonio McDyess.

—The Knicks are an extremely perimeter-oriented team. They are soft & small on the frontline

—The Stones were very unselfish and featured good passing throughout the 1st H

—Darko was seen <u>eating an energy bar on the bench</u> in the 1st H

—The Pistons got to the line a lot: 15 times in the 1st H and 37 overall

—In the 3rd Q, Chauncey drained a jumper while falling sideways

—Also in the 3rd, Chauncey took off on the break and <u>dunked it 2-handed!</u>

—After building a good lead in the 3rd Q, the Pistons squandered most of it by going into a lull

The 4th Q was highlighted by altercations featuring Ben and Kurt Thomas. Thomas was clearly the instigator coming after Ben and giving him periodic shoves and stares. Ben got a tech. for yelling about the no-calls to the refs.

Then, they both got in each other's face, staring at each other, nose to nose. Later, Ben was fouled underneath by a converging Knicks defense and Thomas got in his face.

Thomas got a tech. as Ben walked away. He then began thumping his chest vociferously for the crowd. And they loved it!

Thomas then fouled out at the 3:54—mark off the 4th Q, having lost both the battle and the war. As Ben said afterwards, teams are going to have to find a different way to beat the Pistons than that.

After Thomas sat down, 3 Pistons fans were all over him, hooting & hollering.

—Chauncey had 23 pts and 9 assts; <u>Ben had 9 blks!</u>

—This was a good win, but <u>the Pistons need to do a better job of putting these types of games away much earlier</u>. Develop the killer instinct!

HORNETS 81 PISTONS 80

(HOME, Sunday, November 23rd)

This was a wild one on every level. The game featured the top 2 scoring PGs in the NBA with Baron Davis who averages over 25 ppg and Chauncey. The Hornets have one of the best starting fives in the NBA and are considered to be one of the top contenders in the East this year.

Elden was out, as he was talking to his very sick grandmother on the phone.

—Memo started in Elden's place

—Tayshaun blocked David Wesley right at the goal on the break

—A 23-6 Hornets run gave them the lead in the 2nd Q. The Pistons were disorganized & out of sync. In the beginning they handled the zone well, but in the 2nd Q it seemed like they couldn't handle it at all.

—The Hornets just <u>attack</u> the off. glass

—The Pistons came back by getting stops on D' and attacking on offense before the end of the half

—On the break, Rip scored & was fouled in a collision that left him down for awhile. He was in terrible pain and left the game with a neck strain.

—A 25-6 Pistons run from the 2nd Q on into the 3rd Q had The Palace rocking

—David Wesley took **horrible** shots all night long

—Baron Davis also took a lot of bad 3-pt atts. shooting from his heels

The end of the game went like this: the Pistons had a 2-pt lead and got a bunch of off. rebs on the same possession, killing a lot of clock. Then, the Hornets trapped Chauncey and got a steal. Wesley made only 1 FT, so the Pistons still had a 1-pt lead with 8.2 secs. left.

Chauncey (a 93% FT shooter coming in) missed 2 FTs! As Ben switched out too far on Baron Davis on the perimeter, Davis drove right down the pipe and dunked it on Bob Sura to win the game. What a bizarre ending to a bizarre game.

—This was just a rugged, low-scoring game. It was a struggle, kind of like a football game featuring a bunch of FGs for both teams and few touchdowns.

PISTONS 94 HAWKS 89

(AWAY, Monday, November 24th)

—Elden was back for this one, but Rip is still out. Lindsey started in his place.

—Another Darko sighting: he got in at 9:35 of the 2nd Q and played for 3.5 mins. He had a sweet pass on a look-off to Corliss on the baseline.

—Great play: Tayshaun soared in with the ball in one hand—Statue of Liberty style—and went right at Theo Ratliff who met him at the summit. Tay was so strong with his dunk attempt that, even though Ratliff got a good chunk of it, the ball still went in. Afterwards, Tay just looked at Ratliff and shook his head, like "You can't stop me!"

—Stephen Jackson, new Atlanta addition, seems to be much worse as a player than last year when he played with the Spurs. Maybe Tim Duncan's presence just makes you a better player than you are otherwise.

—A huge Pistons run completely vanquished Atlanta's lead and gave them a lead of their own in the 4th Q

—A lot of the run was based on 2 things: huge Pistons' determination & intensity and steals. They got a bunch of steals in the 4th Q.

—Darvin Ham made a terrible play right near the end as he jumped in the air to pass it, threw it away, then allowed a lay-up on the ensuing break when he should have fouled. Now Atlanta had a 1-pt lead with 18 secs. left!

—Next, Chauncey drew a foul on a hard baseline drive and made both FTs. (this was big since he missed 2 key ones last night)

—On Atlanta's next possession, they threw it away on the inbounds pass, in what was either a mis-communication or just a bad play.

—Tayshaun hit 2 FTs to give the Stones a 3-pt lead and Chauncey then hits 2 more to ice it, baby!

After losing last night in the final moments and Chauncey missing 2 key FTs, this game played out just the way you would like: the Pistons pulling it out in the clutch, refusing to wilt on the road when down many points, and Chauncey as a key leader on this team, making all 4 FTs in the last 18 secs.

76ERS 90 PISTONS 86

(AWAY, Wednesday, November 26th)

It was Larry Brown's first game against the team he coached for the last 6 years. The fans both booed and cheered him. Philly fans were not happy that he left and went to the team that eliminated them from the playoffs last year. Also, he had been misunderstood in the media when he said that he had coached a lot of jerks in his career. They thought he was referring to Allen Iverson; he maintains he was talking about other players.

Being that Philly fans are known to boo their own players (and sometimes even Santa Claus) you have to give these things their proper perspective.

Coach Brown did receive big hugs from both Iverson and Eric Snow before the game, showing their appreciation for what he was able to do for their careers. Iverson even said that he might not be an All-Star or have become the MVP of the league were it not for Coach Brown.

—The Sixers were without Glenn "Big Dog" Robinson who was out with injury

—Ben stopped a 2 on 1 fast break by himself when he blocked Eric Snow's lay-up

—Then Tayshaun blocked an Iverson lay-up

—At one point the crowd started chanting "Larry Sucks!"

—Chauncey had serious foul trouble throughout

—A lot of bad 1st H turnovers led to easy Philly scores and their lead

—Down 56-48 at the half, the Pistons had given up 40 pts in the paint. That is unheard of for a half.

—Iverson committed 3 off. fouls tonight

—Rip fouled out at the 3:50 mark of the 4th Q and Chauncey fouled out a minute later. With the score tight, this made it hard to score in the stretch run.

—The Pistons just couldn't score in the 4th Q at all

PISTONS 92 CAVS 88

(HOME, Friday, November 28th)

Lebron James was in the house for a national broadcast on ESPN. And he scored..... 6 points.

—Elden got off to a good, quick start

—Ricky Davis, as he did many times last year, torched the Pistons. He had 10 pts in the 1st Q and 25 overall.

—The Pistons were up 33-24 after 1 Q

—Tommy "Hit Man" Hearns was in the house wearing a "CIA" hat. Uncle Kracker was also kickin' it at The Palace.

—Memo had a great baseline drive & dunk

—This was a high scoring game early

—Cavs are winless in their last 30 road games

—Rip had 22 pts at the half and 44 for the game (career high) on 15-23 FGs. This is truly being in the zone.

—Lot of 1st H assts and good passing and just good team offense in the 1st H

—Ben blocked a Zydrunas Ilgauskas lay-up attempt

PISTONS 80 WIZARDS 69

(AWAY, Friday, November 29th)

This is part one in our defensive lock-down series. This is what "Goin' To Work" is all about.

—Both Jerry Stackhouse and Gilbert Arenas were out for Washington with injuries

—It was a Larry Hughes kind of 1st H

—In the 2nd H, the defense was much better and just %$&# good!

—The Pistons only allowed 9 pts in the 3rd Q, but couldn't convert enough of their own and thus only led by 2 going into the 4th Q. It should have been a much larger lead.

—Ben, in the 4th Q, took the ball, ran right down the pipe, and threw down a serious, 1-handed dunk with authority!

—Christian Laettner has the most ridiculous hair now. It's curly on the ends, but straight otherwise. And the headband doesn't help.

—The Pistons have tired legs, playing their 3rd game in 4 nights

—Memo wasn't getting any calls in this game

—Rip shot 11-16, staying hot for the 2nd straight game. He had 25 pts.

—The Pistons shut the Wizards down and allowed only 23 pts in the 2nd H!

3

December

12/4/03—A 4-1 Week And The Debut of Dr. Fever

This was a fun week: Rip was completely in a zone for 2 straight games and scored 69 points in 2 days; Chauncey got his second dunk of the year; and we saw the return of the "Defensive Lock-down." You may remember this term from last year. It's used when the Pistons just completely shut down an opponent for key stretches of a given game.

Consider this: the Pistons gave up 23 pts in the second half of 2 consecutive games! This is unheard of. Twenty games into the season (with a record of 14-6) the Pistons have yet to give up 100 pts for a game.

◆ ◆ ◆

We have a new feature this week at Pistonsfever.com. It's called, "Ask Dr. Fever". This is where we take a question or issue that's on Pistons' fans minds and answer it or address it.

So, this week we'll look at what seems to be everybody's favorite topic: Darko Milicic.

ASK DR. FEVER

Question: Dr. Fever, did the Pistons make the wrong choice by drafting Darko over Carmelo Anthony?

Dr. Fever: No, for several reasons. First of all, drafting Carmelo would be fun in the short-term. He'd score some fabulous buckets, the team would have an immediate return on their investment of a draft choice, and the media would favor the choice. But, keep in mind that if Denver had the #2 pick, they would have taken Darko as well.

Here's the main point: talented big men are about as rare to find as an honest politician. When the potential is very promising from a given big man, an NBA franchise has to take that player. If a guy like Darko even becomes half of what most scouts believe he can become, the Pistons frontline will have huge advantages game in and game out.

Consider this: even now, with an older veteran in Elden Campbell, a center who's in & out of the lineup with health issues in Zeljko Rebraca, and the inexperience of second year player Mehmet Okur, the Pistons still have one of the biggest and most effective frontlines in the East. Granted, the East is small top to bottom. But, imagine what would happen if Darko develops into even just a good player, and joins forces with Ben Wallace, and the multi-talented Okur on the frontline.

People sometimes forget that if the Pistons had Carmelo and invested in his future, they'd have no use for one of either Tayshaun Prince or Rip Hamilton. There just isn't enough shots to go around on that perimeter. And the Pistons would still have to find help on the frontline.

Yeah Carmelo is scoring some points right now (18 per game). But he's also shooting 39% from the field and at the moment, does not defend in a way that is useful to a Detroit Pistons team.

Playing for a bad team allows a guy to get major minutes. In Darko's case, he's going to play less anyway since his team is much better and thus has a lot more at stake when rookie mistakes occur. But also, big men always take longer to develop in the NBA. Think about it. Who was the last 7-footer that you can think of who was considered an impact player at age 18?

In fact, of all the guys who have come into our league with no college experience at a young age (like Darko), only Kevin Garnett averaged double figures (at about 10 pts per game) in his first year. Kobe Bryant didn't. Tracy McGrady didn't. Jermaine O'Neal didn't. They're just not ready right away.

O'Neal began to shine a few years into the league when his body and mind had matured enough. This is what we're looking for with Darko. He might not contribute right away (though I would hope he would get more regular season playing time than Tayshaun got last year), but the idea is to have him playing at a high level in the next 2-3 years. As has been mentioned in this newsletter before, this should be about the time the Pistons are developed enough as a team and ready to go for the NBA championship.

In the grand scheme of things, that's all that matters anyway: NBA championships. Carmelo can score all the points he wants to. Ask Dominique Wilkins and Tracy McGrady how it feels to pour in tons of points and not win the title.

So, if as fans we can just be patient and look at the big picture of what it takes to win in this league, we have a good chance of being happy with the Darko pick overall.

In the game notes for the Knicks victory this week, you find Magic Johnson's comments on the matter. He believes the Pistons made the right choice.

Also, Monday's Detroit News has a story talking about how much Darko has already improved since he first got here. And he's learning it all without playing in games. Hopefully soon he will see more game action.

12/11/03—Sputtering Offensive Performances

Well, Chucky Atkins and Zeljko Rebraca are back from the injured list. Also, in an interesting side note, Bill Laimbeer's daughter's team won the state basketball championship this past week.

Other than that, the only significant thing going on in the world of the Pistons right now is poor, poor offense.

Hey, what's this? Oh I see that someone has brought a high-back leather chair for Dr. Fever to use as he helps fans with questions and concerns that they have about the team. Sitting in it today makes him feel thoughtful, even reflective.

ASK DR. FEVER

Question: Dr. Fever, what is up with the Pistons offense? It has been very ineffective and many times, just doesn't look right. What is your diagnosis?

Dr. Fever: There are several issues right now. Coach Brown wants the guys to work the ball inside and get high percentage shots, share the ball, and work it from side to side. Instead, the Pistons show lack of patience, and try to do too much individually. They also show an amazing lack of movement off the ball.

What it boils down to is that they're relying too much on their talent to carry them through and are not helping each other enough as a team on offense. Sometimes they don't even play with the proper energy, intensity, or heart. They are playing hard, but not with the right sense of urgency.

Question: Weren't the Pistons supposed to be more of a running team this year? How come they rarely reach double digits in fast-break pts?

Dr. Fever: They haven't really generated a lot of turnovers. Normally, you can score on the break off of steals, which lead to automatic numbers advantages and broken floor opportunities.

Also, the guys seem to be impatient on the break and settle for quick jumpshots, instead of waiting for trailers and hitting the second and third waves of offensive players.

Question: Are all of these offensive problems correctable?

Dr. Fever: Absolutely. Why they don't make the adjustments and improve on these things right away or even game to game is unclear. The same issues keep coming up.

But, it is a new system, with new coaches, some new players, and some old players in new positions. So, once everybody gets on the same page, and the players start to relax and just play, instead of over-thinking, the offense will be much better.

12/19/03—Terrible Performances and Darko is an Accountant?

Greetings from Pistonsfever.com! This was a rough week as the offense continued to spiral out of control, and losses piled up.

We have a number of questions for Dr. Fever this week from a group of "patients" who just entered the "clinic". And, it seems that people can't get enough Darko—Carmelo talk.

ASK DR. FEVER

Patient 1: "Dr. Fever, is it true that before the Pistons—Cavs game last week, the Pistons were forced to practice in the dark, courtesy of Cavs management?"

Dr. Fever: Yes, this is true. In all my years following this great game, this was one of the most childish incidents involving an organization as a whole.

Apparently back around Thanksgiving when these 2 teams squared off at The Palace, the Cavs were forced to practice in the dark due to facility problems since the building was shutdown during the holiday. Now with the Cavs hosting the next game, they figured they'd get revenge by intentionally shutting off all the main lights, forcing the Pistons to have their shoot-around and walk-through in very dim lighting.

This is a clear example of an organization thinking it is more important than it is. Sure the Celtics used to pull similar tricks when they would mess around with the hot & cold settings in the visitors' locker room at the old Boston Garden. But you know what? The Celtics were actually a winning organization; one with several championship banners hanging from the rafters. The Cleveland Cavaliers are not.

Just having Lebron James does not raise your status as a franchise to an untouchable level. Get over yourselves.

Patient 2: Dr. Fever, I know you discussed the Darko vs. Carmelo debate 2 issues ago, but I can't get this subject off my mind.

Dr. Fever: Well at least that shows you have Pistonsfever.

Patient 2: I thought so. I knew I felt different this time of year than I did in the summer time.

Dr. Fever: That's usually the first symptom.

Patient 2: I guess what I really want to know is not so much why was Darko taken over Carmelo in the draft, but why isn't Darko playing more? Isn't the best way to develop a guy to play him?

Dr. Fever: Excellent question, young fella. The answer is "yes" and "no". Yes for some players, but no for others.

Some really young players do very well being thrown right into the fire and become better because of it. Others don't. It's sort of like how some business professionals will be hired in corporate America with no prior business experience and do very well. But, many are only hired after extensive business training and experience.

Each company will usually only hire someone without a business background if they're actually ready to step in right away and contribute (and show they have a knack for fitting right in). Otherwise they're not brought into that situation.

In Darko's case, he's kind of like a kid (let's call him Darren) who was brought on as an intern for a Big 6 accounting firm immediately after high school. He has no college training, and certainly no CPA.

But, he took a couple of accounting classes in high school, and is good in math, is very left-brained, and has a quantitative and analytical mind. Oh, and he reads the Wall Street Journal.

So he's got all the natural ability and tremendous potential. But, does this mean he's ready to handle the books of Fortune 500 companies? No way. However, he is going to be able to learn so much over the next year as an intern, by simply being around and observing everything the more experienced accountants do. And, every once in awhile he'll be able to contribute by assisting one of the other CPAs with balance sheets.

If he keeps working hard, Darren will be able to become a full-fledged accountant within the next couple of years and will be part of the success of a major accounting firm.

Patient 2: So what professional-type is Carmelo like?

Dr. Fever: Well, he's more like a Computer Network Administrator named Carlos. Carlos has a 2-yr Associate's degree, which is all you need to work in the field, and is already making a good salary. But, it doesn't look like he's going to be doing networking for an industry leader, like Darren is doing accounting for a major accounting firm.

Patient 2: So you're saying that Carmelo is more ready now, but Darren, or I mean Darko, could be the better player on a championship team in the near future.

Dr. Fever: Yes, because as we discussed in a prior issue, big men always take longer to develop in our league. A perimeter player like Carmelo can rely on quickness and athleticism to get him by and help him overcome his young player weaknesses. But a big man cannot. If he makes a mistake down low, no amount of quickness is going to save him. He's going to give up dunk after dunk and several offensive rebounds.

Patient 2: Wow, Dr. Fever this is deep! Thank you.

12/24/03—Merry Christmas!

This week saw several extremes for the Pistons and their play. Playing like true warriors on the road in Indy for three quarters, they then collapsed and lost the game.

Playing like world-beaters against the Jazz, they then turned in a terrible offensive performance against the Bucks.

They're getting a little bit better, but they're still a long ways off from where they need to be.

◆ ◆ ◆

Like many doctors at this time of year, Dr. Fever is using the week of Christmas as a vacation week. As such, there is no "Ask Dr. Fever" column this week. But, he did want to pass along some friendly medical, er basketball, advice to everybody.

Several fans and patients have asked if eggnog helps treat Pistonsfever. The Good Doctor says that there really is no cure for it, and I can neither confirm, nor deny the rumor that a spiked glass can help in easing the pain of seeing the offense struggle so much night in and night out.

◆ ◆ ◆

A rumored trade featuring Bob Sura for Ron Mercer has been floating around this past week.

Speaking of the trade, it would be interesting since Bobby is playing great defense and giving us a lot of energy off the bench, but can't score a lick right now. Mercer, meanwhile could provide some points.

But keep in mind, that it's very possible that neither player will be back after this year. They're both in the last year of their contracts and either one would have to prove that they're a good fit with this team.

◆ ◆ ◆

This week saw a lineup change for the current squad. Mehmet Okur is now starting in place of Elden Campbell. Memo seems to really want this opportunity to start and show what he can do.

At this point, it's unclear whether Elden's minutes will go to Zeljko Rebraca or whether he'll stay as a major part of the rotation. One thing's for sure though, he's a great guy to have around come playoff time.

Merry Christmas!

THE GAMES OF DECEMBER

Knicks: Chauncey Billups did something incredible and Magic Johnson gave some words of wisdom.

Sonics: One of the lowest moments of the season.

Jazz: Darko Milicic feels the ups and downs of being a rookie in the NBA.

Hawks: Two very unusual scenes in this game with Atlanta.

PISTONS 79 KNICKS 78 (OT)

(AWAY, Monday, December 1st)

This is part 2 of our defensive lock-down series. Remember, that score you see above is an OT score.

This game also marked the return of Antonio McDyess, who had never played for the Knicks up till now, going through 3 knee surgeries.

—Chauncey got his 2nd dunk of the year with a 2-handed one on the break in the 1st Q

—The Pistons were down 27-16 after 1 Q and 47-37 at the H

—McDyess looks real rusty

—The Pistons also had 10 1st H turnovers

—Then, in the 3rd Q, they had 9 turnovers, just playing awful

—The Piston D' was superb in the 4th Q

—Chauncey had one of those amazing NBA plays, where he got fouled, lost control of the ball, grabbed it while in the air, and threw it in for a 3-pt play

—Out of a time-out near the end, Ben was guarding Allan Houston! Houston made a tough shot to tie it up.

—The game ended like this: Tayshaun was all over Houston. He knocked the ball away and caused Houston to fumble it around. Houston then had to pass it away. Michael Doleac had to shoot a 17-fter and Memo rejected it. Ball game.

—The Pistons once again gave up exactly 23 pts in the 3rd & 4th Q's combined

Magic Johnson joined the Fox Sports Detroit crew in the 4th Q and OT with analysis. Magic was going nuts watching this game! He was fired up! The Pistons D' had a lot to do with it.

He also said some interesting things. First, he said that the Pistons play the best team defense in the league. Second, he said that both the Lakers and Pistons would be playing their best ball by February. Both have had adjustments to make early in the season.

Magic also said that he understands why the Pistons did not select Carmelo Anthony in the draft. It's because of Tayshaun. He can do so many things well and defends at such a high level, whereas Carmelo does not.

PISTONS 87 HEAT 73

(HOME, Wednesday, December 3rd)

Part 3 of the defensive lock-down series.

—Elden was attending his grandmother's funeral. Memo started in his place

—9 1st Q fast break pts for the Pistons; a very high number

—Memo had 11 pts, 5 rebs, and 3 blks in the 1st Q and was everywhere. Coach Brown hated how he started settling for jumpers in the 2nd Q, though.

—The Pistons were 14-17 on FTs in the 1st Q

—Their lead of 32-18 after 1 Q, gave them control of the game pretty much throughout

—Tayshaun threw a lay-up attempt by the Heat into the stands in the 3rd Q

—The Pistons were blocking everything and had 14 blocks for the game! Ben, of course, had 6 himself.

—Miami had the energy and momentum going in the last part of the 3rd Q and cut into the lead

—The 1st part of the 4th Q had nothing going right for the Pistons. Then they restored order and put this one away.

—Ben had 20 rebs and 3 Pistons had double-doubles: Ben, Tayshaun, and Memo

ROCKETS 86 PISTONS 80

(AWAY, Saturday, December 6th)

—The Pistons were giving up a lot of dunks and lay-ups and off. rebs in the 2nd Q

—Maurice Taylor was hitting a lot early for them

—Pistons were kinda sloppy with the ball in the 2nd Q

—Memo had his own scoring run in the 3rd Q, shooting, scoring inside, and sticking a triple

—Down 14 pts going into the 4th Q, the game was getting out of control

—Memo was good all night

—Yao Ming had 20 pts and 20 rebs

—The Rockets had 44 pts in the paint: <u>not good</u>

76ERS 78 PISTONS 76

(HOME, Tuesday, December 9th)

This game featured both great defense and poor Pistons' offense. With Allen Iverson and Glenn Robinson out with injury, it's really not acceptable that our guys didn't just go out there and jump on this team early and knock them out.

—Tayshaun blocked (and saved) a fast-break lay-up in an amazing sequence in the 2nd Q

—The Pistons had 7 blks in the 1st Q and 14 for the game. <u>That's a heckuva lot.</u>

—Samuel Dalembert even got blocked twice in a row by first Ben, and then Elden; Tayshaun blocked a Kyle Korver triple attempt and he got Aaron Mckie on the break

—It was odd that not many fouls were called, even though it was such a defensive battle. Normally big defense means a lot of physical contact, and thus fouls.

—A lot of Pistons shots rolled off the rim and out

—Chauncey hit for 5 triples

—McKie was just solid on offense for them throughout

—Though a close game right down to the wire, a bad sequence of events ended the contest: McKie made a shot after the shot-clock expired that was ruled good, then Eric Snow hit a jumper just before the shot-clock. Then Rip stole the ball out front from Snow for a key lay-up. But, the Pistons missed the last shot of the game and it was over.

—Chauncey was the only guy to consistently score for the Stones, with 29 pts

This was a fun game if you like defense, but the Pistons offense isn't flowing at all the way Larry Brown has designed it. They're too impatient and some players go off on their own for offense too much.

CAVS 95 PISTONS 86

(AWAY, Thursday, December 11th)

The Cavs had lost 9 of 10 coming into this game. It definitely seems different to see the stands full in Cleveland. Normally they would draw about 25 people per home game. Due exclusively to the Lebron influence, the place is constantly packed now.

—The Pistons seem to be over-thinking each possession on offense

—The game was close at the half, but the Pistons were really not playing well

—Lebron James had 16 pts at the half, while Rip had 14 pts

—With only 15 pts in the 3rd Q, the Piston offense began to really go into the tank

—In fact, they went something like 10 mins without a FG: **that's sick**

—I never realized before that Cleveland's court is raised off the ground (like the Minnesota Golden Gophers' in college)

—The Cavs shot 53% on FGs for the game: way too high

—They also got 46 points in the paint: that's ridiculous

—Lebron finished with 23 pts and 9 assts

—Carlos Boozer killed us with 28 pts on 11-16 FGs

SONICS 93 PISTONS 72

(HOME, Friday, December 12th)

This was by far the worst performance of the year. The Pistons played uninspired and just terrible on every level.

—Seattle really took control right out of the gate, opening up with a 15-6 lead and were at 25-15 after 1 Q

—Coach Tubby Smith and his Kentucky Wildcats were in the house. Their team was playing MSU at Ford Field the next day, and thus were in town. Tayshaun would return the favor, attending the Ford Field game to root on his alma mater, Kentucky.

—When both Rashard Lewis and Brent Barry score the way they did, with 16 and 13 pts respectively, you know you're probably not going to win.

—The Pistons, to their credit, were somewhat trying to do the right things on the basketball floor by being way more selective with their shot atts. than in recent games and looking to work the ball inside more than out on the perimeter. But they also began to press too hard out there.

—Rip was 1 for his first 10 on FGs

—Seattle had good spacing, passing, and execution all night

—As the Pistons went down 18 going into the 4th Q, the boo birds came out at The Palace, letting the team have it for their pitiful performance. Then as they continued to stink the place up in the 4th Q, boos rained down on them.

—Rashard Lewis finished with 33 pts

—Darko got in at the 3:30 mark of the 4th Q and scored his first ever NBA regular season basket. He posted big and went strong to his left hand for a jump-hook.

The Pistons offense has been so bad for so long (at least a couple of weeks) and the same problems happen every game, that it seems like they have an illness that just stays and lingers. And it affects everybody on the team. It's kind of like the current flu outbreak that is hurting so many communities throughout the country right now. For some unknown reason, they can't get out of this funk they're in.

PISTONS 77 BULLS 73

(HOME, Wednesday, December 17th)

A lineup change featured Memo starting in place of Elden Campbell. The Pistons have had 4 days off to practice and get things right, whereas the Bulls are in the 2nd night of a back-to-back.

—Eddie Curry, Tyson Chandler, and Scottie Pippen were out for the Bulls with injury

—Ben had 5 blks in the 1st H

—Chicago was 9-40 on FGs and 0-10 on triples in 1st H: just terrible

—The Pistons led 35-25 at half. What kind of a score is that?

—In the 3rd Q, Ben had a 1-handed alley-oop slam! You don't see that too often!

—Also in the 3rd Q, Tayshaun blocked a Gill lay-up attempt on the break

—Amazingly, the Pistons gave a half-assed effort in the first half of the

4th Q

—This helped contribute to the Pistons losing the 16 point lead they had earlier in the 2nd H

—Then, they made a couple of plays and won the game

—Ben blocked a Jerome Williams shot from at the rim all the way to half-court with 2 mins. left in the game

PACERS 80 PISTONS 75

(AWAY, Friday, December 19th)

This game featured the only 2 teams in the league who have not yet given up 100 pts in a game this year. The Pistons played great for 3 Q's, then just caved in.

—Ben had a major power post move and dunk in the 1st Q

—The bench was big in the 2nd Q and had 21 pts in the 1st H

—The Pistons gave up a ton of off. rebs all night

—Up 44-33 at the half, the Pistons looked like they were in control; they were even shooting 59% from the field at that point.

—Kenny Anderson missed the 2nd H with injury

—O'Neal got his stuff blocked by all 3 of our centers over the course of this game and Ben got him 3 times by himself!

—The Pistons went to a 2-3 zone that frustrated Indiana all night

—There were a lot of Pistons fans who made the trip to Indy for this game

—Bad shots and no defensive rebounds led to the Pistons demise in the 4th Q. It was a basic collapse.

—The Pistons gave up a lot of 4th Q pts after not giving up much all night

PISTONS 96 JAZZ 75

(HOME, Sunday, December 21st)

In this game, the Pistons finally got their offense going. It was a sight for sore eyes, let me tell you. The half-court offense was efficient, the fast-break was performing at a high level, and Chucky was superb.

—Excellent start for the whole team, everyone playing with a lot of energy

—Chauncey was hot in the 1st H, scoring from <u>everywhere</u> and finishing with 17 pts in the half

—In the spirit of the season, Automotion Dancers were wearing Santa hats

—The Pistons fast-break offense is much better and more active tonight

—Chucky had 19 pts in 25 mins on 7-10 FGs and 3-5 on triples. Now that's stroking it!

—Tayshaun Prince was 7-9 on FGs

—The Stones shot over 54% for the game, a very good number for them

—Darko got called for a lot of fouls in the time he was in there

—When he went off on his own and broke a play, Coach Brown pulled him out, sat him in the chair right next to him, made a point to him, then put him right back in the game

—Darko then scored out of the post and got a 3-pt play. It was a quick move.

BUCKS 83 PISTONS 78

(AWAY, Tuesday, December 23rd)

—Corliss was attending a family matter and thus not at the game

—The Pistons had a lot of off. rebs in the 1st H (especially Memo)

—The Pistons can't make any shots; they had 31 pts at the half

—Ben blocked a Joe Smith jumpshot in the 3rd Q

—Ben had a missed dunk in the 3rd Q, where the force was so hard that he just completely rocked the rim

—Behind the whole night, the Pistons cut it to 4 with about a minute to go

—This was just an **ugly, poor performance** by the Pistons

—After the game was already decided, Ben actually hit a triple! He shot it like a guard.

NETS 82 PISTONS 79
(HOME, Friday, December 26th)

—The first 3 mins. of this game were odd: both teams went 0-5 on FGs

—Memo had 2 excellent blocks early; both on Kenyon Martin dunk attempts. One was a 1-handed attempt and the other was a 2-handed attempt. That's great when you block a guy's 2-handed dunk!

—Down 22-12 going into the 2nd Q, the off. looked like it was in disarray

—Both Dave Bing and Kid Rock were in attendance

—The Pistons had 0 FT atts in the 1st H. You're just not going to win if you don't play aggressive and get to the line.

—Down 34-27 going into the half, things were not looking good

The 2nd H was totally different than the 1st, as the Pistons came out and played very aggressive and with good energy. Good D' led to fast-break offense, and 31 pts in the 3rd Q. The aggression led to 12 FT atts in the 3rd Q.

The Pistons led 58-54 going into the 4th Q.

—Tight right down to the end, this game ended when Chauncey missed 2 triples that could have tied it

—Jason Kidd had a triple-double and Ben had 18 rebs

PISTONS 87 HAWKS 84

(AWAY, Saturday, December 27th)

—The Hawks wore lime-green retro jerseys to pay homage to the '70–'72 seasons. This is definitely a 1970's color! The players also had their names listed at the bottom of the jerseys instead of the top.

—This was an actual Hawks sell-out, which is very rare and was possibly induced by it being holiday time. Normally they draw about 38 fans to their home games.

—The Pistons had good effort, energy, aggression, and played good defense in the 1st H

—The offense also featured good balanced scoring and produced 55 1st H pts

—It was a Bobby Sura kind of 2nd Q: he was scoring from everywhere and had 12 pts in the 1st H

—In the 3rd Q, the Pistons just couldn't make shots; they were forced into mainly perimeter shots by the Hawks defense; with 9 pts for the quarter, it allowed Atlanta to go on a 20-4 run and take a 3 pt lead into the 4th Q

—Weird scene: Bobby Sura had Jason Terry all over him and couldn't do anything with the ball. He thought he was fouled, so he called a timeout, to both save the possession and make a point that he was being fouled throughout the possession.

—Rip had great, big-time shooting in the 2nd H; he scored 14 pts in the 4th Q alone and 28 pts for the game

—In the stretch run, Ben also blocked a Shareef Abdur-Rahim dunk attempt from behind! Just a great play!

—Chauncey & Rip combined for 11 guard rebs: a very good number

PISTONS 108 HORNETS 99
(HOME, Monday, December 29th)

With this game, the Pistons tied the record for most consecutive games holding opponents under 100 pts. Since the inception of the shot clock, only one other team has done this 33 times in a row as the Pistons now have, dating back to last season.

—Ben had 7 rebs in 10 1st Q mins

—The Pistons had a 29-11 run to close out the 1st Q and led 31-21

—Memo had 12 pts in 9 1st Q mins

—Bob Sura blocked a Stacey Augmon jump-shot in the 2nd Q

—Augmon, a non-offensive player, had 12 pts in the 1st H

—Chauncey had 17 pts in the 1st H and 31 pts for the game

—The Pistons shot 55% on FGs for the game: a very good number for them

—The Pistons had a very good quarter with 29 pts in the 3rd Q and led 83-71 going into the 4th Q

—Then, they inexplicably showed the worst ball-handling and passing ever which meant a 14-2 Hornets run to tie it in the first 3.5 mins of the 4th Q

—Finally they settled down and took care of business and the Hornets

PISTONS 78 BLAZERS 71

(HOME, Wednesday, December 31st)

This was a rare occurrence, as the Pistons played on New Year's Eve. It was only like their 4th game on New Year's in their history. Luckily, it was a victory!

—This was a close game all night

—Rasheed Wallace was raining in 3's in the 3rd Q for the Blazers

—Rip & Zach Randolph really struggled shooting the ball all night. Rip stayed aggressive in the 4th Q though, and helped pace the team to victory.

—Ben was clearly in Randolph's head, blocking his shots and making him shy away from being aggressive. He finished 8-24 on FGs.

—The Blazers were held to 40% on FGs for the game

—Their were so many ties and lead changes all night (over 30)

—In the 3rd Q, Ben soared up & over Ruben Patterson on the break for an awesome dunk

—Corliss had a double—double: 12 pts and 10 rebs

—Good Piston D' and just making plays in the 4th Q completed this Piston win

4

January

01/01/04—Happy New Year!

Going 3-1 this week and playing a very good 2nd H in the one game they lost, the Pistons are finally playing better again. It's nice to see a return to aggressive play and more of a "lock-down" attitude on defense.

Speaking of defense, the Pistons set an NBA record this week by holding their 34th straight opponent to under 100 pts, dating back to last season. Since the shot-clock was added to NBA games, this is the top streak of under 100 pts for any team. No wonder Magic Johnson is impressed with the Pistons team D'.

◆ ◆ ◆

With the holidays in full swing, Dr. Fever has been out of his office for much of this week, but I did come in for a few hours one day to complete some paperwork. It's a good thing too.

Sitting in the waiting room was a long-time Pistons fan who seemed to be fairly stressed out. When asked what exactly it was that was stressing him out, he said that the typical holiday pressures were getting to him and the fact that Larry Brown and Mehmet Okur seem to be developing a combustible relationship is worrying him tremendously.

As you may be aware, there have been 2 occasions already this year (and one last week) where Brown stressed getting the ball inside and not settling for jump-shots during a time-out or at half-time, and Memo promptly goes out and shoots one anyway. Then he gets pulled. This means Brown is frustrated and Memo is frustrated.

ASK DR. FEVER

Patient: Dr. Fever, why is Memo at times defying Larry Brown? There are some games where it doesn't even seem like he's shooting that many jumpers early in the game, and then he just shoots up a triple right when Brown told him not to.

Dr. Fever: It's unclear why Memo is defying Coach Brown. Being a great outside shooter for much of his professional career, including over in Europe, it is understandable that Memo would naturally fall back to that part of his game.

Brown is trying to get our players to understand that a deep perimeter shot should normally only come after the interior has been explored. Post-up, drive, work for a better shot first, then shoot the jumper.

For a young player like Memo, it may be a little more difficult to get that point across.

Patient: Well, if he keeps getting pulled out of games, he's bound to get the point eventually. Is some of this Brown's fault though? He's known to really press some players' buttons and at times alienate them. As a young guy, can't we cut Memo some slack?

Dr. Fever: It is true that Brown has alienated some players over the years and has even exposed their faults publicly to media personnel. Last year, while coaching the Sixers, he exposed the weaknesses in Keith Van Horn's game during the playoffs. This made Van Horn get motivated and he played better in the short-term. Then he reverted back to his old ways (which are that of a weak player). In Van Horn's case, he's never going to get better because he doesn't have the inner fortitude to become a truly strong impact player.

For Memo, I think Brown sees a kid with a world of potential. He has so many skills and tools that he can use. He could become a real prime-time player in our league. Remember the vision of him stroking big-time jumpers in the 4th quarter of a couple of playoff games last year? He plays well in the clutch, is the second best rebounder on the team, and has shown flexibility in scoring off the drive, in the post, and from the perimeter.

Part of this is that Brown wants to make sure that Memo develops all these other parts of his game further so that he doesn't just become another big man shooting jumpers (like Terry Mills).

Patient: With Memo becoming a restricted free agent this summer, are the Pistons running a real risk of losing him to another team? What if he says, "Forget Brown; I can go elsewhere."

Dr. Fever: It could happen, but right now it's too early to tell. Maybe we'll see a case where Memo plays a big 2nd half in a key playoff victory in the spring, doing the exact things that Brown has harped on all along and everybody is smiling and everybody moves forward in a positive manner.

With Memo playing so far away from home and his family living in a hotbed of violent unrest (the suicide bomb that went off in Turkey a few weeks back was within 10 miles of where his family lives) may have him behaving unlike himself.

Patient: Is it possible that Brown could have some similar issues with Chauncey Billups before this is all said and done? Chauncey seems to shoot a lot of ill-advised jumpers.

Dr. Fever: It is very possible. Brown is known to be very difficult on point guards, mainly because he was one himself. He knows what he wants out of that position.

Brown is a perfectionist. He knows how he wants things done.

This can push some players to greatness and others, like Van Horn, will never meet his expectations.

Evaluation Point

The Pistons recently passed the one-third point of the season. Those of you who were subscribers with us last year remember the reports that were developed after each third of the season was complete.

These reports were designed to evaluate the team on what it's achieved so far and what areas are potential for improvement.

At Pistonsfever.com, we feel that NBA seasons and teams are best evaluated in thirds. This is because halves are too long and only allow for a broad interpretation of team performance and quarters are just too short for consistent trends to emerge.

Right now, in a nutshell, the Pistons are still an evolving work in progress. A group with new players, some of the same players in new roles, and a new system from a new coach, have made this first third of the season into a transitional one.

The progress hasn't always developed as fast as it should. The team and the organization do deserve a lot of credit, however, for attempting to do something difficult: go from becoming a good team to a great team. A great team is one that competes for NBA championships year in and year out. Some of the challenges this team has encountered thus far this year are a result of the growing pains of development that is necessary when trying to reach greatness.

Right now this team is very good defensively and needs a lot of improvement on offense.

This report was prepared prior to the January 3rd game vs. the Golden State Warriors, so the statistics and trends mentioned here are not inclusive of that game.

The links from NBA.com for all the statistical information mentioned here, as well as much that was not mentioned, are available at the very end of this report, under "Appendix."

THE 1/3 REPORT

The Pistons, at the point of this analysis are 20-13, 3.5 games behind Indiana for the top spot in the Eastern Conference. Last year at this time, they were 23-10.

This year, they have had a winning streak of 5 games and three 4-game winning streaks. They've had two bad losing streaks: one of 4 games and one of 3 games. Many of their wins have come against weak teams, though they did beat the powerful Lakers.

The Pistons have a pretty large target on their back this year as a result of getting to the Eastern Conference Finals last year. Everybody wants to beat them and thus, they get everyone's best game and effort.

THE PLAYERS

Here we discuss only certain key players. Some don't really require comment. For example, Lindsey Hunter hasn't played enough to discuss his contribution. Zeljko Rebraca is playing the same as he always had.

There has been talk that the Pistons miss Jon Barry, Michael Curry, and Clifford Robinson from last year's team. On some levels (most notably Curry and Robinson's defense) this is true. That will happen anytime you replace 2 starters and 3 key contributors to a successful team and replace them with players that have different strengths and weaknesses.

As the current group of players continues to develop, they should be able to more than compensate for the 3 that are no longer here.

Chauncey Billups & Richard Hamilton

These 2 are both the straw that stirs the drink and the ice that keeps it cold. The Pistons' offensive success is directly tied to how these 2 guys perform. Normally if at least one of them scores at least 20 pts, the team wins.

Chauncey's shooting has been up & down as he's been transitioning to Coach Larry Brown's system and learning when to go for his own offense and when to set up others. He seems to be really coming on in the past few games now.

Rip is just being Rip. Scoring consistently and shooting the ball well. Imagine what will happen for him as the team gets more of the offense down and fast-break opportunities increase!

These 2 average over 37 ppg combined, putting them right near the top of the list of NBA guard tandems. And as Rip has pointed out on many occasions, he believes that they are <u>the best</u> backcourt in the NBA.

Ben Wallace

While we're on the subject of offense, it's interesting to see that Ben is averaging almost 10 ppg. If he would average 10-12 ppg for the season, the Pistons' offense would be so much more effective.

He is only shooting 40% on FGs, which is terrible for a big man, but in watching him game in and game out, there is definitely a marked level of improvement this year when compared to the past. He has post moves he can go to now. He's shown a higher comfort level in driving the ball, making a move & faking, and shooting from outside. He even made a triple recently. Ben's FT % is up 10% over last year, meaning he now makes 55% from the line (which is higher than Shaquille O'Neal).

A key issue in the development of Ben as a true, big-time player is that of becoming a leader. He recognizes this, as he recently said that he needs to be the one to make the players more accountable to playing with the right effort and doing what is expected of them.

Chauncey is the more natural leader and probably does more of the daily leadership duties, but Ben can be effective too. Recall last year's playoffs when the Pistons went down 3 games to 1 to the Orlando Magic and Ben called out his teammates for their lack of effort. The Pistons went on and demolished the Magic in three straight games.

When Ben speaks the rest of the team will listen.

Mehmet Okur

Of all the frontline players not named Darko Milicic, Memo has the most diverse and dynamic set of skills. There's really not much that he can't do or can't develop as part of his game. He can shoot it, pass it, drive it, post it up, block it, and rebound it. In fact, he's averaging almost 7 rebs per game, while only playing 23 mins. That's impressive.

Add to that over 9 ppg from a variety of angles on the floor and Memo is only scratching the surface of what he can become. He and Coach Brown have had their moments so far this year. If Memo can keep his emotions under control and just keep working to get better, he's going to be real good.

He also needs to continue to get bigger in the upper body area (probably won't happen till the off-season) and learn how to protect the ball inside. He has the ball knocked away from him too often.

Tayshaun Prince

He's done a relatively good job transitioning from not playing much at all during the regular season last year to becoming a starter and playing over 35 mins per game this year. Tayshaun is averaging over 10 ppg without really commanding the ball or forcing activity. Defensively, he's done a good job replacing Michael Curry at his position.

As the season goes along, Tayshaun will probably see more time at point-forward. This will allow the offense to become more dynamic in its attack, give the opponents' defense another look to have to defend against, and allow Chauncey to run off screens and become a scorer.

This ability to play multiple positions speaks to Tayshaun's versatility. If Memo has the most diverse skills on the frontline, Tayshaun is the most diverse player on the entire team. The one thing that he really needs to work on is being more aggressive on offense. The guy can score out of the post, off the drive, on the perimeter, and needs to go after it. You can only defer to the veterans so much.

Darko Milicic

There is no way to evaluate Darko based on his play in games, because he has had no consistent playing time. Big men are a different type of player and always take longer to develop than perimeter players do. There hasn't been an 18 year-old big man, not named Kevin Garnett, that has made a real impact in their first NBA season in recent NBA history.

Those that are around Darko in practice and the physical training sessions the players go through, say he has improved significantly since he first got here. He's much stronger and is more ready to do battle in the NBA than he first was.

Darko is the Pistons' hope for the future, a guy that they feel will be able to dominate several phases of the game in due time.

For the rest of this season what he needs to do is keep working very hard and taking time to learn from the veterans. Ben can teach him so much about defense and rebounding; Elden Campbell about post moves; and Memo about being patient in waiting for your opportunity, especially coming over from a foreign country.

Also, he needs to stop acting offended when put in the game at garbage time. He's winning 0 points with Coach Brown when he does that and whether Darko likes the decisions or not, Larry's the boss.

Elden Campbell and Bob Sura

Both of these players haven't played at the same level that they have throughout their NBA careers with other teams. Sura still plays the same tough defense and makes a lot of activity happen from several areas of the court on offense (including his patented draw & dish move), but his jump-shot has left him. He used to shoot a real flat shot that was effective, even out to 3-pt range. This year, both he and the coaching staff desired to change his shooting stroke to one with better mechanics and he did so in training camp. Unfortunately, his new stroke has provided him with little success.

Elden's game is in the post. A good defender down there, he also has excellent court savvy moves down low. For whatever reason—always being in foul trouble; lack of conditioning; the team struggling to find offensive cohesion and balance (which includes using your post players wisely); he has not been the type of force down low that the Pistons need and that he was in the past.

THE TEAM AS A WHOLE

Shown below are the Pistons' rankings in a few key statistical categories:

Defense

Pts:	4th,	85.3 pg
FG%	6th,	42.4%
Opp. 3-pt%	1st,	26.2%
Assists:	5th,	19.9 pg
Steals:	15th,	7.5 pg
Blocks:	5th,	6.7 pg

Analysis: The Pistons remain one of the best defensive teams in the league. Their points allowed and FG% against are low. Their defense against the 3-pt shot and limiting opponents assists show that they are very good at taking an opponent out of what that opponent wants to do. They keep teams from getting into a strong offensive flow and from playing to their strengths.

They also now hold the single season record for keeping teams under 100 pts. Despite all of this, Coach Brown and the team believe that they can actually play even better on defense, particularly on breakdowns off of penetration and occasional double-teams.

Once they shore up these areas, they are going to be very dominating on the defensive end of the floor.

Rebounding

Total rebs.	14th,	42.7 pg
Opp. rebs.	7th,	41.0 pg

Analysis: The Pistons are out-rebounding their opponent which is what you want. This has been an area of improvement over last year: they finished -0.7 in 2003 and are now +1.7 in rebs per game. That's almost 2.5 rebs per game more than last year (vs. their opponent), which means 2.5 more possessions they have to score and that the other team does not. This is very good.

It's due to several factors: Elden's inside presence and Memo (who's been great on the glass) playing more, and Coach Brown's insistence on the team having all 5 players commit to the defensive boards and 3 to the offensive boards on every possession. Now, we have guys like Tayshaun and Rip going to the glass in areas where they would not have before.

Offense

Pts:	25th, 88.5 pg
FG%:	24th, 42.3%
3-pt%:	21st, 33.0%
FT%:	7th, 77.0%
Assists:	26th, 18.9 pg
Turnovers:	19th, 15.5 pg

Analysis: A lot of work is needed here. With 2 new starters and an unsettled rotation, it's taken awhile for cohesion and consistency to develop. Finding the proper balance inside and out and defining new roles has also played a part.

This has also been an area that Coach Brown has completely re-done over last year. Under Rick Carlisle, the Pistons' offense was designed to play to the strengths of individual players. If a player was a great 3-pt shooter, he'd get a lot of those types of shots. If he liked it on the block in certain situations, he'd get those shots. As each individual flourished, so too would the entire offense.

Brown's system is designed with a philosophy predicated on team offense. Everyone helping each other to score. Brown always talks about playing the right way. What he means is to work the ball inside first, before going to a perimeter jumpshot. Share the ball, get a high-percentage shot, and get to the foul line. The Pistons are actually averaging only about half as many 3-pt attempts as last year, showing this type of commitment.

Rather than simply playing to individuals' strengths, he wants the team's offensive weapons to develop multiple parts of their game so that they can become true players: guys who can make plays in a variety of situations. This way the team will have less "specialists" and more true basketball "players." Players make plays.

A successful implementation of this offense should mean that the Pistons will become a more difficult team to defend than before and have a more dynamic attack.

There are still several aspects of the offense that haven't even been installed yet and Coach Brown is still learning his personnel: what each one's tendencies are and how they can be most successful on the floor. One thing he needs to do is feature Tayshaun more so that he can maximize the offensive potential of his various offensive skills.

Season Splits

The Pistons are 12-5 at home and 8-8 on the road. That's fairly typical and expected.

In their wins, the Pistons are slightly better in many categories than when they lose, which is also to be expected. Interestingly, they shoot 4% better on FG attempts and 6.5% better on three-point attempts. They average an amazing 11.1 more points per game when they win!

This basically proves what most of us who watch the team regularly already knew: when they score they win. The defense is fairly consistent.

CONCLUSION

The Pistons are a work in progress. This was to be expected with personnel changes and coaching changes.

As much as Jon Barry, Michael Curry, and Cliff Robinson might be missed now, it is safe to say that they will not be missed in a year or two. They're all getting older and the moves to replace them were very pro-active in nature.

The personnel and coaching changes as well as the different style of play are designed to help the Pistons in the long-run better compete for a championship.

The players have been slow to adapt to many of these changes this year. However, in the last handful of games it appears that many things are coming together and the team is playing much better. The key will be to continue to define roles, develop Tayshaun, Memo, and Darko, and become a consistently potent offense.

APPENDIX

From NBA.com, the following links were accessed when analyzing statistical data:

Team rankings and stats:
http://www.nba.com/statistics/sortable_team_statistics/00002.html

Team splits: http://www.nba.com/pistons//stats/team_splits.html

NBA standings: http://www.nba.com/standings/by_division.html

Pistons' player stats: http://www.nba.com/pistons/stats/

01/10/04—Wins, wins, and more wins!

It's been a great week as the Pistons went 4-0! They have now won 7 straight games, their best streak since the 1991–92 season. In addition, they've held all 36 opponents this year under 100 pts—an NBA record.

The Pistons are 23-13, 4 games behind Indiana in the standings.

The Pistons are playing better now for 3 simple reasons: their team defense has cleaned up a few key areas (like keeping perimeter players out of the lane and better help-side defense), the team offense is flowing better and in a much smoother pattern than before, and individual players are playing much better (in fact Ben Wallace was named Eastern Conference Player Of The Week last week).

The guys are not only getting Larry Brown's system down better now, but they are also learning how to use it successfully.

◆ ◆ ◆

A Pistons fan recently caught up with Dr. Fever on the street. I had just taken a shower, so my hair was still slightly damp. As cold as it's been this week, I've been lamenting (and cursing) the fact that I lost my blue and red winter hat.

With the wind ripping through us, we only had a chance to discuss one topic. So, we talked about how former Piston-legend Isiah Thomas recently took over the New York Knicks.

ASK DR. FEVER

Dr. Fever: Isiah taking over the Knicks is interesting. It's seems a little odd that he would take over a front office position after he recently said that he wanted badly to get back into coaching. But it only seems that way if you don't know Isiah.

Isiah is a competitive, focused, and restless soul. He's always been that way ever since he was a young boy growing up on the tough west side of Chicago. There, he had to fight every day to survive. As a player in the NBA it was no different. He was a small player in a land of giants. To this day he is the only guy his size to ever lead his team to the NBA championship.

So, Isiah cannot rest, especially for the game that he loves. His last stint in the player personnel business was with Toronto. The reviews are mixed on the job that he did there. Some people say he left the team a mess. Others point to how he had the vision to draft future stars like Damon Stoudamire and Tracy McGrady.

Certainly how he does in New York could very well define his legacy as a team-builder. In New York the pressure is very intense. If he makes mistakes, both the regular media and the tabloids will be all over it. However, he could bring on a massive amount of support if he turns that franchise around.

One thing's for sure: he's got a significant juggling act on his hands. The Knicks' owner is not particularly liked by many of his players who see him as more of a corporate guy and not a basketball guy. Isiah could get caught between these two factions.

The trade for Stephon Marbury was huge. Huge in 3 ways: the basketball sense, the excitement it brings to New York fans, and in terms of dollars and cents. From a basketball sense, he's one of the best point guards in the NBA. For that matter, him and Allan Houston now make such a powerful backcourt duo that they can challenge Richard Hamilton's and Chauncey Billups' assertion that they are the best backcourt tandem in the league.

Being that New York is Marbury's home town, it makes everyone over there excited. However, both he and Penny Hardaway, who was also brought over in the trade, have very large contracts. Add this to an already enormous payroll and Isiah is going to have a huge challenge on his hands when it comes to cap flexibility relative to other personnel changes.

But, only time will tell how this plays out. Well, if you'll excuse me I've got to be going. This cold air is causing icicles to form in my hair.

01/18/04—A Beautiful Winning Streak

The Pistons are quite simply, on a roll. They got 5 more wins this week and have now won 12 straight games. They are now one victory away from their franchise record.

This is also Larry Brown's best-ever winning streak as a coach in the NBA. That's quite remarkable considering that he's won over 900 games!

This week featured several interesting happenings in the world of Pistons basketball. Ben Wallace was ejected from a game against Toronto, weather delayed the start of that same game, and the Pistons won their 12th straight by beating a Milwaukee team that had won 10 straight at home.

All of these things are chronicled in the game notes below. In fact, the game in Milwaukee was attended by some Pistonsfever.com subscribers and yours truly. We give an interesting review of the Bradley Center and its' fans in the game notes.

Unfortunately there is no "Ask Dr. Fever" feature this week. Dr. Fever's flight back from Milwaukee (via Chicago) didn't get in till late on Sunday. We apologize for any inconvenience this may have caused.

01/25/04—3 Games Against 3 of the NBA's Best

This week the Pistons played the Spurs, Pacers, and T-Wolves, meaning they played some of the best competition that the NBA has to offer. After beating the defending champion Spurs, they lost the next 2, halting their winning streak at 13.

This tied their franchise record. To put this all in perspective, consider this: the last time the team won 13 straight, it was the 1989–90 season. After the streak was snapped that year with one loss, they then went on to win 12 more in a row. That means that they had a stretch in which they were 25-1, which at the time was the second greatest stretch of any team in the history of the NBA. The only team to do better was the Lakers of Jerry West and Wilt Chamberlain when they won 33 straight back in the day.

The '89–'90 team won the NBA championship that year, their second in a row. This team is not quite at that level yet, but the streak is still a nice accomplishment nonetheless.

◆ ◆ ◆

Right now the Pistons are 29-15, 3 games behind Indiana for the top spot in the East.

◆ ◆ ◆

The Pistons this week waived guard Hubert Davis. Hubert ranks as the second best 3-pt shooter in the history of the NBA. That's pretty good!

There simply was no role for Hubert here for the last 2 years. He was brought here with Rip Hamilton in the Jerry Stackhouse trade. With guards Lindsey Hunter, Bob Sura, and Chucky Atkins on the Pistons' bench, there was just no room for Hubert. He requested to be released so that he'd have a chance to latch on with another team before people around the league completely forgot about him.

◆ ◆ ◆

This week, Chris McCosky of the Detroit News wrote a great story about the toll that playing for Team USA has on NBA players. Injuries and affected performance levels are the result more often than not. Make sure you check it out!

◆ ◆ ◆

Dr. Fever recently met a man named Chuck, who is very frustrated over the Pistons' inability to beat the Pacers.

ASK DR. FEVER

Chuck: Dr. Fever I was so upset when the Pistons lost to Indy this week! The win could have meant a team record! Plus, we've now lost all 3 games to the Pacers this year. Why can't we beat this team?

Dr. Fever: Well, keep in mind that the other two losses were by 2 points and 5 points. So they were close games and the Pistons were right there. In Tuesday's game they were playing their 6th game in 8 nights which showed in the 2nd H.

Shots were falling off the rim the way that they do when a team is fatigued and playing with tired legs.

Having said that, they shouldn't just allow Indiana to dictate the style and physicality of the game the way they did on Tuesday. Some of the local media has pointed out that it is in these areas that the Pistons miss Michael Curry and Cliff Robinson. Those guys set a tone defensively and physically against the Pacers. Now our team is trying to counteract the likes of bruising Ron Artest and extremely talented Jermaine O'Neal, with Tayshaun Prince and Mehmet Okur, two guys who didn't play a lot last year.

Chuck: Are the Pacers just gonna kill us in the playoffs this year? They seem to have our number, plus Rick Carlisle knows the Piston players' strengths and weaknesses inside and out.

Dr. Fever: I doubt it. If the Pistons and Pacers meet in a 7-game playoff series, especially if it's in the Eastern Conference Finals, it'll be a battle and a war. These are the 2 deepest and most-talented teams in the East.

Keep in mind that neither Rip nor Chauncey has yet had a decent game against the Pacers. Once they do, then the Pistons will find the going a lot easier against them.

Also, don't put too much stock into regular season head to head battles. In many cases, it has nothing to do with what happens when those same teams meet in the playoffs. Remember the '97 season?

The Pistons had just come off a 54-win regular season and had handled the Atlanta Hawks, winning 3 out of the 4 times they met that year. When they drew the Hawks in the first round of the playoffs, many people said the Pistons should have no problem with them. After all, look at how easily they handled them in the regular season.

So, then the Hawks beat them 3-2 in the playoffs.

The moral is that the playoffs are completely different than the regular season. It probably doesn't matter that the Pistons are 0-3 vs. the Pacers this year anymore than it would if they were 3-0 against them.

The only real bad thing about this is that Indy is improving their positioning for the playoffs and now own the tiebreaker in case the Pistons tie them in overall record. That will hurt if they play each other in the playoffs and the Pacers have the home-court advantage.

THE GAMES OF JANUARY

Warriors: This game featured Larry Brown achieving a career milestone and a bizarre occurrence involving an ejection that was later reversed.

Rockets: Darko Milicic causes a sensation.

Raptors (first game): This one had it all: referees stuck in a snow storm, an ejection for Ben Wallace, and a fan wearing one of the best T-shirts ever.

Bucks: This was one of the best regular season games of the year.

Spurs: A team record was achieved vs. San Antonio and Dr. Ben Paolucci had a great time.

T-Wolves: Ben Wallace's amazing defense against Kevin Garnett and a bad call that Pistons fans will remember for a long time were highlights of the game with Minnesota.

Raptors (second game): Here was more great defense by Ben Wallace in an overtime win.

PISTONS 93 SUNS 81

(HOME, Friday, January 2nd)

—Amare Stoudemire was out with injury

—There was a fan that was sporting one of the largest 'fros I've ever seen. It was a fake one worn by a white guy. It was like a small tree! His belly was equally large and said "Pistons" across it.

—Great play: Chucky & Stephon Marbury were going for a jump-ball. Chucky didn't even jump, so Stephon taps it out and Chucky sprints after it, tracks it down, and gets a lay-up on the break!

—The Pistons had 17 assts in the 1st H

—It was a Penny Hardaway kind of game. He was making all those mid-range jumpers he likes.

—Corliss had to leave the game in the 1st H with back spasms

—Ben had 22 rebs

—The Pistons as a team had 21 off. rebs.

—Just a good, solid win by the Pistons!

PISTONS 99 WARRIORS 93

(HOME, Saturday, January 3rd)

This was Larry Brown's 900th career victory. However, he would not be around to see the end of it.

—Memo blocked an Erick Dampier dunk in the 1st Q

—Brian Cardinal made a 3/4—court shot to end the 1st Q

—Corliss was out with back spasms; Calbert Cheaney was also out for them with the flu

—Weird play: Cliff Robinson took the ball out of the basket after a Piston FT and threw it in. The only problem was that he wasn't out of bounds when he threw it! After a few seconds of Golden State dribbling, the refs caught it and ruled a violation.

—Tayshaun had 14 pts in the 1st H, while Brian Cardinal had 11 and Cliff Robinson had 10

—Jason Richardson is amazing in the open floor and off the drive. That's what made 2 Piston defensive plays so exciting: Tayshaun caught his lay-up on the break and Darvin Ham blocked his reverse dunk attempt. That first one is true: he actually caught the shot. That is very rare.

In the 3rd Q, Rip was called for a debatable foul. Rip then argued the call and got a technical foul. According to the Detroit Free Press the next day, the ref told Rip that he couldn't talk to him unless he was the team captain. (What??!!)

This made Larry Brown crazy. He voiced his displeasure about how his player was talked to and got a technical of his own. One ref mistakenly thought it was his second technical and ejected him. Larry also had punched the ball out of one ref's hand and stormed all over the court.

As The Palace crowd was rocking, Larry left the court. After the officials realized their mistake and that Larry only had 1 technical, he was summoned back to the floor. He said thanks, but no thanks.

So, Assistant Coach Mike Woodson took over the team.

—The Pistons had what appeared to be a safe, good lead in the 4th Q. Then a furious Golden State rally saw them take the lead away. A big Darvin Ham three-point play and some made FTs gave the Pistons back the lead and the victory.

—Tayshaun had 20 pts and shot over 50% on FGs for the game

PISTONS 78 CELTICS 68

(AWAY, Monday, January 5th)

—It was a sloppy and ugly start for both teams

—Darvin Ham had one of the most incredible reverse dunks you're ever going to see in the 2nd Q. It went down fast and with authority!

—Boston shot 29% on FGs for the game

—Elden Campbell was hot throughout: 13 pts & 5 rebs in 15 mins.

—Boston shot a tremendous number of triples: 34 for the game! If you take the Pistons' average number of 3-pt atts. per game, it would take them about 4 games to match the number of triples Boston took tonight.

—Oh by the way, Boston was 9-34 on triples for the game. That's repulsive.

—Still no Corliss

PISTONS 85 ROCKETS 66

(HOME, Wednesday, January 7th)

Houston led the league in FG% allowed coming into the game at 39%. But, the Pistons defense was even more impressive tonight.

—The Rockets went away from Yao Ming on offense for long stretches. Why is unclear.

—A 20-8 Pistons' run in the 2nd Q broke the game open

—The Pistons had a bunch of assts., showing good team basketball and passing

—The Pistons played fantastic D' all night, just locking down and limiting everything the Rockets tried to do

—With a huge 3rd Q, the Pistons blew the game wide open and gave the Pistons a 74-51 lead going into the 4th Q

—Rip hit his first 7 shots in a row

—The Rockets were held to 33% on FGs

With the crowd chanting his name, Darko entered the game at the 6-min. mark of the 4th Q. He then proceeded to block Clarence Weatherspoon's shot, got 2 dunks while battling inside, and scored out of the post on a baseline scoop. The baseline scoop was a total European move.

In a blowout game like this, it was kind of wild to see the crowd staying pretty much to the end and making all kinds of noise whenever Darko touched the ball. The bench was really fired up too. It's clear that his teammates really like the kid and are pulling for him.

Darko looked different today. He has dyed his hair completely blonde.

PISTONS 115 MAVERICKS 102

(HOME, Sunday, January 11th)

—This started the 1st of 7 games in 10 nights

—Dallas started Marquis Daniels in a typical Don Nelson mis-match ploy. Daniels, a non-drafted rookie, came through with 9 pts in the 1st Q being guarded by smaller point guards. He then did nothing the rest of the game.

—Ben was everywhere in the 1st Q, getting his hands on a lot of loose balls and rebs.

—Chucky had 4 triples in the 1st H to go along with 15 pts

—The Piston offense comes much easier against this Dallas "sieve-like" defense. They just aggressively attack it.

—The Pistons had a ton of 1st H off. rebs

—The Pistons had a huge 3rd Q with 35 pts and a huge 2nd H with 60 pts

—Chauncey hit 3 straight triples on 3 consecutive possessions in the 4th Q

—Chauncey finished with 27 pts and was 7-10 on triples!

—Darko got about 3 mins. of action and scored a hook shot

PISTONS 105 BULLS 89

(AWAY, Tuesday, January 13th)

—This game was the first of 3 sets of back to backs

—Rip was hot early, and played with a pep in his step, scoring 10 pts in the 1st Q

—Ben had 10 rebs in the 1st Q

—Ben had a great, aggressive move, driving the ball right at Eddy Curry and scoring over him in the 1st Q

—It was a Darvin Ham kind of 2nd Q: he was dunking, rebounding, out-leaping people

—Kirk Hinrich played a fantastic game for them all night

—Chucky hit 3 straight triples in the 4th Q

—Great play: in the 4th Q, Chucky threw a no-look alley-oop pass to Tayshaun on the break, where he soared, then dunked and drew a foul

—Darko played about 2 mins.

—Pistons are now 17-1 when scoring at least 90 pts

PISTONS 95 RAPTORS 91

(HOME, Wednesday, January 14th)

On one of the worst days of the winter season, the Pistons beat Toronto in a game before a crowd that was smaller than normal. But as one young girl's sign read, "We risked our lives to see (win) #10".

The game was delayed by about a half-hour, since the officials did not arrive at The Palace until 7:45. It took them 4 hours get to the arena from Detroit Metro Airport. Jim Clark was at the wheel when their car finally pulled into The Palace, and his partners on this night were Sean Corbin and Derrick Collins.

—The Raptors started all 3 of their new guys: Donyell Marshall, Jalen Rose, and Lonny Baxter. They were all acquired in the Antonio Davis and Jerome Williams trade with the Bulls.

—Memo blocked a Baxter dunk attempt

—Tayshaun had a great play: dunking the ball on a put-back while being fouled! And doing it all in one motion!

—Ben got ejected with 2 techs just before the 1st H ended.

—Down 11 at the half, and only shooting 33% from the field, the Pistons looked like they were in trouble. Especially without Ben Wallace for the 2nd H.

—One guy wore a shirt that read, "I was a Pistons' fan before it was cool."

—Memo was scoring, hitting FTs, and rebounding. He finished with 27 pts and 14 rebs.

—Rip made all the big shots in the last 2 mins. to win the game

PISTONS 98 WIZARDS 77

(HOME, Friday, January 16th)

—The Pistons had a lot of turnovers and dropping of the ball early

—Rip was lighting up his former team, with 8 pts in the 1st Q

—A 14-2 Pistons run opened things up in the 2nd Q. It just snowballed from there, and the clearly overmatched Wizards got crushed.

—Tayshaun blocked a Kwame Brown dunk

—The Pistons shot 64% on FGs in the 1st H

—The starters played most of the 3rd Q, then got to rest in the 4th Q with the big lead. This is good with a game the very next night.

—A huge Pistons run in that 3rd Q gave them a 80-54 lead going into the 4th Q

—Chauncey had 12 pts in the 3rd Q

—Darko got in at the 9-min. mark of the 4th Q

—The Pistons had a bunch of assts

The Famous Chicken made his only appearance of the year at The Palace for this game. Entertaining the crowd in a variety of ways, the best one was when a fake Wizards' Assistant Coach got mad at him for trying to peak into their huddle on numerous occasions. The coach chased him down and "skinned" him.

<u>PISTONS 99 BUCKS 94</u>

(AWAY, Saturday, January 17th)

Some Pistonsfever.com subscribers made the trip up to Milwaukee for this game and were treated to a great road performance by the guys. It was the 12th straight victory and came over a good (and dangerous) team that had won 10 straight at home.

We ran into a good number of other Pistons' fans who were very boisterous and fired up (especially afterwards).

The Bradley Center is a decent enough arena. Most of us felt like one word described it: "functional". There was nothing spectacular or really that unique about it. It seemed to have less suite boxes than you would expect.

One thing about it though: the Bradley Center did get loud very easy. It's small enough where the noise and energy just surges throughout the building. The crowd responds very quickly to appeals for noise by the scoreboard and mascot.

—The Pistons had a sloppy start: turning the ball over and mis-handling it on several occasions

—They also gave up a bit too much drive penetration early on

—Brian Skinner got his dunk blocked by Ben

—Tim Thomas hit a half-court shot to end the 1st H

—Chauncey & Rip were simply fabulous throughout

—<u>This was just a great NBA game</u>, especially in the 2nd H.

—The Pistons led & had control most of the way, but Milwaukee pulled close in the 4th Q

Down the stretch, the Bucks would hit a big shot to pull close (usually a 3), the crowd would surge with energy, and the place would become very loud. The Pistons, every time down, would stay calm, and confidently execute their offense. Then, they would

hit a "silencer". Chauncey & Rip were particularly impressive, hitting big shot after big shot.

This victory is a sign that shows that the Pistons are just a very good team. To make those types of shots, in that type of environment, on the road, against a team that had won 10 straight at home, while playing their 4th game in 5 nights, means the Pistons are becoming a force in this league.

PISTONS 85 SPURS 77

(HOME, Monday, January 19th)

This was the game that tied the team record for victories with 13. It was a 3:00 matinee game before a packed house on Martin Luther King Jr. Day. It's always fun to beat the defending NBA champs!

—Memo blocked Tim Duncan on a post move. Remarkable, considering it was a play that he was guarding!

—Actually, the Piston D' was solid on Duncan all game. Double-teams and good 1 on 1 defense held him to only 8 pts at the half and 17 for the game.

—Rip was a bit out of control and too excited through the 1st 3 Q's. He was so hyped up for this big game. He did play great defense though, chasing his man all over the floor and even blocking a shot or two!

—At the half it was just a dead-even game all the way around. Virtually all the team stats were close on both sides.

—Tony Parker was held down. He had 5 pts.

—Elden Campbell just can't make a jump-shot anymore

—Down the stretch it was both Chucky Atkins and Charlie Ward hitting all the big 3-pt shots. They kept coming fast and furious.

—Much like Memo earlier in the game, Ben blocked a Duncan post-move shot

—In the critical moments, Chauncey hit 2 huge, deep, knock-down triples. Then he got a 3-pt play the old-fashioned way. Once that third shot went down, it was pure euphoria at The Palace. Chauncey was tackled by his teammates and even team doctor Ben Paolucci was all smiles and high-fiving Chauncey. That's rare! Dr. Paolucci never gets caught up in the emotion of the game like that!

—Chauncey finished with 13 pts in the 4th Q

PACERS 81 PISTONS 69

(AWAY, Tuesday, January 20th)

This was a big game, because the Pistons were going for the team record with 14 straight wins. Plus Indy leads the East and had won 11 of 12 coming in. As a result, the Pistons only gained 2 games over this stretch.

Being that it was the Pistons 6th game in 8 days, they seemed both fatigued and lethargic. They also allowed Indy to dictate the style and physicality of the game.

—In the beginning, the Stones just simply could not score. They were down 8-0 and 12-2 early. The score was 20-9 after 1 Q. You usually don't win on the road playing that way.

—There were a lot of Pistons' sales staffers that made the trip down for the game

—With Ron Artest going to the bench at the 8:35—mark of the 2nd Q with 3 early fouls, the Pistons were able to cut into the lead and had the lead down to 44-40 at the half. A bunch of Indy turnovers also contributed to the Pistons surge.

—Tony Dungy, a Jackson native, was in attendance

—Corliss was effective with 17 pts on 7-11 FGs

—Due to fatigue, good Indiana D', or just poor play, Chauncey shot 2-13 on FGs and Rip shot 4-13 on FGs

—Jermaine O'Neal had 28 pts and 15 rebs for them

—The Pistons couldn't score at all in the 2nd H. It was good Indiana D', a tired team, and not controlling the style of the game that cost the Pistons.

T-WOLVES 80 PISTONS 79

(AWAY, Friday, January 23rd)

Minnesota had won 9 straight at home coming in. They also held the #2 record in the West. Bizarre officiating would mar an otherwise great playoff-like game.

—Ervin Johnson missed the game for them due to a death in the family. Mark Madsen started in his place.

—Cold shooting early for both teams; in fact, the score was 18-13 in favor of Minnesota after the 1st Q

—The Pistons had some poor shot selection tonight, especially early

—Latrell Sprewell was hot for them early with 11 pts in the 1st Q, but the Pistons just shut him down in the 2nd H.

—Hey, what do you know…former Piston big-man Oliver Miller plays for Minnesota

—Memo had 19 pts in the 2nd H

—As the guys said on the UPN broadcast of the game, this was like a playoff game. There was all sorts of defense being played, and other big-time plays being made in the 4th Q.

DEFENSE

Speaking of defense, consider this (all courtesy of Ben Wallace):

He blocked Kevin Garnett at the rim, stripped Garnett inside, blocked a fade-away jump-shot in the critical last few mins. of the 4th Q by Garnett, and blocked Sam Cassell at the rim. Ben is truly a special player.

The ***worst call of the year:***

Down 1 pt with less than 5 secs to go, Chauncey drove the lane and got both his man, Sam Cassell, and Garnett into the air with a fake. He then drained a 7-footer while falling down. The whistle blew and you knew it had to be a 3-pt play opportunity.

But no! Referee James Capers called an offensive foul. Chauncey barely caused any contact and in a situation like that, no foul is generally called anyway. It's the last shot of the game, so the officials usually let the players determine the outcome and let a lot of little things go. What's more is that the officials had not called much of anything all game long on various levels of contact that occurred all night. You can't let everything go, then make a call like that on the last shot.

What's more is that they wouldn't call a foul when the Pistons were intentionally fouling on the ensuing inbounds, causing the remaining 0.8 secs to evaporate and with it a great opportunity to get a high quality road win.

Afterwards, a couple of Pistons fans (and it looked like they were on cell phones), said into the UPN cameras "We were robbed!" This is reminiscent of last year's game down at Conseco Fieldhouse in Indiana when Jermaine O'Neal's last second shot was counted when it was actually late. You might recall that subscriber, "The Great Baldetto", and I were down at the game and had Indiana fans rubbing it in to us. Then as we were leaving, other Piston fans who were on cell phones called down the concourse to us saying we were robbed.

Ah, such is life on the road in the NBA.

HAWKS 91 PISTONS 82

(HOME, Sunday, January 25th)

There really isn't much to say here, except that the Pistons played like crap. Maybe it was a letdown from the Minnesota game, featuring the worst call of the year.

—Tayshaun blocked a Jacque Vaughan lay-up on the break

—Jason Terry had 12 pts in the 1st Q

—The Pistons were featuring a lot of alley-oop plays to Ben in the 1st H, from all angles

—Corliss had 12 pts in the 2nd Q, and 20 pts for the game in 26 mins

—This team was just in a funk all game long. Only Ben and Corliss played well.

—Poor effort displayed by the Pistons throughout

PISTONS 106 CELTICS 103

(AWAY, Wednesday, January 28th)

Jim O'Brien had just resigned, so this was John Carroll's first game as head coach. This was a great win because normally teams play out of their minds in their first few games with a new coach.

—It was a slow start: the Pistons were down 11-1 early

—They were giving up way too much in the paint in the 1st H

—Walter McCarty shot a double-clutch fling with the shot-clock running out that went in during the 1st H

—A good, solid Piston run to end the 1st H, gave them a 2 pt lead

—In the 3rd Q, the Pistons surged and the lead swelled to 14. Then Boston pushed back and cut it to 5 to end the quarter.

—Memo had 21 pts

—Ben made 4 straight huge FTs in the last 3 mins.

—At the end, Boston kept making big shots and the Pistons kept making FTs

—There were a lot of FTs tonight; the two teams combined to shoot 76 FTs!

—The 4th Q saw both teams pour in over 30 pts apiece

PISTONS 90 RAPTORS 89 (OT)

(AWAY, Friday, January 30th)

—Memo and Vince Carter, and really both teams, were hot early. In the first 8 mins. everything went in.

—The Pistons played poor on several levels in the 1st H: no ball movement or inside play, and a lack of defense

—Bob Sura was playing great in the 2nd H, especially with his defense on Carter and just making plays on the basketball court. He was rewarded with major crunch-time minutes.

—From the second part of the 3rd Q into much of the 4th Q, the Pistons took control of the game and had all the momentum. The Toronto crowd was booing and was not real pleased with Carter's play. Then, he began to take over and got the game close.

—With a 2 pt lead, Rip went to the FT line with just seconds left. He only made 1 FT, which gave Toronto a chance.

—On the next possession after the timeout, Vince Carter came off a baseline curl on the right side, received the pass, and drained a triple to tie it.

—Chauncey missed a shot to win the game, and overtime was upon us

—In the OT, Rip scored all 8 Piston pts, making up for missing the critical FT

—Ben Wallace played 50 man-sized minutes tonight (including 18 rebs)

With a 1 pt Piston lead and little time left in the OT, check out this sequence:

Ben caused an inside player to miss a shot, Morris Peterson grabbed the rebound and went to stick it back, and Ben blocked it. There was a scramble underneath for the ball and Darvin Ham and Donyell Marshall were tied up for a jump-ball.

The Raptors won the tip and Carter got it. He rose up for the game winning shot, and Ben blocked it! Three blocked or changed shots on the last possession of the game to preserve the victory. Ben is clearly the most dominant defensive player in the game today.

—As the buzzer sounded, a jubilant Larry Brown was running out onto the court with a big smile on his face

PISTONS 80 GRIZZLIES 78

(HOME, Saturday, January 31st)

—After giving up a bunch of pts (27) in the 1st Q, the Pistons held them to 11 in the 2nd Q

—Pau Gasol, Jason Williams, and Bonzi Wells were all held down below what they normally do

—The Pistons generated a bunch of steals tonight, especially in the lane

—Corliss scored 13 pts in 16 mins.

—Larry Brown gave an ominous presence with a dark coat, dark shirt, and dark tie on

—Hooper was seen at one point without a jersey on. Just a naked horse running around.

—The Pistons had solidly built the lead up to 11 with about 3 mins left. They then proceeded to squander the entire lead. Here, we saw good Memphis urgency and a lack thereof for the Pistons.

—With mere seconds remaining, Bonzi Wells milked the clock, then shot a ball from his heels to try to beat the Pistons. He air-balled it. (Hubie Brown thought there was a foul.) This is great because Bonzi usually kills the Pistons. He's always been upset that they traded him to Portland not long after drafting him.

On the next possession with 5 secs left, the Pistons went to Chauncey isolated on the left side. He backed Earl Watson down a little bit, almost waited too long, then went into his shot and drew a foul. The shot was short. The officials ruled contact and Hubie Brown was ticked. Chauncey hit both FTs and the game was over.

Hubie was still incensed with the refs afterwards. But hey, that's life in the NBA. Chauncey was on the other end of a call at the end of the Minnesota game that decided the outcome. So, it's good that our guys got an opportunity to win a game like this.

5

February

02/01/04—Back on Track With a 3-Game Winning Streak

The Pistons are back to playing good solid winning basketball after a 3-game losing streak. They've now won 3 in a row and 16 of their last 19. That's "*Goin' To Work*"!

A couple of very positive things that have contributed to this success are Corliss Williamson playing great and Bobby Sura fitting into his role in a successful way.

Right now, the Pistons are 32-16, 3 games behind Indiana.

◆ ◆ ◆

The All-Star starters were announced this week and Ben Wallace will be starting on the frontline for the second straight year.

Tayshaun Prince will compete in the Rookie—Sophomore Game and Mehmet Okur was chosen as an alternate.

And, Chauncey Billups was selected to compete in the Three-Point Shootout. This is great since Chauncey has been #2 in the league in 3-pt shooting for awhile.

It's about time too for a Piston to be represented since Jon Barry not being selected the last 2 years was a complete crime.

◆ ◆ ◆

ASK DR. FEVER

Question: Dr. Fever, this week Jim O'Brien resigned as coach of the Celtics, marking the 14th team to change coaches since the end of last season. And this is just in the Eastern Conference! Only Terry Stotts of Atlanta is still in the same position he was when the season ended last year. What is going on?

Dr. Fever: It's a league and a conference in transition. The East being as bad as it is has several teams trying to make change to become better. In the NBA the most common solution to problems with a team is to replace the head coach. The players have all the power anyway and it's much easier to replace one head coach than it is 12 players.

Plus, it's the nature of the business. I think it was Chuck Daly who said that when a coach signs his contract to join a team, that he's also signing his termination papers.

It is interesting to look at the changes that have taken place in the last year on a case by case basis. Many of which have more to do with personality clashes or politics than anything else.

We know all about why Rick Carlisle was replaced with the Pistons. Meanwhile, Larry Brown desired to not have to deal with Allen Iverson anymore, so he left Philadelphia. That's 2 coaching changes.

Larry Bird wasn't particularly fond of Isiah Thomas running his Pacers, plus he thinks his friend, Rick Carlisle, is the greatest thing since sliced bread. So, out with Isiah. Jason Kidd didn't like Byron Scott and almost didn't re-sign with the Nets because of it. It was just a matter of time, and now Scott is gone. That's 4 coaching changes.

In Washington, they've tried to get rid of everything connected to the Jordan era and that included Doug Collins, whose whole reason for being there was Jordan. In Orlando, they've fallen on hard times and have currently won only 27% of their games. This is really due to management failing to surround Tracy McGrady with enough talent to win. But, they needed a scapegoat, so they fired Doc Rivers. That's 6 changes.

In Miami, it was well past due for Pat Riley to resign. There's nothing more he could do with that team as coach. Plus, he needs the time off. In certain phases, the game has passed him by. Similarly in Milwaukee, George Karl couldn't have done much more with the Bucks. Though he tried to prevent it (he had dismissed assistant coaches that could have succeeded him as head coach last summer) the handwriting was on the wall: it was time to go. That's 8.

In Boston, Jim O'Brien and Danny Ainge were not even remotely on the same page for how to turn the Celtics into a success and could not co-exist (there were even rumors last year that Ainge liked Carlisle to replace O'Brien). New Orleans replaced Paul Silas for apparently no reason at all, other than that management was bored. That's 10.

In Toronto, Lenny Wilkens had worn out his welcome and the Raptors couldn't seem to get over the hump and become the contender in the East that they had appeared to be threatening to do for years. And New York, Cleveland, and Chicago are just flat-out awful and have been so for multiple years. So in those 3 cases it was very natural to replace the coaches. That's 14.

Thanks for being part of our coaching carousel! Watch your step getting off. Hope you're not so dizzy that you fall over!

02/09/04—3 Losses in a Row, Bogus Trade Rumors, and Darko Looking for Time

It was a very eventful week in Pistons basketball. Unfortunately several losses were part of the mix. The team went 1-3 for the week, including 2 losses by 3 pts each.

The Pistons are 33-19, 4.5 games behind Indiana.

Larry Brown was named NBA Coach of the Month for January. The Pistons went 13-3 for the month.

◆ ◆ ◆

Now, to show you that you can't believe everything you read **(especially when it comes to NBA trade rumors!),** check out how the Detroit Free Press and Detroit News reported this story about a potential trade with the Bulls.

On Saturday, the Free Press said the trade was being discussed, featuring Marcus Fizer and Kendall Gill for either Corliss Williamson or Bob Sura. The very next day, the News reported that Joe Dumars had said that the story was untrue.

◆ ◆ ◆

This week, a couple of fans (we'll call them Ron and Ed) have some good questions for Dr. Fever about a few different topics, including, you guessed it—Darko.

ASK DR. FEVER

Ron: Dr. Fever, it seems like Chauncey & Rip are All-Star worthy. Does it surprise you that they did not make the team?

Dr. Fever: No, not really. The Eastern Conference is stacked with guards having great years and they couldn't all make the team. Rip referred this week to the fact that his team's success this year and in the playoffs last year should count for something and help the chances of either him or his backcourt mate in being selected.

Unfortunately, though, that is not normally the case. Usually the coaches vote based on the current year's contributions of individuals. Plus, Chauncey & Rip have been so up & down and haven't really had a lot of dominating performances this year. Those types of things tend to stick in coaches' heads and can influence them.

But, both guys need not worry. They'll both make the All-Star team in the near future.

Ed: I heard Larry Brown visited his old team in Philly and it created a lot of media attention. Why did he go down there to visit his old team, especially in the middle of the season?

Dr. Fever: He had some time available between games, so he used it to visit both his family and Sixers' Coach Randy Ayers and General Manager Billy King. His wife and young children still live in the Philadelphia area, so he misses them a lot.

As far as the Sixers go, it's interesting. Out of all the teams that Larry Brown has coached in the NBA, this was the one that he spent the most time with (6 years) and he had developed some strong relationships with several people there.

To be honest, I'm not really sure why the Philly media was so fired up by this occurrence. Larry looks at Randy Ayers as one of his protégés and wants to offer him some advice. That's just the way he is: loyal to those who have been loyal to him.

Now, if he was consulted by Billy King for potential personnel moves regarding the Sixers' roster, that's another matter entirely.

Ron and Ed (shouting simultaneously): What about Darko? He said this week he wants playing time!

Dr. Fever: Yeah, that was interesting. Both Detroit dailies reported this story about Darko saying he was going to ask Larry Brown what his status was. Then, Larry said that both he and Joe Dumars agreed that Darko wasn't going to be ready to play this year (at least not many real minutes).

Darko, to his credit, did not seem upset by this and has not been a distraction to the team. He did say that he wants to play next year.

It's tough for Darko because he's young and at 18 you feel like you're invincible. He thinks, "If Carmelo and Lebron can do it, then so can I."

The problem is that big men always take longer to develop than perimeter guys do. There hasn't been an 18-year old big man to play at an impact level yet in our league.

Larry Brown, who has been in coaching for as many years as Darko is old (plus 13 more), understands this. He is bringing Darko along the way that he believes is best for both himself and the team.

02/14/04—An Extended Losing Streak & the All-Star Break

Well, the Pistons lost 2 more this week, taking their streak to 5 straight going into the All-Star break. Maybe having 5 days off before their next game will do them well. Chauncey has already talked about having a player's only meeting on

Monday to sort some things out and get everyone on the same page as we go into the last one-third of the season.

The Pistons are 33-21, 7 games behind Indiana in the loss column and now 1 behind New Jersey. Their next game is Tuesday at New York.

This week, Coach Brown went with a couple of changes in the starting unit for the Sacramento game. Zeljko Rebraca started in place of Elden Campbell who was starting for the injured Mehmet Okur. And, Darvin Ham started over Tayshaun Prince. It is unclear whether these moves will stay in place into the next several games or not.

◆ ◆ ◆

As you know, Ben Wallace will start in the NBA All-Star game on Sunday at 8:30. He received the second most votes of anyone next to Vince Carter. That's great to see. Fans of the NBA do appreciate more than just scoring. They do understand the finer points of the game.

You might recall that last year, Ben played in this game with a heavy heart after having lost his mother only days before. It's great to see that he's back this year and can enjoy himself for a much deserved honor. <u>And the word is that he's going with the 'fro!</u>

Chauncey will compete in the 3-pt shootout on Saturday night. Tayshaun played in the Rookies vs. Sophomores team on Friday and scored 18 pts, including 3 triples in the 1st H and a windmill, between-the-legs jam in the 2nd H. Rock on, Tayshaun.

All NBA All-Star coverage is on TNT.

◆ ◆ ◆

ASK DR. FEVER

Fan (of the Pistons and all things Detroit): Dr. Fever, the Motor City's own "The White Stripes", who rock by the way, have a song called "Girl, You Have No Faith in Medicine". Being that you're a doctor, is there any type of medicine that you are aware of that can cure the Pistons of this current losing skid and all the streakiness that marks their play?

Dr. Fever: You're right "The White Stripes" do rock. But, no there's no simple cure for the Pistons' slide. It would be nice though if we could see them play every game like their last one vs. Sacramento.

There you had a team playing very hard and giving a maximum effort to try to get the victory. In the other recent losses, this is something that has been lacking from the Pistons' performance.

Fan: Well, what about the lineup change for that Sac game? Darvin Ham & Zelly in the starting unit. Is that something that you think Larry Brown will stick with for awhile?

Dr. Fever: It's hard to say. With the All-Star break upon us, that's a lot of time for Larry to think about what he wants to do with this team to fix its problems.

The insertion of Ham was interesting because he has nowhere near the offensive ability of Tayshaun Prince. But, he brings a high level of energy and an ability to make things happen.

Also, Larry said that he likes how Tayshaun played coming off the bench. It does seem to give him more scoring opportunities. The first unit features Rip and our post players primarily. The idea is to get them going and established right from the beginning.

The second unit though, goes out and plays with a lot of energy and good defense while playing a bit more of a free-lance style on offense. Tayshaun can shine in that environment.

However, I doubt if Ham will still be starting over Tayshaun when the playoffs begin. You need more offense early in playoff games than Ham can provide.

02/23/04—Rasheed Wallace!

This was truly a historic week in Pistons basketball. Joe Dumars pulled the trigger on perhaps the biggest blockbuster trade in the history of the franchise. (This one is considered bigger than trading Grant Hill for Ben Wallace and Chucky Atkins simply because all those players would have signed with the teams they ended up with anyway. The trade was done to facilitate a better cap position for the Pistons at that time.)

The deal started a wave of excitement and euphoria all over Metro Detroit as Pistons fans began to imagine what the team is now capable of with Rasheed in the lineup. 'Sheed was the talk all over sports radio in Detroit for several days this week, as he was around office water coolers, and at the gym. Just hours after the trade was complete, ballers at places like Basketball America in Lake Orion were buzzing about the deal.

No wonder they're excited! Rasheed brings many elements that the Pistons have been lacking for years. Namely a serious post presence on offense, the ability to dominate games, a big body that is utilized to the fullest in all aspects of the game, forceful aggression to succeed, and star-power. He's also another dominant defensive force to put on the frontline. This will help make Ben's job so much easier.

This trade truly came at the perfect time for the Pistons. Over the last several weeks many disturbing trends have been developing. This is a team that continually gets off to terrible starts almost every game (mainly due to the fact that there's a lack of post options to go to in the starting lineup). This is also a team that goes through many stretches where points are about as hard to find as weapons of mass destruction (also due to the fact that with little post options the team has to continue to try to score most of its points out of the perimeter).

In addition, the Pistons sometimes haven't played with the proper aggression level for 48 mins. to win. And when Ben goes out of the game, opposing teams see it as a free pass to drive to the basket.

Rasheed answers all these needs for the Pistons.

Is he controversial? You bet he is. Does he fly off the handle at officials at critical times in games? You better believe it. Has he been caught with possession of marijuana? Yes, but at least he didn't say something stupid like "I did not inhale."

Rasheed is an enigma. He has more basketball talent in his little finger than 99% of the population has in their whole bodies. He also has set the record for most technical fouls in a season and has threatened an official after a game.

Rasheed Wallace is quite simply the largest personality the Pistons have had since the Bad Boys. Back in those days, Rick Mahorn, Bill Laimbeer, and Dennis Rodman weren't exactly well-loved by officials either.

Or opposing players and coaches. Michael Jordan once called Bill Laimbeer "The dirtiest player in basketball." During a brawl with Chicago, Rick Mahorn once threw Bulls' coach Doug Collins on top of the scorers table twice. When Bill Laimbeer and Charles Barkley squared off in what became known as "The Palace Malice" in 1990, the team and its players were fined a total of $90,000.

Now, Joe Dumars was not involved in any of these incidents and very rarely was ever involved in "Bad Boy behavior". But he knows that in order to win, certain things have to be in place for a team.

Is bringing Rasheed here a risk to the Pistons' chemistry? Yes, though more so in the long-term than the short term (Dr. Fever will talk more about this below). However, it has been often pointed out that in the business world, personal life, and in sports success is most often bred out of risk. The saying goes, "The greater the risk, the greater the potential reward."

Joe Dumars has proven that he's willing to make bold moves in order to turn the Pistons into champions. Were it not for Matt Geiger's refusal to waive a trade-kicker clause in his contract a few years ago, Allen Iverson would have been wearing Piston red, white, & blue. Joe also had the guts to trade established-star Jerry Stackhouse for Rip Hamilton.

The amazing thing is that Joe gave up very little in order to get Wallace. The trade went like this: Chucky Atkins, Lindsey Hunter, a first round draft pick, and cash to Boston; Bob Sura, Zeljko Rebraca, Chris Mills, and a first round draft pick to Atlanta; Rasheed Wallace and Mike James to the Pistons.

The reason Atlanta did this deal is because they wanted players in the last year of their contracts so that they could clear up major salary cap space to go after free agents in the summer. The reason Boston did it is because they want first round draft picks.

Now consider this: due to many legalities involving player contracts and the uniqueness of the salary cap, the Pistons will actually be in a position to clear some $9 to $10 million off their salary cap for this summer as a result of this deal. What this essentially means is that they can re-sign both Mehmet Okur and Rasheed. Certain things will have to fall in to play for that to successfully happen. The details are covered in Sunday's Detroit News column by Chris McCosky.

Since the Pistons own Rasheed's "Larry Bird rights" they can go over the cap to re-sign him and offer him more than any other NBA team. They can also use those "Larry Bird rights" to sign and trade Wallace for another high caliber talent.

So how did Joe do this? Well the key was trading Chucky's multi-year contract and the draft picks. All first round draft picks get a guaranteed 3-4 year deal for a set amount of money that automatically counts against the cap.

By trading what would have been lower 1st round picks anyway, the team eliminated the requirement to tie up salary cap space to players that would have had very little chance of making the regular rotation anyway. The early analysis from draft experts is that this year is supposed to be a pretty weak draft anyway.

Really the Pistons only lost one key player in the whole deal: Chucky Atkins. The other players probably would not have been back next year anyway. None of them made a big contribution.

Chucky was the exception. Remember when he hit the game winning shot on that driving lay-up vs. Philadelphia in the playoffs last year? He's a good 3-pt shooter and energy guy.

He will be missed, but he's got to be excited about the extended playing time he'll get in Boston. He's probably going to start, whereas here Chauncey is always going to play 35-40 mins. per night in front of him.

Mike James will take Chucky's spot in the rotation (and wear the same jersey number). As a starter in Boston he was averaging over 10 ppg and 4 assts. He also shoots the triple quite well.

◆ ◆ ◆

More on Rasheed

Rasheed Wallace showed up at the press conference Friday wearing a Kansas City Chiefs hat and a Derrick Thomas throwback jersey.

Larry Brown was talking a lot in the press conference about how exciting it was to add someone from the North Carolina fraternity to his team. Larry played for Coach Dean Smith many years before Wallace did. One of the first things Larry said was, "Coach Smith is smiling right now."

Rasheed also referred to the relationship that Carolina players and coaches past and present share by saying, "You are family for life."

Assistant Coaches Dave Hanners, John Kuester, and video coordinator Pat Sullivan are all from Carolina as well, making for a large extended family of Carolina guys here in "Rock City."

Larry said that everyone that you talk to who has played with Rasheed calls him a great teammate. Portland Coach Maurice Cheeks said that Rasheed was his favorite player. He's also considered to be a very unselfish player.

Larry had pressed Joe to get Rasheed ever since he first learned that he would be available several weeks ago.

◆ ◆ ◆

Here at Pistonsfever.com, we recently added a guy—Bob—who's going to assist with the "Ask Dr. Fever" column. Bob's main duty will be to collect and consolidate the questions that fans have for Dr. Fever. On this day, he helps out with all the questions that people have about Rasheed.

<u>Bob:</u> Hey, here comes Dr. Fever. He has a gleam in his eye and a smile on his face.

The excitement has been brewing wildly for fans since Tuesday when the news first broke that Rasheed might be coming to Detroit.

We've collected everyone's questions on paper and will now read them off for Dr. Fever to answer.

Take your places everyone.

ASK DR. FEVER

<u>Question:</u> In one sentence, how would you describe Rasheed's presence on the basketball floor?

<u>Dr. Fever:</u> If he were a rock star, he would be a cross between Kid Rock and Metallica.

(the rest of the room erupts into laughter)

<u>Bob:</u> What exactly do you mean by that?

<u>Dr. Fever:</u> Well, he's all out aggression and power while he's on the floor. He has that certain "kick-ass mentality" that those 2 bands have. Rasheed is also supremely confident, talented, and successful while he's on stage, er I mean on the court!

He also puts on a show. With all his energy, anger, smiles, and technical fouls, it makes for quite a viewing experience.

<u>Question:</u> I think the biggest question on everyone's mind right now is what the $%&*# is "agent certification."

<u>Dr. Fever:</u> (Laughing) Yeah that was something wasn't it? In all my years being associated with this great game of basketball that was the first time I had ever seen anything like that.

Rasheed and Mike James couldn't return to the game in the 2nd half on Friday because there were some player-agent certification papers not into the league office on time. It appears that the missing papers were not those of either Rasheed or Mike James, but were for other players involved in the deal.

All the papers weren't in until Saturday afternoon, costing both players a chance to practice that day too.

Question: How much can Rasheed help the Pistons this year?

Dr. Fever: I told some people this on Thursday as soon as the trade was complete: **they're going to the NBA Finals.**

This powerful post presence that is Rasheed counters the one area that Indiana had a real advantage over the Pistons. They had Jermaine O'Neal tearing it up inside whereas our Stones did not.

Also, the Pistons can now counter New Jersey's team speed with size and power. Imagine a frontline featuring Memo, Ben, and Rasheed all playing together.

Question: Can 'Sheed's combustible behavior hurt the Pistons' chemistry?

Dr. Fever: Only time will tell. However, I think that Joe D pointed out something interesting when he said that Rasheed is not surrounded with "knuckleheads" here in Detroit. The inference there of course is that in Portland he was.

This is true. Portland didn't have any strong leaders and not many classy players when he was there. Here he joins a team full of high character guys, that while their presence won't transform Rasheed's behavior, it may have a bit of a calming effect on him.

Also, don't discount Larry Brown's role in all this. He guided Allen Iverson to channel all his energy and anger into driving his team to the Finals a couple years ago. The hope is that Larry can do the same here.

Question: What about the talk of wanting to play in New York? Will Rasheed just leave us as a free agent this summer anyway?

Dr. Fever: It's possible. But keep in mind that New York is way over the salary cap and thus would only be able to offer him the mid-level cap exception of about $5 million. That's a huge discount for a guy who's making $17 million this year alone.

The Pistons with their "Larry Bird rights" can offer him the most money. Plus if 'Sheed likes the winning atmosphere around here, then he could be excited about the prospect of staying.

That's rare that you have the opportunity to give a free agent-to-be a chance to try out your team for a little while to see how he likes it. The "D" might not have all the glitz & glam of New York, but it may give him the best chance of his career to win the NBA title. And as Rasheed said recently, if he retires and hasn't won a title, then he's going to feel like his career was a failure.

THE GAMES OF FEBRUARY

Heat: During overtime, one Pistons player had "an out of body experience."

Cavs: Seeing Lebron James up close and personal.

Kings: There was a lot of physical play involving Pistons players and Brad Miller in this game with Sacramento.

Knicks: In New York, there was a buzz in the air about the big impending trade, two Piston Bad Boys chatted extensively, and the second very poor call of the year was made by a familiar face.

T-Wolves: Rasheed Wallace made his debut for the Pistons and The Palace was rocking.

PISTONS 102 HEAT 100 (OT)

(AWAY, Monday, February 2nd)

Miami is much improved and is a hot basketball team right now, having won 5 of their last 6 coming in.

—Tayshaun was very aggressive right from the start, and attacking on every level. He had 13 pts in the 1st Q alone!

—Brian Grant is out with injury

—Rafer Alston made 3 first H triples for them

—Udonis Haslem just played amazing all night

—Good job by the Pistons of controlling the lead for much of the game. The Heat cut it down to even though with just a couple of mins. left in regulation.

—Chauncey was dead-solid on many of his 3-point attempts all night

—Dwayne Wade had a foot injury in the 4th Q and missed the OT

—A huge block by Ben right under the basket saved a sure lay-up right at a key time in the OT. He covered so much ground on this play. He would later say that it was like "an out of body experience."

—Then, Rip hit a huge jumper coming off a screen to give the Pistons a 2-pt lead

—After the timeout, Rafer Alston missed a very deep triple and the game was over

CAVS 85 PISTONS 82

(HOME, Tuesday, February 3rd)

Seeing Lebron James in person was an eye-opener. He had some fantastic plays in this game. Though he didn't score much tonight, you can see where his potential lies and how good he can become.

The most amazing thing is his build. His body looks like that of a 25 year-old. He is big and strong. One other weird observation: he walks like a duck!

Next time you see one of his games, watch his feet during a timeout or break in the action. But, he doesn't waddle. It looks more like a duck strutting around.

—Memo missed the game with back spasms

—The Pistons gave up a lot of baskets off penetration in the 1st H

—Newly-signed Tiger, Ivan "Pudge" Rodriguez, was in attendance and got a big ovation from the crowd

—The Pistons got off to a bad start and were down 32-20 after 1 Q

—In the 3rd Q, the Pistons were able to secure a lead that they held for awhile into the 4th Q. Then they proceeded to score only 11 pts in the 4th Q.

—The game went down to the final possession, but the Pistons' inability to score, coupled with 39% on FGs and 10 missed FTs were their undoing

—Elden Campbell, though Coach Brown felt he played good D' on Zydrunas Ilgauskus, was unable to be even remotely effective offensively in the 2nd H

—Ben had 17 rebs

—Carlos Boozer, who has really come into his own as an NBA player now, had 21 pts and 15 rebs

—Lebron James, one game after scoring 38 pts, scored 12 pts and was only 5-19 from the field

HORNETS 92 PISTONS 81

(AWAY, Friday, February 6th)

—Memo was still out with back spasms, so Elden started again; Jamal Mashburn is back for them after having missed a ton of time due to injury

—Ben had a great move, posting on the right side then using a power dribble to the baseline, and dunking 1-handed on the opposite side of the lane

—Ben blocked a Robert Traylor dunk attempt in a major defensive help-out & recovery play in the 3rd Q

—The game became very physical with a lot of defense being played on both sides in the 3rd and 4th Q's

—Darvin Ham threw down a serious dunk in the 4th Q; he was everywhere, getting loose balls, and leaping & soaring for rebounds. He even lost a tooth in the process!

—Good battle by the Pistons in the 2nd H, but the mountain was too high to climb after getting down by 8 pts in the 1st Q and down by 14 pts going into the 4th Q

—The Pistons shot 38% for the game. That's not going to cut it.

MAVERICKS 111 PISTONS 108

(AWAY, Saturday, February 7th)

—The Pistons had a great start, scoring 22 pts very quickly by attacking the Dallas interior defense. It's pretty weak anyway, and the Pistons' aggression led to lots of pts in the paint.

—Up 15 at one point in the 1st H, the Pistons took only a 58-55 lead into halftime, due to a good Dallas run and Pistons turnovers at the end of the half

—In a typical Don Nelson ploy, Danny Fortson, who didn't even play in the 1st H, started for the Mavs in the 2nd H

—The Pistons were getting no calls in the 3rd Q; in fact, Darvin Ham was called for a tech. for simply making contact with a guy's arm! That's ridiculous.

—Dallas led by 1 pt going into the 4th Q

—Just a great basketball game: it was playoff-like. The teams kept matching each other with big shot after big shot in the 4th Q.

—Steve Nash could not and would not miss in the 4th Q

—There were too many defensive mistakes in the last few mins. Steve Nash & Nowitzki kept running the pick & roll and the Pistons were always leaving one of them open. They were both too hot to allow that.

—Nowitzki played like Larry Bird. He just made everything. He finished with 40 pts.

—The Pistons had 56 points in the paint. It's rare to lose when you have that type of production inside.

NETS 89 PISTONS 78
(AWAY, Tuesday, February 10th)

—The Nets are 7-0 since Lawrence Frank took over for the fired Byron Scott

—Memo is out again with back spasms and Jason Collins missed the game for them with injury

—Ben blocked a Kenyon Martin dunk attempt in the 1st Q

—A sight for sore eyes: the Pistons got off to a good, solid start. They led 29-16 after 1 Q

—To end the half, the Nets went on a 14-0 run by getting out & running and alley-ooping out of the half-court. In other words, they were playing true Nets basketball and the Pistons were letting them.

—The Nets' zone hurt the Pistons a lot in the 2nd H

—The Pistons just couldn't score at all in the 2nd H. They put in just 36 pts.

—Meanwhile, they allowed New Jersey to play their game: giving up fast-break buckets and the alley-oops out of the half-court. They finished with 25 fast-break pts. That's totally Nets basketball.

—Richard Jefferson had 27 pts and 10 rebs

—Props need to be given out to the Nets arena staff for playing the music to "Rapper's Delight" (also known as "Good Times") at various times while New Jersey had the ball. Now that's some old-school hip hop!

KINGS 96 PISTONS 94
(HOME, Wednesday, February 11th)

—In order to change things up and try to create a spark, Coach Brown started Darvin Ham & Zeljko Rebraca in place of Tayshaun and Elden Campbell (for the injured Memo)

—It didn't work at first: the Pistons were down 16-4 out of the gate and 32-20 after 1 Q

—The Pistons gave up a lot of dunks early on Sacramento back-door cuts: their calling card

—It was the tale of 2 Q's in the first H: bad start, but good Piston energy and scoring, coupled with better D' meant a surge in the 2nd Q. They outscored the Kings 30-17 in the 2nd Q.

—Darko got in at the beginning of the 2nd Q. He got to face his idol growing up: fellow countryman, Vlade Divac.

—20 1st H Kings assists: an incredible number. All their baskets had assists attached in the 1st H.

PHYSICAL PLAY

There were some extracurriculars involving Brad Miller tonight. Zeljko Rebraca got tangled up with him in the 3rd Q on a rebound and then seemed to go after him. He hit him with an open-handed punch. So, Z got tossed.

Then just before the end of the 3rd Q, Corliss hammered Miller pretty hard on a drive to the basket. The officials gave him a "Flagrant 2" meaning automatic ejection. This seemed excessive. After all, Corliss made contact with Miller's arms, so it wasn't like he completely avoided going for the ball. A "Flagrant 1" would have sufficed.

—Rip had great, smooth shooting all night

—Chauncey's first FG came at the 1:05—mark of the 4th Q: a dead-eye triple to tie up the game

—Weird goal-tending call on Tayshaun with 2:30 to go. Maybe it was goal-tending, but maybe it should have been let go within the context of the play.

—Then, after the timeout, Peja Stojakovic hit a triple coming off a screen on the right side with 0.4 secs left to win it

Although it was a bad start, this was the best Pistons' effort in awhile. The 2nd H was a great basketball game. There's no shame in losing to Sacramento with the best record in the league. But, it does hurt more after dropping the last several games in the fashion that the Pistons have.

KNICKS 92 PISTONS 88

(AWAY, Tuesday, February 17th)

Rumors were swirling around New York as Peter Vescey's column in the New York Post suggesting that Rasheed could be coming to the Pistons hit newsstands the morning of the game.

This was the Knicks' first game with Tim Thomas & Nazr Mohammed. Darvin Ham was still starting for Tayshaun and Memo was back from his back spasms. Allan Houston was out with injury for the Knicks.

—Ben blocked Dikembe Mutombo right at the rim; Memo blocked a Stephon Marbury lay-up

—Memo had a great start with 10 pts & 5 rebs in the 1st Q. He was everywhere.

—A big New York run, coupled with sloppy Pistons play allowed the Knicks to open up a 9 pt lead after 1 Q

—The 2 Presidents: Isiah Thomas & Joe Dumars were talking together throughout the game and looking smooth in their sports jackets

—The Pistons gave up a ton of 1st H fast-break pts: 19! That's terrible.

—The Pistons shot 29% on FGs in the 1st H. That's also terrible.

—Good Pistons' surge in the 3rd Q that included fast-breaks, defensive stops, and more energy

—The Pistons only shot 36% on FGs for the game

—With the game tied with 1:08 left, Chauncey had a clean blk on a Marbury 3-pt attempt, but James Capers called a foul on Chauncey. He's the same guy who called Chauncey for the off. (phantom) foul at the end of the Minnesota game earlier in the year.

—After 2 Chauncey FTs, Marbury buried a 3 with 2 secs left on the shot-clock

PISTONS 102 BUCKS 98

(HOME, Wednesday February 18th)

—Keith Van Horn has not yet reported to the Bucks after being traded from New York for Tim Thomas

—Tayshaun is back in the starting lineup

—Milwaukee had a bunch of 1st H turnovers: 15+

—The Pistons were down 33-20 after 1 Q. That's just sick.

—Pistons used the Buck turnovers and some 30 pts of offense in the 2nd Q to give themselves a 50-47 lead at the H

—Ben was blocking everything in the paint in the 3rd Q

—The Pistons' D' allowed only 14 pts in the 3rd Q; they had 10 blks as a team in the Q: a team record

—Chauncey & Rip combined for 43 pts

—The game ended up much closer than it should have been as a result of timely and potent Milwaukee shooting and 17 missed Piston FTs

—This was a very long game due to all the fouls that happened throughout

T-WOLVES 88 PISTONS 87

(HOME, Friday, February 20th)

Rasheed Wallace's first game meant an electric atmosphere at The Palace. He didn't start, but got a huge ovation when he first came in.

—Rasheed had 2 quick buckets early, the first one being a smooth jumper from the right baseline

—The Pistons had quite a bit of turnovers early, just seeming to rush things a bit with all the excitement going on in the building

—Minn. shot 49% on FGs in the 1st H

—It was great to watch Rasheed go at it with Kevin Garnett in the 1st H. They were just battling each other in the post. We finally have someone to match up with those kinds of players!

—Ben dunked it with authority right over Kevin Garnett at the beginning of the 2nd H

—Due to "agent certification" (?) Rasheed and Mike James were unable to play in the 2nd H

—Chauncey got his 2nd career triple-double tonight

—Chauncey & Rip combined for 44 pts

—Unaware that Rasheed was not allowed to play in the 2nd H by the league, the crowd began chanting, "We want Rasheed" about mid-way through the 4th Q

—Rasheed was leading the cheers in the 4th Q, waving the crowd into a frenzy

MAGIC 87 PISTONS 86

(HOME, Sunday, February 22nd)

—'Sheed started tonight for the first time; Memo sat so that Tayshaun could guard McGrady

—Orlando was wearing their retro black pinstripe uniforms from when they were an expansion team

—Rasheed hit a triple immediately, right off the opening tip, coming off a screen & curl on the right side; then he hit another triple right away

—Ben blocked a T-Mac jumper early and then got him again out by the 3-pt line as time was running out in the 3rd Q

—Rasheed untied Tyronne Lue's shoe at the scorer's table as he checked in

—Mike James had an excellent start: hitting a triple, driving, and setting up others, including an alley-oop to Rasheed. He threw it down with 1-hand.

—Orlando stayed resilient from the 3rd Q into the 4th Q and tied it up by the 8:41—mark

—Orlando shot a lot of FTs tonight

With a 2-pt lead and about 10 secs left, the inbound went to Chauncey and T-Mac stole the ball. Juwon Howard got it and Rip grabbed for the ball; it looked like it could have been a jump ball situation. Instead Howard powered it up and in and drew the foul! He made the FT giving Orlando a 1-pt lead. Rasheed missed a triple at the end and it was over.

—Rasheed finished with 14 pts, 7 rebs, and 2 blks in his first full game with the Pistons

—The Pistons had just 38 pts in the 2nd H, while Orlando had 29 pts in the 4th Q alone. That's just sick.

Good job by Orlando tonight, but if you're the Pistons, you can't allow this to happen to a team this bad, when their best player goes 3-20 on FGs as T-Mac did. The Pistons' lack of killer instinct hurt them again as they failed to put this team away earlier when they had the game under control.

<u>PISTONS 76 SIXERS 66</u>

(AWAY, Monday, February 23rd)

—Allen Iverson did not play due to a shoulder injury. The last time he missed a Pistons game earlier in the year, the Sixers still won.

—Ben was blocking everything in the 1st H. And he was covering so much ground to do it!

—Ben was also just attacking the rim on offense. Scoring with power time & again in the 1st Q. He had 8 pts in the Q.

—The Pistons led by as many as 18 pts in the 1st H, but only by 8 at the H

—Rasheed's first technical as a Piston came at the 8:35—mark of the 3rd Q

—Rasheed joined Ben in the block party, getting some great blks inside

—Pistons had way too many turnovers tonight

—Tayshaun had the most amazing block in the 4th Q: Eric Snow had what looked like a sure lay-up for a fast-break bucket. He was way out in front on the field. <u>Tayshaun chased him down from out of nowhere and blocked the lay-up!</u>

—There were a lot of techs tonight: 7 total

—Philly kept it close through their infamous resilient play and threatened to take the game in the 4th Q, but the Pistons survived and got a much needed win

<u>PISTONS 107 BULLS 88</u>

(AWAY, Wednesday, February 25th)

—No Memo tonight: back spasms

—The Pistons had a ton of 1st Q turnovers: 7

—Rasheed was in foul trouble throughout 1st H, as was Ronald Dupree who had 4 1st H fouls

—Tayshaun had a great play in the 1st H when he stole an inbounds pass from Eddie Robinson. He was guarding the baseline and when Robinson threw it, Tay stopped it and grabbed it with his long arms.

—After only scoring 17 pts in the 1st Q, they got 34 in the 2nd Q

—Then, 33 in the 3rd Q was real nice!

—On a screen that featured "big for big", Rasheed for Ben, Ben caught the pass by the foul line and actually did a sweet cross-over dribble and left Antonio Davis in the dust while scoring at the rack

—Tayshaun played real well all night, scoring from all over the place; Elden Campbell, who hadn't played much in recent games, had a real nice game, doing everything on offense and defense well.

—Tayshaun had an unbelievable pass in the 4th Q: he threw it from half-court, on the run, and off-balance to Rasheed for an alley-oop throw down!

—A "We want Darko" chant started with 5 mins. left. In Chicago? You bet. First it was Pistons fans, then Chicago ones got into it. He entered the game at the next dead ball.

PISTONS 105 HAWKS 83

(HOME, Friday, February 27th)

This game was over as soon as the Hawks got off their team bus. The Pistons overwhelmed them right out of the gate, leading 38-21 after 1 Q and 66-38 at the H.

—The Pistons' size did them in from the opening tip. There were many blocked shots and steals in the lane.

—The Pistons had 18 fast-break pts in the 1st Q! They just ran it right down the Hawks' throats all night long.

The officials tonight wore their shirts inside-out and wrote the number "62" on them. It was part of a protest that was done at various games tonight to show solidarity for their colleague, #62, Michael Henderson. He was suspended for 3 games for blowing a call at the end of the Nuggets—Lakers game this week. The fact that the referees have an expiring labor contract with the league ought to make this an interesting summer!

—Chauncey was fabulous with 20 pts and 8 assts

—Due to injuries & recent trades, Atlanta just doesn't have much left. They only dressed 9 players tonight.

—Bob Sura played for the Hawks, but our good friend, Zeljko Rebraca was sidelined with injury

—The Pistons finished with a 30-4 edge in fast-break pts

Some Pistonsfever.com subscribers were in attendance for this game. None of them were too impressed with Darko's performance tonight. He got a lot of time with the blowout but didn't do much. Except foul. In fact, he had 5 fouls in 12 mins.

PISTONS 100 CLIPPERS 88

(AWAY, Sunday, February 29th)

The 1st game of a long West Coast trip is always a good one to get. It helps to set the tone for the rest of the games on the trip. The Pistons had blown big leads and lost the last 2 years playing the Clippers in LA. It was finally the Pistons' time to break through.

—This game was marred by technical fouls early. Rasheed & Larry Brown got one each real early, then Rip got one and Coach Brown got a 2nd one right after Rip's when he said simply, "Call the darn foul then you won't have that." He actually did say "darn" and yet was still T-ed up and ejected. So for more than 3 Q's the Pistons were without him. Mike Woodson took over the team.

—The Pistons were down 9 after 1 Q and gave up way too much penetration. 33 pts in the 1st Q is just too much period.

—Chauncey had smooth shooting all night long. He was totally in rhythm and made big shots throughout. He ended up 7-11 on FGs and scored 28 pts.

—The Pistons only had 1 turnover in the 1st H

—The game got closer in the 2nd & 3rd Q's, but it was the 4th Q where the Pistons took over. A great surge, featuring fantastic D' on all levels and Chauncey & Rasheed led the way on offense from all over the place.

—Rasheed had started 1-12 on FGs, but finished very strong with 15 pts, 10 rebs, and 2 blks

—The Clippers fell apart in the 4th Q, turning it over basically every other time down the floor.

—The Pistons finished up 30-39 on FTs

—Elton Brand finished with 26 & 10, while Quentin Richardson had 22 & 10 (pts & rebs)

6

March

03/01/04—Four Wins, the Legendary Will Robinson Honored, and Rod Thorn Causing Trouble

The Pistons went 4-0 this week and hammered Chicago and Atlanta in the process. This is exactly what they needed going into a tough 5-games-in-8-nights West Coast trip. The Pistons appear to finally be learning how to play with an edge and develop the killer instinct necessary to not only put away lowly teams, but also to be able to win and be successful in the playoffs.

The Pistons are 38-24, which puts them 2 games behind New Jersey in the loss column for the 2nd best record in the East. The Pistons are not going to catch the Pacers for the best record in the conference since there's so few games left. But, if they catch the Nets, they will have home-court advantage in a potential second round play-off match-up.

The Nets would still hold the #2 seed by virtue of being a division winner, but the home-court advantage would actually go to the Pistons in the event that they hold the better record. So, that's the objective from here on out.

◆ ◆ ◆

The Pistons were fined $200,000 this week for allowing Rasheed and Mike James to play vs. Minnesota when the trade paperwork wasn't all complete. This is ridiculous. It wasn't like the Pistons gained an advantage by playing those guys, nor were they attempting to fraudulently steal that game. In the end they lost the game anyway.

It's still up for debate whether it was more the Pistons' fault or the league's for the fact that those players played in the first place. So in a case like this, why would the league add insult to injury by imposing this fine? It is ludicrous.

◆ ◆ ◆

What's up Rod Thorn? You've been a thorn in the Pistons' sides many times before (including several fines & suspensions levied towards the Bad Boys when he worked in the league office). Now you're trying to strongly urge the Hawks not to trade Rasheed to the Pistons right as the deal is close to completion? This is terrible and you should be both fined and suspended for it.

This was a case of Rod Thorn clearly overstepping his bounds as a team executive. Chris McCosky talked about it in Sunday's Detroit News column, but of course it's not getting much national play in the media.

◆ ◆ ◆

Will Robinson was honored at halftime of the Hawks game this week. After 28 years with the Pistons organization, Will is clearly a franchise legend. The stories of him helping the Pistons get great talent like Dennis Rodman and Joe Dumars are well-known.

But, what a lot of people don't know is that Will actually coached former Pistons' head coach Doug Collins in college. He was the first-ever black head coach at a Division 1 college.

At 92 years old, Will is amazing in that he only just retired last year. And he doesn't look a year over 72, let alone 92.

Many of us can only hope that we'll still be as involved in Pistons' basketball at his age!

◆ ◆ ◆

Kenny Thomas was quoted in Thursday's Detroit Free Press as saying that playing the Pistons now is like playing a Western Conference team because of how big they are on the frontline since the addition of Rasheed. You might recall that Thomas killed the Pistons on the glass in multiple games in the second round of the playoffs last year with the Sixers.

◆ ◆ ◆

Rip had suffered a broken nose in the pre-season and after having it get hit in a game last week, will now need surgery. He will have it done after Monday night's game in Utah. It's unclear whether or not he'll have to miss time while it heals.

Memo is on the injured list with back spasms.

◆ ◆ ◆

ASK DR. FEVER

Fan: Dr. Fever, what the heck is Rod Thorn doing? How can he do that?

Dr. Fever: That is pretty shady. But, you can feel good in the knowledge that the reason why he attempted to prevent the Pistons from acquiring Rasheed is that he knows that the Pistons now represent a huge obstacle to the Nets' goal of getting back to a third straight NBA Finals. Now Kenyon Martin is going to not only have to deal with Ben Wallace, but also Rasheed Wallace on that frontline.

In some ways it was Martin's aggression that was the difference in last year's Conference Finals. Now Rasheed brings that same all out aggressive approach to the Pistons.

Then when you realize that Rod Thorn is a former general manager for the hated Chicago Bulls, you find that it's not that surprising that he'd pull a stunt like this.

Fan #2: With 2 recent crushing victories over the Bulls and the Hawks, it looks like the Pistons are developing that necessary killer instinct. Do you think so?

Dr. Fever: It's too early to tell, but it looks like these are definite steps in the right direction. Up to this point the Pistons always displayed an amazing ability to have every single game played close. This included games against inferior opposition.

By allowing these bad teams to stay close though, they ended up giving those teams the opportunity to win, and it has at times this year meant losses that didn't have to be.

So you're absolutely right that developing the killer instinct is going to be very necessary for this team going forward. They need to knock out bad teams early in games and be able to take on—and take out—the high level of competition that they'll face in the playoffs.

Evaluation Point

THE 2/3 REPORT

This report was prepared prior to the March 6th game vs. the Denver Nuggets, so the statistics and trends mentioned are unreflective of this game.

The Pistons are 39-25 for a .609 winning percentage. Last year at this point in the season, they were 41-23. This season, they sit 9 games behind Indiana in the loss column and 2 behind New Jersey.

With only 18 games left, it's imperative that they keep winning games, not just to catch New Jersey for home court advantage in a possible second round playoff match-up with them, but also to hold off Milwaukee and New Orleans. Those teams are only 3 and 4 games behind in the loss column, respectively.

In terms of wins and losses, the team has played almost identical to the 1st third, when they were 20-13. They have been 19-12 since. (With 82 games the NBA regular season is actually split into thirds at the 27 game mark. This year the reports have come out after 33 games and 31 games, so it's important to take that into consideration when reviewing the stats that are provided here.)

While the Pistons' winning percentage is virtually identical in both thirds so far (at about 61%), there have been wide variances in their wins and losses. Check out the following won-loss streaks so far this year (in succession unless otherwise noted):

5 Game Winning Streak,
3 Game Losing Streak,
4 GM Win St, (then a few games later),
4 GM Win St,
4 GM Loss St, (then a few games later)
13 GM Win St,
3 GM Loss St,
4 GM Win St,
6 GM Loss St, (then a few games later)
4 GM Win St

This is quite remarkable! They had a great 13 game winning streak, which was a franchise record, but have been very up & down overall. This is very unusual for an NBA team to be this inconsistent.

On the other hand, it is not that surprising given the fact that the team has been going through so much transition since last spring. A team that went to the Eastern Conference Finals lost 2 starters in Michael Curry and Cliff Robinson, along with a key reserve in Jon Barry and has had to make several adjustments. Tayshaun Prince and Mehmet Okur, who are so young and inexperienced that Coach Larry Brown calls them "rookies", have been starting in Mike and Cliff's places and have been so up & down in their play that it mirrors the team's streakiness.

Larry has also recently said that the Pistons have been in 23 of the 25 games that they've lost and thus had the opportunity to win. To be perfectly honest, they should have won many of those games.

Coach Brown has been trying to get his players (especially Chauncey Billups, Mehmet Okur, Ben Wallace and Tayshaun Prince) to push themselves and develop their games so that they are multi-faceted. This way the team is more dynamic in its attack on both offense and defense and harder for opponents to counteract.

Rick Carlisle was fantastic for this team for 2 years, but he primarily played to players strengths and tried to mask their weaknesses as much as possible. Coach Brown's stance is that if you have a weakness in your game, work on it until it becomes a strength. This way teams can't just not guard Ben Wallace and double our other players off him. Similarly, opponents then know that Chauncey is not going to try and get his own offense a majority of the time. He will run the club as a floor leader and get everyone involved in the offense and control the tempo and style of the game.

These efforts have had mixed results all year. The idea though is that if the team has to take a hit in the regular season for wins and losses, they will be stronger come play-off time. The last 2 seasons opponents could pretty easily analyze the Pistons' strengths and weakness and develop their plan of attack accordingly.

That's why it's duly noted that even though the Pistons got to the Conference Finals last year and were one of the last 4 teams standing in the entire league, they actually had an 8-9 won-loss record in the playoffs.

They need to be tougher to defend, more dominant, harder to plan for, and have a stronger killer instinct if they're going to take the next step and win the NBA championship in the near future.

THE PLAYERS

Chauncey Billups, Mehmet Okur, Tayshaun Prince

Each of these 3 young players have had both good and bad moments when adjusting to how Larry wants them to play. In a nutshell, he wants Chauncey to run the team and not take bad shots, he wants Memo to work inside more and not just defer to his always reliable jump-shot, and he wants Tayshaun to be more aggressive with his own offense.

For Chauncey, it's all about knowing the "time and score" as Larry likes to say. As a point guard he has to do what's right for that particular time and situation in the game. Chauncey's natural tendency is to try and score on his own.

Memo has responded the poorest of the 3, in that he gets so moody. He's young and hasn't yet grasped the big picture. Larry gets on him when he "settles" for jump-shots.

Sometimes Memo will be having a great 1st Q statistically, getting a lot of pts and rebs, but will be benched for a long stretch because he's not doing certain things like posting up or driving the ball to the basket. If he and Larry can co-exist on these issues, he could become one heck of a ball player, able to score inside or out.

Tayshaun has been fairly solid in many areas all year. Larry likes his defense and how he works within the offense. Recently though, he really got on Tayshaun for deferring too much to the veterans. Larry's right: Tayshaun needs to demand the ball at times and command a presence on offense.

Elden Campbell

He has been quite simply, a disappointment. This is the worst he's played in the NBA in a long time. His jump-shots don't fall, his post game is disappearing, and he doesn't finish around the basket.

What happened? He used to be one of the most effective post players in the Eastern Conference when he played for the Hornets. Every time the Pistons went up against the Hornets, he would kill them.

Elden is older now, he's coming off a knee injury, and is apparently not in the best shape. Maybe all these things add up to his deteriorating offensive game. On the positive side, his defense has been pretty solid down low.

Rasheed Wallace

There's not much to say yet. He hasn't been here long enough. Not much other than, "Welcome, Rasheed. We need everything that you bring to this team."

His outlet passes are already becoming legendary for spearheading Piston fast-breaks, his shot-blocking and big presence inside combines with Ben Wallace to make a formidable defensive front-line, and his inside-out ability makes the Pistons so much more dynamic in their offensive attack.

Bob Sura and Zjelko Rebraca

These guys are no longer Pistons, since they were dealt away in the Rasheed trade. But, it's important to note that they wouldn't have been here much longer anyway. Both players were in the last year of their contracts and not making a significant contribution. So, they would not have been back next year.

Zelly played a lot like Elden Campbell, only worse.

THE TEAM AS A WHOLE

Shown below are the Pistons' rankings in a few key statistical categories, both now and as of the 1/3 report:

Defense

	2/3		1/3	
Pts:	5th,	86.3 pg	4th,	85.3 pg
FG%	4th,	41.8%	6th,	42.4%
Opp. 3-pt%	1st,	30.3%	1st,	26.2%
Assists:	5th,	19.7 pg	5th,	19.9 pg
Steals:	15th,	7.5 pg	15th,	7.5 pg
Blocks:	2nd,	7.0 pg	5th,	6.7 pg

Analysis: The team has stayed very consistent on this end of the floor all year. This was the part of the team's game that was easiest to transition from last year to this year. Outstanding defensive principles were already in place from Rick Carlisle's regime.

The Pistons have had some full-court pressure and trapping sets that they use periodically to affect the style and tempo of the game. This, along with occasional doubling-down, are changes over last year. The Pistons never double-teamed under Carlisle and defensive guru Kevin O'neill.

There seems to be less defensive breakdowns than earlier in the year and the team remains outstanding on the perimeter, as evidenced by their #1 ranking for 3-pt % allowed.

Rebounding

	2/3		1/3	
Total rebs.	6th,	43.5 pg	14th,	42.7 pg
Opp. rebs.	6th,	41.0 pg	7th,	41.0 pg

Analysis: The Pistons are now +2.5 rebs. per game on the year. This is very good. After so many years of struggling with this area, it is now becoming a strength of the team.

Offense

	2/3		1/3	
Pts:	21st,	89.9 pg	25th,	88.5 pg
FG%:	22nd,	42.8%	24th,	42.3%
3-pt%:	16th,	34.0%	21st,	33.0%
FT%:	13th,	75.8%	7th,	77.0%
Assists:	25th,	19.5 pg	26th,	18.9 pg
Turnovers:	19th,	15.3 pg	19th,	15.5 pg

Analysis: Things have stayed pretty much the same all year in these categories. They are up 1.4 pts per game though, which is good. Overall, the offense still needs work.

The addition of Rasheed Wallace should help all of these offensive categories. It will take time to get him acclimated to his new teammates and to the Pistons' system. The goal over the last third of the season will be to have him and everyone else on the same page and hitting on all cylinders (or pistons) by the first part of April when the playoffs begin.

Season Splits

The Pistons are 12-1 when they score 100 or more pts and 3-1 when they give up that many. They average 2 pts per game more at home than away.

Just as was the case at the 1/3 report, the Pistons average 11 pts per game more when they win than when they lose.

Conclusion

For the Pistons right now it's all about preparing for the playoffs and gaining a good playoff seed. The offense especially needs fine-tuning before April.

Getting Rasheed acclimated is key, but the same is true of new-comer Mike James. Both he and the newly re-acquired Lindsey Hunter have key roles backing up Chauncey & Rip. One may end up winning a larger role before it's all said and done.

Chauncey's decision-making needs to continue to evolve as the point guard and Tayshaun needs to be energized and aggressive by the time the playoffs start.

If all these things occur, it should be a fun April and May.

APPENDIX

From NBA.com, the following links were accessed when analyzing statistical data:

Team rankings and stats:
http://www.nba.com/statistics/sortable_team_statistics/sortable1.html?cnf=1&prd=1

Team splits: http://www.nba.com/pistons//stats/team_splits.html

NBA standings: http://www.nba.com/standings/by_division.html

Pistons' player stats: http://www.nba.com/pistons/stats/

03/14/04—The Pistons' Defense Takes Over the League

What a great time to be a Pistons fan! After a West Coast trip in which they went 4-1 in 8 nights, while traveling over 8,700 miles, they come home and thrash both Chicago and Philadelphia.

By the end of the road trip, the Pistons had held 3 consecutive opponents under 70 pts, which was an NBA record. Then they did the same to Chicago and Philly, meaning 5 straight games under 70!

The Pistons defense is truly remarkable. Heck, the Nuggets couldn't even find one player to hit double figures for them!

But the offense hasn't been too shabby either. Each of these last 5 wins has been in complete blow-out fashion, as the game summaries below indicate.

◆ ◆ ◆

As you have undoubtedly noticed, Lindsey Hunter has been a big part of the Pistons' resurgence, particularly on defense. Lindsey was traded to Boston in the Rasheed deal for salary cap reasons, but since he was not in their plans, they waived him.

So, the Pistons re-signed him. People have asked how he became such a big part of the team now, whereas he really wasn't playing much before the trade.

Part of it is due to injury. He was out for awhile. But also with Chucky Atkins and Bob Sura now gone, the Pistons had a real need for solid backup guard play. It will take a little while for Mike James to learn the plays and get acclimated, plus Larry Brown just loves Lindsey's defense. So, he's been getting good playing time.

◆ ◆ ◆

ASK DR. FEVER

Question: Hey, what's up with the Pistons D'? They're just killing people.

Dr. Fever: Well, since Chucky Atkins was traded, it opened up an opportunity in the backcourt for somebody. Interestingly, one of the players included in the trade from Detroit, Lindsey Hunter, is playing a big role in the Pistons' defensive dominance, since he was reacquired back from the Celtics.

Actually, both he and Mike James are a big part of this because both do an excellent job in limiting guard penetration into the lane. This is one thing that Chucky was not particularly good at. Many guards, especially bigger ones, would break him down off the dribble. By cutting this off, the current Pistons' guards are only making their frontline defense that much stronger because the big guys don't have to come off their own men and help.

Lindsey Hunter has been particularly impressive with his on-the-ball defense. He creates so many steals and wreaks havoc on the perimeter. Opposing guards just can't get comfortable when he's around. Larry Brown recently said that Allen Iverson once told him that Lindsey is the toughest on-the-ball defender he's ever played against.

Question #2: What about Rasheed Wallace? The ABC broadcast crew on Sunday was practically hyperventilating with excitement at how the 2 Wallaces play defense together inside.

Dr. Fever: Oh, he's been huge. When Rasheed was first acquired, I think most people were hyped about his offensive prowess. But his defense has simply bolstered an already strong team defense.

He blocks and changes a lot of shots inside, and guards his own men very well one on one. He covers a lot of ground on defense too. He can be trapping out on the perimeter one second, then contesting a shot inside on the same play the next.

One of the best things that Rasheed does on defense however, is that he communicates. He calls out what's happening in front of him. This way guys know when they're about to be screened or if the defense needs to adjust to something that the offense is executing.

With Ben and Rasheed playing together inside, it's like every penetrating guard's, (as well as frontline players with weak moves) worst nightmare.

03/25/04—The Defensive Lock-down

Welcome to this week's Pistons update, where our theme is blowouts, domination, and more blowouts.

The Pistons' defense has been completely shutting down virtually every opponent they've played within the last couple of weeks. In fact, before Tuesday's 82-81 loss to the Hornets, the Pistons had won 8 straight games by 15 pts or more. And that, ladies & gentlemen, is an NBA record!

The Pistons are now 46-26. With 10 games to go, they'll easily win 50 games for the third straight year. They are now up 2 games on New Jersey in the loss column for the second best record in the East.

Speaking of the Nets, did you catch K-Mart & J. Kidd's comments following the Pistons' demolition of them last week? Reported in both the Detroit News & Detroit Free Press, it basically sounded like this (not verbatim):

> They're not better than us. If we were 100% healthy it would be a different outcome. They're still crying over our sweep against them in last year's playoffs. They used excuses back then, saying they were hurt. We don't do that.

This is, of course, revisionist history. The Pistons have never said that injuries were the reason that they lost to the Nets last year. What's more is that these comments don't really sound like that of an elite team that truly feels like they are the best team in the East.

It actually sounds like the type of comments that are usually made when a group of guys are truly concerned that another team has passed them by. In fact, these comments bring back memories of last year's first round of the playoffs vs. Orlando, when a vociferous Doc Rivers was yelling something about the Pistons "better get their asses ready to play" in Game 7. The Pistons had just finished up mauling the Magic at home in Game 5 and killing them in a big win in Game 6 at Orlando. These were the obvious words of a desperate man who deep down knew that time was running out on his team.

It looks like the Nets are starting to feel the same way.

◆ ◆ ◆

RIP

An interesting observation regarding Rip Hamilton: despite playing with a surgically repaired broken nose, he relentlessly attacks the basket. This was especially evident in the New Jersey game.

Sure he wears a mask to protect his face, but a lot of guys would be hesitant either consciously or subconsciously, to go inside and take hits after an injury like his. His attitude of not backing down shows a toughness that is necessary to become a champion.

◆ ◆ ◆

PATIENCE

One of the reasons that the Pistons defense has been so unstoppable of late, is that they are so much more patient on offense. They're not taking quick, deep shots anymore. Thus, they don't give up long rebounds and fast-break buckets, and they have time to get back and set up their defense.

The patience also means better shots, which has improved offensive production. Good defense leads to good offense and vice versa. The cycle is a wicked one: for opponents.

◆ ◆ ◆

CARMELO

Well Carmelo Anthony was at The Palace on Friday, and what a deplorable showing by the young kid. No I'm not talking about his stats: he was actually pretty lethal in the 1st H. But, after scoring 16 pts by halftime, he disappeared in the 2nd H, both literally and figuratively.

As reported in Sunday's Detroit News by Chris McCosky, his selfish play and lack of complete effort had his teammates furious with him. Then, he would not go back in the game when called upon.

As he walked off the court after the game, head down, towel over his head, and pouting, a fan reached over and snatched the towel right off his head. Welcome to Detroit Melo!

◆ ◆ ◆

The Punch

I just finished reading an incredible basketball book that was submitted by long-time subscriber, "The Great Baldetto". The book is called *The Punch* by John Feinstein.

This is truly an amazing book and a must-read for anyone who considers himself a basketball junkie. *The Punch* talks about a lot of little things in NBA life that many people never consider or are aware of.

It is timely to talk about *The Punch* now since the Todd Bertuzzi incident in the NHL from a couple of weeks ago is still fresh in so many fans' minds.

The Punch tells the story of the Rockets' Rudy Tomjanovich (from Hamtramck, right here in Detroit Rock City) basically getting the crap beat out of him with one single punch from Kermit Washington of the L.A. Lakers. It was such a strong blow that Rudy's face bones became mis-aligned with the rest of his head, while spinal fluid began leaking into his mouth.

As astonishing as this is, it is not nearly as astonishing as the tale of how this one single event would go on to completely affect both men's lives forever from that day in 1977 forward.

The book also makes mention of a young Moses Malone. Understanding Malone's lot in the league at that time, can also help in understanding the challenges of a young Piston that we all know.

Malone jumped to the pros straight out of high school. This is a guy who scored over 27,000 pts in the NBA. He averaged over 20 points per game and over 12 rebounds per game. But, he wasn't always dominant.

Apparently, he struggled in the beginning:

> "As talented as he was, Malone found the transition to life in the pros difficult. He was a boy living among men. And although he was big and strong, he didn't really know how to play the game, certainly not at the pro level. He struggled in Utah and continued to have difficulties after signing with the Buffalo Braves in the NBA after 2 seasons in the ABA. At times his potential was apparent. At other times, he appeared to be years away from being a competent player." (chapter 13, pg. 202)

This description of Malone seems to fit Darko Milicic to a tee. It's been said many times, both in this newsletter and throughout NBA circles, that big men take the longest of any type of player to develop. Feinstein's description of Malone's early days in the pros is a direct example.

◆ ◆ ◆

ASK DR. FEVER

Bob: *A Pistons fan, we'll call him "Steve", just walked in to visit Dr. Fever. He seems very excited!*

Steve: Dr. Fever, the way the Pistons are playing right now is unbelievable! I am getting so fired up every time I watch the team play! How do I know if I have Pistonsfever?

Dr. Fever: Well, let me ask you this: are you a fan of many different types of basketball or just the Pistons?

Steve: Actually I love basketball on all levels: college; pro; I even like to play the game myself.

Dr. Fever: I see, I see. So did you watch the NCAA tournament this weekend?

Steve: Of course! I never miss it!

Dr. Fever: Now, the Pistons were pretty busy this weekend. They played on 3 of the 4 tournament days. When they were on did you flip back & forth, or just watch the Pistons, or just watch the tournament?

Steve: The first day, Thursday, I was checking the internet all day at work, keeping up on the early scores of the tournament. When I got home, I turned on the Pistons & Nets then started flipping back & forth to and from the tournament.

It's interesting though: when the Pistons opened up a 19-pt lead by halftime, I had a funny feeling. I think it was this sense of destiny, like the Pistons are truly for real and are a title contender in the truest sense of the word.

The rest of that weekend, I watched many NCAA games, but only when the Pistons weren't on. I made sure that the Denver & Cleveland games received my whole attention.

That has never happened to me during the tournament before.

Dr. Fever: Well we see that happen a lot in this clinic. How many games have you been to in person this year?

Steve: Pistons games?

Dr. Fever: Yes.

Steve: About 6.

Dr. Fever: How many do you usually attend per year?

Steve: Oh, let's see……2 or 3.

Dr. Fever: Do you normally stay till the final buzzer or leave with a couple of minutes to go to beat the traffic?

Steve: Now that you mention it…I have been staying till the very end lately. In the past if it were a blow-out, I would leave a little early. But now, I find myself very interested in waiting so I can see how Darko plays!

Dr. Fever: Okay, now for the big question Steve. Have you at any time this year, bought an Afro wig?

Steve: Yes, a black one for me and a red, white, & blue one for my wife.

Dr. Fever: Well it's official Steve. You have a full-blown case of Pistonsfever. At first it was minor, but then it grew. Kind of like when someone carries a virus in their bloodstream.

As time has gone by and this team has gotten better, it became more intense. You probably felt it spike up a bit when Rasheed Wallace was acquired and then when the Pistons started holding everybody under 70 points, it took full hold.

Your next challenge is going to be staying focused while at work when the playoffs begin and you're thinking about that night's opponent. Don't hesitate to call if you struggle with it and need help.

Steve: I won't Dr. Fever! And thank you.

THE GAMES OF MARCH

Nuggets (first game): Carmelo Anthony tried to show the Pistons up and got embarrassed in the process.

Bulls: The killer instinct was surfacing vs. Chicago.

Sixers: Controversy involving Allen Iverson and Rasheed Wallace dominating were the themes of the Philadelphia game.

Nets: This game was an outstanding performance by the Pistons. In it the Nets went out of their way to avoid embarrassment.

Nuggets (second game): Rasheed Wallace achieved a milestone in this game and there were a whole lot of wigs.

Spurs: Tempers were flaring in this one against San Antonio.

Clippers: Present at this game were great defense and an octopus.

JAZZ 94 PISTONS 86

(AWAY, Monday, March 1st)

This was Rasheed Wallace's coming out party as a Piston. He scored 27 pts. and had 4 blks.

—New acquisitions Tom Gugliotta & Gordon Giricek were in the lineup for the Jazz

—Raja Bell was jacking up shots all over the place in the 1st H

—It is really strange to see the Jazz without Stockton & Malone

—Rip's 3rd foul came at the 6:04—mark of the 2nd Q, sidelining him for extended time in the 1st H

—Ben just blocked & stole everything all night

—In the 4th Q, Tayshaun threw a long alley-oop pass to Rasheed. He reached back, grabbed it with one hand and threw it down with authority and drew a foul! It was a 3-pt. play and quite simply one of the most amazing highlights of basketball athleticism that you'll ever see.

—Giricek was tough and was a consistent threat for them all night

—Pistons couldn't contain Carlos Arroyo's penetration in 2nd H

—Utah was playing out of its mind, raising its' level to match an elite team

—A couple of Piston turnovers hurt them in the last couple of mins.

PISTONS 83 BLAZERS 68
(AWAY, Thursday, March 4th)

It was the return of Rasheed to the city that he played in for 7.5 years. There was excitement in the air!

—Rip's out due to nose surgery; Lindsey Hunter started in his place

—Rasheed was booed by the Portland crowd each time he touched the ball early, but also had a large share of supporters

—Ben had 9 rebs in the 1st Q

—Rasheed got another of his specialties: a 1-handed alley-oop in the 2nd Q

—Portland had cold shooting and several FG droughts in the 1st H

—The Pistons had only given up 29 pts in the 1st H, baby!

—Larry Brown left the game in the 3rd Q with the Pistons comfortably ahead, due to back probs.; Mike Woodson took over the team

—Ben was rebounding everything at an amazing level; just capturing everything!

—Nobody appeared to be guarding Corliss in the 4th Q; he was just scoring every time down the floor

—The Blazers played with a lack of heart and effort tonight

PISTONS 97 NUGGETS 66
(AWAY, Saturday, March 6th)

Carmelo Anthony is upset because he thinks that the Pistons mis-led him last summer when they didn't bring him in for a workout. He says that they led him to believe that he would be.

This sounds like a typical case of revisionist history. If memory serves, it was Anthony's agent who cancelled the workout, citing that it was obvious that the Pistons were going to draft Darko.

—Carmelo decided he would try to take it to the Pistons in this game. Immediately he drove to the basket……and Ben blocked his shot. Three straight times, he tried to take it right into the teeth of the Pistons' defense, and 3 straight times he was blocked and denied.

—The Pistons had 16 fast-break pts in the 1st H

—Early in the 3rd Q, Tayshaun Prince, apparently fired up by his match-up with Carmelo, took him off the dribble, broke him down, and jammed it fast!

—After a Ben alley-oop, Rasheed got another of his patented 1-handed alley-oops! Then Ben got another one of his own!

—Denver doesn't appear to be guarding anyone

—A 23-3 run to end the 1st H, coupled with a 17-4 run to start the 2nd H, meant the Pistons outscored Denver 40-7 during that stretch

—Rick Carlisle, wearing a Pacers hat and black leather jacket, was in attendance scouting the Nuggets for their next game

—Darko got in at the 9:24—mark of the 4th Q for some extended time

—No Nuggets player reached double figures. It's the first time that's happened since the shot-clock was brought into the league.

—Carmelo Anthony started 0-7 on FGs and finished 3-17 with 8 pts

PISTONS 86 SONICS 65

(AWAY, Sunday, March 7th)

—Ray Allen was out with the flu and Brent Barry was out with a finger injury

—The Pistons got off to a great start with a 12-4 lead out of the gate

—Tayshaun was raining in shots early

—Lindsey was stealing everything and wreaking havoc on defense

—The Pistons just took control of this game early, stomped on the Sonics and never looked back

—Darko got in at the 3:45—mark

PISTONS 98 BULLS 65

(HOME, Wednesday, March 10th)

This was the Pistons' 4th straight win without allowing 70 pts or more: an NBA record. This is simply amazing!

—The Pistons built a big lead right out of the gate and took complete control early: <u>the first sign within a game of a killer instinct</u>

—Rasheed scored <u>16 pts in a heartbeat</u> early in the game. <u>He had 3 alley-oops in the 1st H!</u>

—Darko got more extended playing time, and didn't do much, but they didn't really go to him much either.

—Rip & Memo were back from injury. Rip was wearing a face mask to protect his broken and newly repaired nose. He doesn't like wearing it.

—The Pistons kept this inferior team down and stomped the life out of them early. This is the 2nd sign of a killer instinct.

PISTONS 85 SIXERS 69

(HOME, Sunday, March 14th)

A nationally televised game on ABC, with no Allen Iverson. Coach Chris Ford said it was due to lack of conditioning for not having played much in the last 20 games or so. Iverson was not happy and wanted to play.

Props to ABC for showing lots of shots of downtown Detroit, including the river walk, and for playing the Kid Rock song, "Son of Detroit" as they went to a commercial in the 1st H. Later, "Detroit Rock City" by Kiss was heard.

—Rasheed was everywhere in the 1st Q: hitting 3's, slamming it, blocking shots, forcing a turnover

—Rasheed also blocked a Kyle Korver jump-shot by closing in amazing fashion and covering a lot of ground

—Glenn Robinson is still out with injury for them, but Derrick Coleman and Marc Jackson are back

—Rip was doing a lot of driving & slicing inside for lay-ups. That's very good; don't just settle for jumpers!

—Talk about great defense: Rasheed on one possession in the 3rd Q, covered 50 feet within about 2 secs when he was part of a trap near half-court, broke over the timeline on the left side of the floor, thinking there was a steal. Then when the Sixers recovered the ball and swung it deep into the corner on the ride side, he was there in time to knock it out of bounds!

—The Pistons' trap has been great today; they keep closing the vice on the Sixers right when they cross half-court

—Corliss scored a lot, especially off of plays taking his man 1 on 1 to the basket

—Willie Green, straight out of Detroit and U-D, scored big for Philly. He got 17 pts on 8-10 FGs.

—A 5th straight opponent under 70 pts! Are you kidding me?

PISTONS 89 NETS 71

(AWAY, Thursday, March 18th)

Richard Jefferson said before the game that the Pistons holding 5 straight teams under 70 pts was not really a big deal because it wasn't coming against the elite teams in the NBA. Jefferson, you'll recall is the same guy who said last year that the Pistons are the most overrated team in the NBA.

Jefferson is making his Alma mater, Arizona, look bad with his lack of intelligence! Either that or he'd have to admit that his own team is not one of the elites after getting held to 71!

—Richard Jefferson got his dunk blocked by Ben in the 1st Q and later got his flying lay-up blocked by Rasheed in the 3rd Q

—Our good friend Hubert Davis got into the game for the Nets

—The Pistons broke this game open by outscoring the Nets in the 2nd Q by 18. It was done in a fairly gradual manner, even though the Pistons scored 34 pts in the Q. On defense, they just stopped New Jersey from getting off. rebs., contested every jump-shot, and pressured the backcourt. And, they didn't allow Jersey to get out and fast-break like they love to do.

—The Pistons led 54-35 at the H

—Rasheed got a tech. early in the 3rd Q. As the Jersey crowd started cheering, he waved his arms up & down, egging them on. They started roaring even louder.

Then he just held his hand in the air, pointing straight up to…what, the sky? No, it was the scoreboard, where the Pistons had a 15 pt. lead.

—Jersey put on a 14-2 run, with Richard Jefferson pumping in some big baskets early in the 4th Q to cut the lead to 7. Here's how the Pistons responded: off a high screen and roll, Rasheed hit a big triple from the top. Then Chauncey hit Corliss for a quick fast-break bucket. Next, Ben drew a charge on Kenyon Martin and the Nets run and chance to get back in the game was over.

The Nets actually committed an intentional foul in the final seconds so that the Pistons couldn't just run out the clock and make their latest victim to be held under 70 pts. At 69, the Nets came down and missed a tough jump-shot, then Aaron Williams tipped it in at the buzzer to push the Nets to over 70.

The Pistons really wanted to keep the streak alive and everyone on the Nets and the crowd was aware of it too. Williams was even pumping his fist after scoring the bucket. Darko had position for the rebound on the play, but got pushed and a bit over-powered by Williams. He's going to have to work on his strength and aggressiveness at pursuing the ball!

◆ ◆ ◆

Great solid win by the Pistons against the team that they most likely will face in the 2nd round of the playoffs.

If this game were a boxing match, it went something like this: after some initial exchanges between the 2 teams early, the Pistons delivered a couple of big roundhouse punches in the 2nd Q that staggered their opponent. From that point on, the match was pretty even in terms of points on the judges' score cards, but the Pistons were wearing Jersey down.

Once the match got into the later rounds, Jersey hit the Pistons with a couple of big blows of their own (when the lead got cut to 7). After weathering that storm, the Pistons gave about 3 solid shots to Jersey, knocking them to the mat and knocking them out.

PISTONS 94 NUGGETS 75

(HOME, Friday, March 19th)

It was a fun-filled night at The Palace. Ronald McDonald was there, in full clown attire. Former baller Spencer Haywood was courtside. Bob Seger, newly inducted into the Rock & Roll Hall of Fame, was wearing a Pistons warm-up shirt and black leather gloves? And, a bunch of people wearing Afro wigs packed The Palace. The fans were encouraged to wear wigs to break the all-time record for wigs at a game. Auto-motion and Palace officials on the scoring crew all wore wigs as well.

—In the 1st H, it was a small forward battle between Corliss and Carmelo Anthony. Carmelo would use his quickness to get open shots and score, while Corliss would back him down and score with power.

—Rodney White has a large portion of his arm covered with tattoo art. That's a lot of tattoos for a guy who seems relatively quiet & docile.

—Former Piston Adrian Dantley is an Assistant Coach with Denver

—Denver had 15 turnovers in the 1st H, while the Pistons had 18 assts

—The Pistons held only a 5-pt lead going into the 4th Q, but then they blew the game open in the 4th Q

—Memo blocked Nene's dunk in the 4th Q

—Rasheed went over 10,000 career pts tonight

—Carmelo, though hot early, with 12 pts in the 1st Q, did nothing in the 2nd H

—The Stones were impressive with 53% on FGs tonight

Since the Pistons held Denver to 66 pts 2 weeks ago, the Nuggets have been averaging 104 pts per game. Now, they play the Pistons again and get held to 75!

And, the wig verdict is in: over 6,200 fans wore Afro-style wigs, some were red, white, & blue and others were the traditional black color. This feat broke the all-time record

for wigs at a sporting venue which was 5,000+ that was apparently achieved in Australia. The Palace will be in the Guinness Book of World Records for this fun night.

PISTONS 96 CAVS 76

(AWAY, Sunday, March 21st)

—The Cavs led at 17-13. Then all heck broke loose for Cleveland as the Pistons went into defensive lock-down mode and started attacking the Cavs on offense from every angle.

—It was a 40-14 run from that point until the end of the H!

—The Stones went to a 2-3 zone for awhile in the 1st H that confused Cleveland and helped take them out of their comfort zone and what they like to do on offense

—Corliss was just attacking & scoring all over the place in the 1st H, especially off the drive!

—Lebron James drove inside and while skying.... got his flying lay-up blocked by Ben in the 1st H

—Making Compton proud: Tayshaun took the ball off a steal out by half-court, went inside on a broken floor situation, faked a pass left, and soared from the dotted line with the ball outstretched and way over his head in his left-hand, jamming it down and drawing a foul! The play put a major surge into the Cleveland crowd.

—It's nice to know that a star like Rasheed could get two quick fouls and only play 8 mins. in the 1st H and the Pistons can still lead by 22. The depth of this team is remarkable!

—Carlos Boozer was solid throughout for the Cavs—as he always is vs. the Pistons

—Lebron James was held to 5-17 on FGs. He hasn't been able to get it going against the Pistons' defense all season.

—Chauncey had 0 turnovers! That's fantastic for a PG. A 25 to 5 assist to turnover ratio for the Pistons as a team on the night is phenomenal

HORNETS 82 PISTONS 81

(AWAY, Tuesday, March 23rd)

—No Monster Mash tonight

—With a 33-21 lead after 1 Q, it looked like the Pistons were continuing their dominance

—A lot of triples by the Hornets got them back into the game in the 2nd Q

—It was just bad Pistons' offense from the 2nd Q on

—The Hornets made everything, absolutely everything in the first half of the 4th Q; this included many triples

—Mike James and the Pistons were struggling in the early parts of the 4th Q. The Hornets' pressure was part of it. Then Mike dropped 2 huge triples to tie it up.

—Down the stretch, Ben blocked, then caught Darrell Armstrong's lay-up!

—As the game got serious in the last couple of mins., Rasheed emerged from the huddle without his headband

—Chauncey, who hadn't made anything all game, hit a huge triple with very little time left to give the Pistons a 1-pt lead

—With the 1-pt lead and just seconds left, Ben blocked David Wesley's jumper. It looked like it would win the game for the Pistons……but Jamal Magloire picked it up and hit a floater to win it for the Hornets!

When it was all over, there was talk of how unfortunate it was to lose on a last second shot by a non-shooter like Magloire. And, it appeared that referee James Capers may have screwed the Pistons for the third time this year on a call at the end of a game. (In this case, a play or 2 before the last shot, it looked like it was out of bounds off the Hornets, but they were allowed to keep it, and thus hit the game winning shot.)

To be honest though, the Pistons never should have been in this position. They just didn't play really well in the 2nd H. Their offense really struggled and it allowed New Orleans to stay close enough to dig it out.

SPURS 84 PISTONS 75

(AWAY, Thursday, March 25th)

With Greg Popovich being a Larry Brown disciple, it is no wonder that their defense locked the Pistons down. This was a battle of 2 strong defenses. They both play the same way.

—Early D': Ben blocked Rasho Nesterovic's dunk attempt and Rasheed blocked Tim Duncan on a lay-up attempt in the 1st Q

—In the 2nd Q, Tony Parker took it in against Rasheed on the break: what was he thinking? Rasheed blocked it, then on the ensuing Pistons' break, hit a triple, baby!

—Using good passing, the Pistons got easy baskets and were out-shooting the Spurs 53% to 36% in the 1st H and held a 42-38 lead. Then in the 2nd H, all heck broke loose as the Pistons couldn't score. The Spurs defense is very good, but the Pistons stopped passing it the way they were in the 1st H, had some bad turnovers, and had several possessions where the shot-clock went down to the final seconds.

—Great defensive play: Ben, after challenging Tony Parker right under the basket, immediately rose up and blocked Tim Duncan, attacking from the side! The ball landed on Duncan out of bounds. Pistons ball!

—Memo went over the back for a rebound in the 3rd Q and a Spur was called for a foul on the ensuing action. Popovich went ballistic. He was all over the floor and got a technical. As animated as he was, and the fact that he went way out on the court should have warranted a second technical and ejection.

—The Pistons could not keep Tony Parker out of the lane all night. Some of it was dribble drive penetration from traditional attacking points for a PG. Other times he was just free-lancing off of the Pistons trap.

—Manu Ginobili got more rebounds out of the swing position than you ever want to see

—Tim Duncan was held to 12 pts

—Rip & Manu went at it. Manu flopped & drew an offensive foul on some Rip cutting action. Rip was not happy and on the next possession, as the ball went out of bounds near the Spurs basket, they went face to face with Rip jawing at him. Double technical: one for each.

—Then Popovich ripped his own scoring crew! They mistakenly re-set the shot clock for the Pistons when a shot missed the rim. So he let them have it!

As Ben was being held going for an offensive rebound, he was called for the foul! Then Ben got ejected at the 6:08—mark with 2 technicals back to back. Steve Javie is always very quick with his trigger finger.

Ben had recently said that he wasn't going to tolerate people grabbing him, holding him, or just flat out cheating to keep him off the boards. This situation has escalated recently and Ben has been patient, but he said earlier in the week that both officials and opposing players are going to have to learn that this is not acceptable.

PISTONS 100 KNICKS 85

(HOME, Saturday, March 27th)

—No Allan Houston, Tim Thomas, or Dikembe Mutombo for the Knicks. No Rasheed for the Pistons, who had some back problems.

—Rasheed was hooked up to a machine, sort of a pack, that gave electronic stimulus to his back. He looked like the Bionic Man. He was dressed in his warm-ups though and gave a lift to his teammates with his presence. Though not playing he was really into the game!

—Memo took a charge on a Demar Johnson dunk attempt in the 1st Q. That's pretty impressive!

—Tayshaun had 3 alley-oops in the 1st H and was just running like a gazelle out there

—He had 18 pts in the 1st H and was very confident as he pumped in pts from all over the floor

—By halftime, the lead had swelled to 67-49, which means the highest scoring 1st H all year for the Pistons

—Memo got a haircut, and it's a good thing. He looks sharper now, whereas before his look was a little sloppy.

—The Pistons got a lot of inside scores, just shredding the Knicks' defense

—Memo blocked a Stephon Marbury lay-up. Marbury finished with only 12 pts.

—Nazr Mohammed had a good game for them with 13 pts and 12 rebs in only 21 mins. of action

PISTONS 108 CLIPPERS 99

(HOME, Wednesday March 31st)

—Rasheed still out with back probs. So Memo started and scored 3 quick early baskets

—Memo does a great job of getting off. rebs by sneaking in there and tipping it away from his opponent

—Mike James hit Rip with an alley-oop pass in the 2nd Q; yeah that's right, Rip jammed an alley-oop!

—Corliss was scoring early & often in the 2nd Q (10 pts) and shredded the Clipper zone

—Lindsey blocked Eddie House's flying dunk attempt right at the summit, then he got the rebound, pushed it up and Rip got a hammer dunk

—Tayshaun blocked Eddie House's 3-pt shot, then as Elton Brand got the off. reb, Corliss & Ben converged on him and swallowed him up. Corliss blocked it.

—A close game throughout, the Pistons pushed it to a 9-pt lead midway through the 4th Q

—An octopus was thrown to mid-court at the 6:55—mark of the 4th Q! This is of course a Red Wings tradition, and you could tell that basketball people didn't know what to make of it. This is why Lindsey gave it a little kick, and then referee Luis Grillo kicked it around till it was over by the scorer's table. Only problem with this is that it spreads slime all over the floor! One of the ball boys then wrapped it with a towel and removed it.

—Rip had 3 triples tonight: very unusual for him

—The Clippers were right there most of the night, but the Pistons won this game because they're just better

7

April

04/04/04—A Third Straight 50 Win Season

With the Pistons' impressive handling of the Pacers on Sunday, they have now achieved 50 victories for the third consecutive year! This is a great job by a very good team. Firmly entrenched in the third spot of the conference and with the #2 best record in the East just about wrapped up, it will be tough for this club to stay focused on the last 5 games.

Speaking of which, it sure is a weird feeling these last few weeks of the regular season. With the enormous potential this team has for post-season success and with the way everyone (even the national media now) is talking about how powerful they really are, it makes you feel like you can't wait for the playoffs to start. These last few games are fun, but let's get to the main attraction!

◆ ◆ ◆

RECORDS

By holding the Pacers under 70 pts (heck, they barely got 60!), the Pistons have now held 73 opponents under 100 pts for the season. That, ladies and gentlemen, is a team record.

◆ ◆ ◆

MR. D AND TRADER JACK

A couple of interesting things happened this week: Pistons owner, Bill Davidson, was inducted into the Michigan Sports Hall of Fame and former Pistons' GM Jack McCloskey was named interim GM for the Toronto Raptors.

Davidson and Mike Illitch, who owns the Tigers and Red Wings, were both part of the same induction class. These are 2 owners that are receiving their just recognition for bringing multiple championships to Metro Detroit and the state of Michigan.

Jack McCloskey was the man who built the Pistons into NBA champions in 1989 and 1990. He drafted or traded for Isiah Thomas, Joe Dumars, Vinnie Johnson, Bill Laimbeer, Dennis Rodman, John Salley, Rick Mahorn, James "Buddha" Edwards, and Mark Aguirre.

Jack fit the team and the city well: he was an underdog, a man who had been around the league awhile but had not found success. He had never been a GM before, but came to the Pistons and made moves that transformed the team from a perennial loser in the '60s, and '70s into the most feared team in the NBA.

Dr. Fever talks a bit about his memories of Jack in the "Ask Dr. Fever" segment below.

◆ ◆ ◆

ASK DR. FEVER

Bob: *Two fans, Jake and Dan, just stopped by to see Dr. Fever. They have been at all the games on the home-stand this week: the Clippers, Heat, and Pacers. While Jake was taunting Elton Brand during the Clipper game, Dan was heaving an octopus onto the court!*

Dan: Dr. Fever, we had a great time at the games this week!

Dr. Fever: Is it true that you were the one who threw the octopus onto the court?

Dan: I can neither confirm nor deny this rumor.

(Dr. Fever column disclaimer: We cannot be certain that we have correctly identified the actual fan who threw the octopus. We think this guy might be trying to steal someone else's thunder.)

Jake: Hey, Doc, what's up with the officiating? It seems like the Pistons are getting screwed a lot lately.

Dr. Fever: Hey, this is a family column!

Jake: Oh, sorry! It seems like the Pistons are getting rooked lately.

Dr. Fever: To answer your question, officiating has been bad throughout the league this year. There seems to be some antagonism between certain refs and the players.

My concern regarding the Pistons is that they are complaining an awful lot. It seems like they feel as though they are entitled to a good whistle all the time. And to be honest, they're not. They have to get to the Finals and establish themselves as a true title contender before they'll get the best whistle that the league has to offer.

Several guys: Chauncey, Rip, and Memo especially, are letting it affect their outlook and approach to the game a bit too much. Let it go and move on.

To be a true champion, you learn how to win no matter what obstacles are in your way: officials included.

Dan: Dr. Fever, tell us your memories of Jack McCloskey, also known as "Trader Jack".

Dr. Fever: You know, Jack was a fierce competitor. An Irishman with a fire inside that burned brightly. A lot of people don't realize that he was just as competitive and intense as Isiah, Bill Laimbeer, you name it. He would do anything to build the Pistons into a winner.

Isiah recently told a story that was widely reported about how when the Pistons were rising in prominence in the late '80s he and Joe were on an elevator with Jack. At this time, Boston was the class of the East.

The door opens and who was standing there, but Celtics' boss Red Auerbach. Jack and Red looked at one another and neither would even say one word to each other during the whole elevator ride. Then the door opened and they got off.

Isiah said that's when he and Joe began to understand what it was all about to have the right mindset to win the championship.

But, you know I'll never forget the summer of '89. The Pistons had just won their first-ever NBA championship. It was only like 2 days later that the league held its expansion draft for 2 new teams. One of those teams, Minnesota, decided they were going to draft Rick Mahorn.

This was of course a huge blow to the Pistons. After all Mahorn was a starter and a big-time leader for the team.

So there Jack was on the phone through all the team celebrations trying to work a deal to keep Mahorn in Detroit. Even on the float during the victory parade downtown he was negotiating with Minnesota. But he was unable to work a deal.

Immediately after the rally at The Palace later that day he had to tell Mahorn he was gone. This was only minutes after Rick thanked Jack for sticking by him through his weight problems. It was a sad time for everyone involved, but especially for Jack.

This team that he built was in some ways never going to be the same now that one of its' key figures was gone. He would say later that he felt like the Pistons were "being penalized for having depth." This was true since each team was only allowed to protect so many players. But all of these players were brought to Detroit by Jack.

04/14/04—Playoff Time!

The Pistons finished the regular season with a record of 54-28, their best record since the '96–'97 season, when they had an identical record. It's truly been an eventful, up and down, and fun year. As we get ready for the playoffs, many in the national media are predicting big things for this team in the post-season.

They will open up with the Milwaukee Bucks on Sunday at 1:00 on ESPN. Get ready to rock!

◆ ◆ ◆

MILESTONES

Many statistical milestones were reached by both individuals and players. For example, Ben Wallace became the first player in NBA history to get 1,000 rebs, 100 blocks, and 100 steals in 4 consecutive seasons. The team held 77 of its 82 opponents under 100 pts for the year—amazing. Their 84.2 ppg allowed led the NBA.

◆ ◆ ◆

GOOD SCHEDULING

After many months of playing several games in a limited number of days, the Pistons played a very favorable schedule down the stretch. Consider this: on March 25th the team returned from San Antonio and did not travel again until April 9th for a game the next day against the Magic. That's over 2 weeks at home, with no travel, and only playing 6 games. Then they got to feel the warmth of Florida.

These things go a long way to helping bodies heal and allowing guys to get rest prior to the playoffs starting. The travel alone can take a big toll on the body.

◆ ◆ ◆

HEALTH REPORT

Going into the playoffs, some guys are a bit banged up, but apparently nothing is too serious. Rasheed and Chauncey sat out the last couple of games with arch and ankle problems respectively, but both could have played if it were at all necessary.

If you remember last year's playoffs and how Chauncey was hobbled with a bad ankle sprain and Ben was battling through a leg brace after MCL damage, you know how big a role injuries can play.

Early indications are that neither Rasheed nor Chauncey are hurt badly and should be ready to rock this weekend.

Other than that, Lindsey has been battling some tendonitis and Mike James a sore groin.

◆ ◆ ◆

AVOIDING DETROIT?

What's interesting is that with the log jam at the bottom of the Eastern Conference, teams have been jockeying for position so that they can stay out of the 6th seed and not have to play the Pistons in the first round of the playoffs.

The word around the conference is that no one wants to play them for fear of getting **shredded.**

This is a great sign of growth for the franchise and proves its' ascension to among the NBA's elite. Teams used to want to play the Pistons. Last year Orlando was glad they drew the Pistons rather than New Jersey in the first round. They felt from the beginning of that series that they could beat Detroit.

◆ ◆ ◆

RASHEED'S FUTURE

Many fans are wondering if Rasheed's going to stay with the Pistons when he becomes a free agent this summer. Right now, the chances look very good and it feels right.

◆ ◆ ◆

ASK DR. FEVER

Question: Dr. Fever, how well do you think the Pistons closed out the regular season?

Dr. Fever: Well, they won virtually every game they played over the last 8 weeks (the Pistons went 20-4 to close the season). That's pretty impressive.

What else is nice to see is that with so much time over the last couple of weeks being spent playing games that are actually meaningless as far as their position for the playoffs, they have for the most part maintained their focus and played at a very high level. Coach Brown has demanded that focus and the guys have delivered.

Also, with Chauncey and Rasheed missing some time over the last week or so, it helped other players to get more playing time and for Coach Brown to experiment with lineups and roles.

Question: Why do you believe the Pistons are better-equipped for success in this year's playoffs than they were in other recent seasons?

Dr. Fever: This team has a certain confidence about it; a swagger; an edge. Those intangibles are so valuable when you're in an opposing arena with the defense locking down on all your primary scorers and the crowd calling for blood.

Last year was about the guys establishing that they had what it takes to win at a high level in the playoffs. Now they can build on that experience: they know what to expect and how to pull out multiple playoff series.

While many people feel that Rasheed was the final piece to the puzzle for this group in terms of his on-the-court contributions and capabilities, what I am excited about is all the playoff experience that he brings with him. He's played in a bunch of big playoff games out West with a powerful Portland team that at one point was battling the Lakers in a Game 7 for a shot at the NBA Finals.

Also, Coach Brown's tremendous coaching experience will help as the Pistons hit some of the rough waters of these playoffs. Nothing against Rick Carlisle, but last year the Pistons were too slow to make adjustments in the Orlando series.

The difference is, he's a young coach learning as he goes, while Larry has already been through these playoff battles many times and will know which buttons to push when.

Alright, enough talk. Let's get it on!

THE GAMES OF APRIL

Heat: The Pistons defense was overwhelming and dominant vs. Miami.

Pacers: Elden Campbell reached a milestone as the Pistons shredded Indiana.

Magic (first game): Chauncey Billups had another one of his amazing plays.

PISTONS 92 HEAT 84

(HOME, Friday, April 2nd)

Block Party

Consider this:

*Ben blocked Brian Grant's dunk attempt from behind in the 1st Q

**Lindsey, knocked down in the lane, got his hands on Dwayne Wade's shot attempt, as he was falling down! Lindsey was just not going to allow a shot attempt!

***Rasheed blocked Lamar Odom right at the rack in the 2nd Q

****Ben destroyed Samaki Walker's reverse dunk attempt near the end of the 2nd Q

*****Ben got 2 blocks on Lamar Odom's flying lay-up atts. in the 3rd Q

******Rasheed took a poor, weak attempt by Brian Grant right under the basket and spiked it right to the floor

*******The Pistons finished with 11 blocks, baby!

—To illustrate how funny the beginning of NBA games typically are, notice how the game started. Miami went up 8-0 right out of the gate. Then the Pistons went on to an 11-2 run.

—Rip got 3 fouls fast in the 1st H and was in foul trouble all night

—The Pistons were down 13 at one point in the 1st H and 45-37 at the H

—Only scoring 37 pts in the 1st H is pretty poor and it was a result of shooting 30% on FGs, the Pistons' inability (or lack of attention to) getting the ball inside, and Miami's very good defensive system

—Rasheed & Bimbo Coles each got a tech. for jawing in the 3rd Q; interesting by Bimbo since he was in street clothes and not even playing!

—Eddie Jones hit 3's for them all night

—Lamar Odom, despite all the times that he personally was blocked inside, kept driving it in there, taking it on down the stretch.

—The pace of this game really picked up in the 4th Q

—Chauncey was a dead-eye tonight on triples. No matter where he was shooting from or what kind of defensive pressure he was under, he shot a smooth ball all night. He finished with a great stat line tonight: <u>31 pts, 7 assts, 7 rebs, 2 turn-overs, 4-7 on triples, and 11-12 on FTs</u>

—Shooting 48% on FGs in the 1st H, the Heat were shut-down in the 2nd H and finished with 39%

PISTONS 79 PACERS 61

(HOME, Sunday, April 4th)

This game was a defensive battle and looked exactly like what it was: a playoff-type game that was played like a year-end regular season game. While it wasn't quite as sharp as both teams will be in the playoffs, this game was fun. It featured a lot of defense which is both teams' calling card.

This victory was big too because you didn't want to have the Pacers sweep the season series and feel invincible against the Pistons going into the playoffs.

—A technical error either by ABC or the local affiliate, Channel 7, had Pistons fans throughout Metro Detroit saying things like "$#%&*" and "!@&$#" when the first 4 mins. of the game were not broadcast. Instead the Sacramento vs. Houston game was being shown.

—No Jamal Tinsley and Jermaine O'Neal was somewhat limited due to his knee probs.

—This was Elden Campbell's $1{,}000^{th}$ career game

—The Pistons led 39-33 at halftime. Later the lead swelled to double digits, before the Pacers closed the gap and pulled even. Then a little Pistons' run gave them a 6 point lead going into the 4th Q.

—Memo blocked an Artest lay-up shot in the 3rd Q

—Rip hit big shots in the 4th Q, running off screens relentlessly to get open. This and the Pistons' D' opened up the game.

—Rip, undoubtedly pumped about his Connecticut Huskies reaching the Championship Game of the NCAA's the night before, finished with 24 pts

—Great moment: with 2:43 left and the Pistons safely ahead, Ben and Artest got into it off a foul shot. Artest got a technical. The Pistons chose Ben to shoot the FT! Ben had already gone 1-4 from the line to that point, but he swished this one home as the crowd roared!

—Indiana was held to 11 pts in the 4th Q and were forced into 19 turnovers for the game

—Only Ron Artest reached double figures for them

PISTONS 102 MAGIC 86

(HOME, Tuesday, April 6th)

As this game began, and it was acknowledged that Orlando had the worst record in the NBA, I thought it was amazing to imagine how far this team had fallen from last year when they were giving the Pistons all kinds of problems in the first round of the playoffs.

—T-Mac is out the rest of the year

—Rasheed blocked a Juwon Howard jump-shot

—It was a Darvin Ham kind of 2nd Q: he was dunking, stealing, and just out-hustling people

—Chauncey underneath the basket shot a flip shot over his head, contorting, while being fouled, while not looking, with a lot of English on the ball and……. it went in for a three-point play

—Chauncey turned his ankle, stepping on Tyrone Lue's foot early in the 3rd Q. It didn't look good. At this time of year, it reminds one of last year when he had the bad ankle sprain that really limited him in the second and third round of the playoffs.

—In the 3rd Q, Rip blocked a Tyronne Lue jump-shot, then did a wind-mill slam at the other end. He's been adding a lot of flair on his dunks lately.

—Rasheed was just raining in triples in the 3rd Q

—Rasheed killed a Briton Johnsen lay-up shot

—By the start of the 4th Q, the Pistons had blown the game open and led 84-65

—This game was played just the way you want to see it: the Pistons leading wire to wire, opening it up, and really flowing with a lot of momentum on both offense and defense. All key things against a much inferior team at this time of year.

PISTONS 74 RAPTORS 66

(HOME, Friday, April 9th)

This is likely to be one of Kevin O'Neill's last games as Raptors' head coach.

—Donyell Marshall tried a lay-up underneath in the 1st Q and……it was smothered by Rasheed

—Great play: in the 1st Q, Darvin Ham missed a FT, but soared in and rebounded his own miss. It led to a Rasheed triple.

—3 technical fouls on the Pistons in the 1st Q: on Rip, Rasheed, and Ben. The Pistons need to understand how to let set-backs like missed calls roll off their back more. Adjust and move on.

—The Pistons seemed to not have the sense of urgency or a killer instinct in the 1st H. The 13 turnovers they had in the 1st H was not fun.

—The lead was pushed up to 14 early in the 3rd Q, but an 8-0 Toronto run got them back in it. Then it was a close game the rest of the way.

—Pistons didn't shoot well in 2nd H, but they also had quite a few unforced turnovers

—Ben missed a bunch of driving lay-ups. He has been shooting worse from the field and FT line as the season has gotten into its' later stages

—Chris Bosh is an impressive rookie that plays like a veteran at times

—The Pistons should have featured Rasheed more in the offense tonight

—Rip was good down the stretch and had 10 pts in the 4th Q

PISTONS 101 MAGIC 89

(AWAY, Saturday, April 10th)

The Pistons just killed them. It looked like the Pistons were auditioning for the role of world beaters while the Magic seemed to be trying very hard to position themselves for the #1 spot in the NBA draft lottery.

—A bunch of early steals, at least 6 in the 1st Q, led to many fast-break buckets

—Rasheed kept finding Tayshaun on the outlets. Tayshaun had 3 dunks in the 1st Q and was soaring on all of them.

—Rasheed had an amazing windmill dunk on the break

—Derek Dial (formerly of EMU) got his lay-up blocked by Tayshaun

—A 26-3 run broke this game open, baby!

—Corliss got several off. rebs in the 3rd Q, just by being around the basket and being opportunistic

—Larry Brown seems to almost coach harder when the game is out of reach and when Darko is in the game

—Rasheed left the game early in the 3rd Q with either an ankle or an arch problem

—Tayshaun finished with a career high 25 pts

—Darko played the entire 4th Q and had some humbling moments out there. He also had a 3-pt play on a dunk.

PISTONS 101 WIZARDS 79

(HOME, Monday, April 12th)

—No Stackhouse or Kwame Brown for Washington and no Chauncey or Rasheed for the Pistons, nursing minor injuries

—Elden and Lindsey started

—16 1st H turnovers for the Pistons

—Tayshaun blocked a 3-pt attempt by Mitchell Butler: return to sender

—Tayshaun had a beautiful reverse alley-oop in the 3rd Q, where he looked over his shoulder as he dunked it!

—A 14-2 run to end the 3rd Q opened this otherwise close game up

—Suddenly the Pistons were playing with a ton of energy and defending the heck out of everyone

—Mike James was a key figure in this as he hit 5 high-arching triples in the 3rd & 4th Q's as the Pistons were making their run. The 3rd Q was just a Mike James kind of Q

—The Pistons defense turned the tide in this game

—Rip was everywhere tonight and finished with 12 assts

RAPTORS 87 PISTONS 78

(AWAY, Tuesday, April 13th)

—Still no Rasheed or Chauncey; Lindsey and Elden again starting in place of them

—Tayshaun, very aggressive early, scored 9 pts in the 1st Q

—The Pistons' traps have become so good and tight over the last several games!

—Kevin O'Neill, coaching his next to last game with the Raptors, looked very relaxed drinking his Diet Coke while directing his team

—The Pistons were down 42-37 at the H

—Toronto surged and pushed the lead to 14 pts in the 3rd Q to take control of the game

—Donyell Marshall had a big game with 27 pts and 16 rebs

—Darko got in at the 9:08—mark of the 4th Q with the game still in doubt and the Pistons down 71-62

—Darvin had a nice dunk in the 4th Q when he went inside and held out the ball in one hand, and paused it in the air before throwing it down

—Mike James, after a great game last night, did nothing in this game on offense

8

The Milwaukee Series 2004 Playoffs Round 1

◆

(The Playoff Diaries: April)

04/26/04—An "Above Average Defense"

That was the phrase that Milwaukee Bucks' Assistant Coach, Sam Mitchell, used to describe the Pistons' D'. This will go down as one of the great understatements of the year.

It is April and you know what that means! Back by popular demand, it's "The Playoff Diaries!"

In this edition, we break down the Milwaukee Bucks and discuss how to beat them.

Due to illness, this particular issue was delayed, so we apologize for any inconvenience this may have caused.

◆ ◆ ◆

ASK DR. FEVER

Bob: *Two fans, Nick & Joe, are here to visit Dr. Fever. Joe looks a little freaky with red spots on his face!*

Nick: Dr. Fever what happened to the Pistons in Game 2? That was a horrible performance.

Dr. Fever: It was disappointing. There were many tactical reasons why the Pistons lost, but the bottom line is that they took the Bucks for granted. After a blow-out performance like they had in the very first game of the series, it made them think that they were just head and shoulders above this team.

Though they didn't appear to be too cocky and overconfident on the outside, the Pistons did in fact take them for granted. This is human nature. It happens on the subconscious level and is a challenge for many teams.

This is one example of many growing pains that we're going to see this year in the playoffs because though the Pistons are mightily talented, they are still inexperienced when it comes to playing in the playoffs as a leader.

In the future, the Pistons will approach a situation like this by literally shutting out their subconscious thoughts and activate the killer instinct to stomp out the opponent.

Nick: You mentioned tactical reasons why the Pistons lost as well. What are some of these reasons? I know that 25 three-point attempts are part of it. Larry Brown hates that.

Dr. Fever: Yes he does. But it illustrates a much larger point. These three-point attempts were not occurring at the end of the shot clock. They were happening early and often. That means there were several opportunities for the ball to go inside for much better shots. Instead the Pistons settled for deep jumpers.

If you work the ball inside, those types of shots, which are higher percentage, give you a much better chance of scoring. Of the 25 triples they tried, they only made 6 for 24%. If they looked inside more, then that percentage could double.

Now not only is your offense functioning at a much higher level, but when you make a team inbound the ball after a score, it gives your defense the chance to set up. Otherwise the opposition is just able to get out and run. And since Milwaukee is the highest scoring team in the East, this is definitely a concern.

Of course this is also true of the foul line. When you get fouled, the action stops and your defense is setup before the opposing team starts their offensive sequence. How do you draw fouls? Get the ball inside!

Joe: Hey Doc, I was at Game 1 and was feeling kind of ill. I had a fever, was achy, and tired. Then the next day, I saw these red spots on my face. Do these symptoms mean I have Pistonsfever?

Dr. Fever: No, they mean that you have chicken pox! Being that you were at the game on Sunday, you probably infected the whole arena! Although most of the people there have more than likely already had it.

Here's what I prescribe for you. Get plenty of rest, have the Aveeno ready for itching, and watch every minute of the Pistons vs. Bucks series. Because while your symptoms indicate chicken pox, it is clear that you do indeed have Pistonsfever as well. Anyone who would go to the game feeling the way that you did is truly a dedicated fan.

◆ ◆ ◆

Playoff Notes

After reviewing the Bucks' stats for the year, the following conclusions were drawn:

—they love to run & score (they are 4th in the league in scoring, 6th in FG% and 10th in 3-pt %)

—they score a lot off of good passing, including from the break

—their record is sterling when they score 100+ pts, but not when their opponents do

—they give up a lot of pts on defense: 97 ppg (to put that in perspective, the Pistons only gave up 84 ppg for the season)

—you can shoot well against them; they gave up 45% on FGs for 23rd in the league

—you can score triples against them and create scoring chances off of passing (ranked 19th & 21st respectively)

—being a relatively small team, with Joe Smith as their biggest presence inside, they are very average at rebounding, and don't block many shots

—they take care of the ball, but don't create many steals

—they draw a lot of fouls

Also, most of these stats are representative of a Buck team featuring TJ Ford starting at PG for them. He is out for the rest of the year with a spinal injury. This really impacts their ability to run, have an efficient set offense, and makes them easier to trap.

Michael Redd is their biggest force. He was 10th in the league in scoring.

The Pistons were 3-1 vs. the Bucks in the regular season, but none of those games featured Rasheed Wallace and many, if not all of them, featured Tim Thomas and not the newly acquired Keith Van Horn (who Thomas was traded for). Plus, TJ Ford was healthy for all of those games. So, those games can't tell us much about how these teams match up now.

The Bucks are a 6th seed in these playoffs, but much of the year they have been near the top of the Eastern Conference. In fact, had they won any of their last 3 games, they would have clinched the 4th seed and home court advantage in the first round.

They lost all 3 and were 10-15 in their last 25 games. This is normally a recipe for disaster in the playoffs. Remember the 1997 Pistons? After an excellent run through the All-Star break, they went 11-14 to end the season and got beat in the 1st round of the playoffs to Atlanta.

Based off all these observations there are **4 Keys To Victory:**

#1—Don't allow non-stars to become stars

#2—Dominate inside scoring, especially of the frontline players

#3—Win rebounding battle by a solid margin

#4—Limit fast-break and secondary break opportunities

05/01/04—Playoff Growth

The Pistons have closed out the Bucks 4-1 in what was truly a fine series for them. They had a little hiccup in Game 2 and lost by 4 pts, but otherwise dictated the tenor, tempo, and style of the entire series.

It's funny how quickly things can change. It was only 2 years ago that the Pistons beat the Raptors 3-2 in a best of 5 series in the first round. At that time it was felt by many, including yours truly, that it was such a satisfying, enjoyable win. It was a big moment. Never mind the fact that the Pistons had to struggle throughout that series and barely pulled it out in Game 5.

But things are different for this team now. They are expected to do well and they do. They also win with style.

Oh sure they still played the same tenacious defense they always have—even like they did 2 years ago. But now they score on the break. They score with flair.

They score with guys like Rasheed jamming the ball down and letting out a loud yell afterwards.

They score with guys like Tayshaun alternating buckets between smooth jumpers and south-paw slams inside.

They score with guys like Chauncey hitting a bank shot off one leg.

This is fun. It's fun because the Pistons are a factor again. They are a true championship contender and a good playoff team.

And it's not like this is uncharted waters for this franchise. Our good friends at UPN 50 and the Pistons Television Network pointed out last week that the Pistons are 5th all-time in playoff winning percentage.

It's good to be back.

◆ ◆ ◆

BIG BEN, THE ACTOR

You've probably noticed all these commercials during the playoffs showing the championship trophy being pursued by star players as if it were a woman that they were trying to court.

The best one, of course, is the Ben Wallace spot. You'll be happy to know that it's authentic too. The spot was filmed at a barbershop in Pontiac. That's also why the picture of a past Pistons' championship in the background of the shop looks so good!

◆ ◆ ◆

CARLISLE & POPOVICH

This week, Spurs Coach, Greg Popovich, criticized the Pacers' Rick Carlisle for openly campaigning for Ron Artest to win "Defensive Player of the Year."

Then, Larry Brown, who both had Popovich as an assistant and is good friends with him, agreed that coaches should not campaign for their own players.

Two key points need to be made here. #1, Ben Wallace is the best and most effective defensive player in the league. Period. End of sentence. And he will continue to be that for the majority of this decade. So any cases made for other players is moot and a waste of time.

#2, Carlisle wasn't so much in the wrong for calling up media members to support his guy, as he was for having his assistant coaches break down film and come up with statistics to show how effective Artest is at things like limiting shot attempts.

If everyone did this, then many players would have a better shot at winning the award. Popovich's guy, Bruce Bowen, would have looked pretty good and heck, Michael Curry from a few years ago would look good for the award also.

It's like when voters go to the polls in November. Many are going to vote for George Bush or John Kerry based solely off the ads they've seen on television. These ads many times contain certain statistics and numbers that can make their candidate look good.

But what if the ad never aired? How would many people know who to vote for? You see, this explains why Ron Artest won the award by such a landslide.

Now, don't get me wrong. He's a great defensive player. But he's not the "hands down" best defender in the league.

◆ ◆ ◆

COACH DETROIT

Did you notice Larry Brown wearing the Charles Rogers jersey this week? He's very supportive of all the Detroit teams. Earlier he was seen wearing a Red Wings jersey and a Tigers jersey and hat.

Alan Trammell returned the favor by wearing a pin stripe suit (a Coach Brown staple) in honor of Larry.

◆ ◆ ◆

ASK DR. FEVER

Question: You mentioned in the last "Ask Dr. Fever" column that the Pistons, like they did in Game 2, would continue to experience some growing pains in this year's playoffs, as they look to go from being a relatively inexperienced playoff team into playoff leaders. Did you see any positive signs of this type of growth in the Bucks series?

Dr. Fever: Yes, and the most important, and potent, aspect of growth they showed was on defense.

Wasn't it fun to watch the Pistons defense attack Michael Redd throughout the series? Rip, though he committed a lot of fouls, did a good job by chasing Redd all over the perimeter. He kept him from getting set, getting to his sweet spots, and getting any rhythm.

So, Redd was left trying to drive the lane, were he encountered what Rip likes to refer to as "the terrordome", as Ben and Rasheed were blocking all his shots.

Notice too that Desmond Mason was rocked down to 34% shooting for the series. And don't even get me started on Keith Van Horn.

The Pistons took the Bucks' top 3 scorers and held them well below what they're capable of. They attacked those guys and didn't allow them to play their game. If your top 3 scorers can't play their game, then your entire team can't play its' game either.

This is one key example of growth for the Pistons at the playoff level. In the past, different guys would shine against us in the playoffs. And that would make winning into a serious struggle.

GAME 1

PISTONS 108 BUCKS 82

(HOME, Sunday, April 18th)

This was the first playoff game of the year, and it felt like an extension of last year's playoffs. The energy in the building was electric, the thunderstix were booming, and the team played so well and at such a high level.

Welcome to the 2004 NBA playoffs!

—The Pistons were ready to rock and so were the fans! Especially after we passed by a band, playing rock covers like "Livin' on a Prayer", on the concourse before the game. Then, Eddie Money, clad in a blue Pistons warm-up, sang the national anthem.

—Also in real rock concert-like atmosphere, there were flames shooting up from atop the 2 backboards during the pre-game. And this wasn't just fireworks; it was real fire, with flames shooting several feet into the air. It was like being at a Kid Rock concert.

—Ben's fro was out, baby!

—Rip is ready for business in these playoffs and opened the game up with 11 pts in the 1st Q

—Tayshaun had a fantastic alley-oop on the break, where he caught it and threw it down, covering a ton of distance

—Leading 27-21 after 1 Q, the Pistons were on their way, and the Bucks did a good job staying close in this volatile atmosphere

—In the 2nd Q, Ben blocked a Keith Van Horn flying lay-up attempt

—Damon Jones committed 3 fouls and Brevin Knight, 4 in the 1st H

—Speaking of Brevin Knight, whatever happened to that guy? When he was in Cleveland, he had game and was effective. Now we haven't seen much out of him the last couple of years and he appears to be the third string PG for Milwaukee (when TJ Ford is healthy)

—Tayshaun swatted Michael Redd's driving lay-up

—With a 52-43 lead at the H, things were going good, but the lead should have been greater for the Pistons at that point

—The Pistons trapped and pressured the Bucks all over the court in the 3rd Q, blowing the game open with steals leading to fast-break buckets

—Then, when Rasheed hit a triple while off balance, with the shot-clock running down, the lead was at 20 pts by the latter stages of the 3rd Q

—The scoreboard read 80-58 in favor of the Pistons going into the 4th Q

—The Bucks were just rattled by the Pistons D' and were throwing the ball all over the place in the 2nd H

—A tell-tale picture of the day: as the Pistons were pouring it on in the 4th Q, and Ben got a jam after dribble-drive penetration broke down the Milwaukee defense, Erick Strickland just put his head down in frustration for a few seconds while the Bucks were in-bounding the ball

—Ben gave his infamous "Fear the 'fro" signal to the bench as he came out of the game for good in the 4th Q

Notable Stats

*Michael Redd was limited to just 11 pts

**Milwaukee only had 7 off. rebs; the Pistons had 19

***The Pistons had 14 stls to contribute to 24 Buck turnovers

****The Pistons (due to turnovers and off. rebs) had 16 more FG atts. than Milwaukee, 91-75

It was a great way to open the playoffs and a stark contrast from last year when the team blew the very first home game vs. Orlando and lost home court advantage right

away. This year's team seems as though they learned their lessons from last year and are not going to let up and allow an inferior team to take control of a playoff series.

GAME 2

BUCKS 92 PISTONS 88

(HOME, Wednesday, April 21st)

Well, maybe I was wrong. The Pistons did let up and did allow the Bucks to take control, if even only momentarily, of the series.

This is too bad because they showed in this game that they took the Bucks lightly. They did not prove their superiority.

—Alley-oop to Rasheed right off the opening tip

—Michael Redd hit 2 quick triples early and had 8 fast pts, looking to be aggressive after a lack-luster performance in Game 1

—Cornrows for Ben tonight

—Larry Brown's favorite official, Bennett Salvatore was doing the game

—The score was tied 25-25 at the H

—Lions coach Steve Mariucci was in attendance

—After being down 7 pts early in the 2nd Q, the Pistons put on an exciting surge—and Rasheed was whipping the crowd into a frenzy!

—Pistons gave up too many (10) off. rebs and missed a lot of inside scores in the 1st H

—Damon Jones had 3 fouls in the 1st H again

—The Bucks were crashing the off. glass throughout 1st H: it was an obvious focus of theirs

—Milwaukee had 11 turnovers in the 1st H

—Down 48-41 at the H, the Pistons were lacking the proper intensity level and only shooting 38% from the field and had 0 bench pts

—Tayshaun and Ben each blocked Joe Smith dunks in the 3rd Q

—Due to Milwaukee resolve, their lead grew to 12 pts at the 5:30—mark of the 3rd Q

—Pistons were down 70-60 going into the 4th Q

—Chauncey in-bounded the ball off of Keith Van Horn's back, caught it and drew a foul early in the 4th Q

—The Pistons featured less trapping tonight than Game 1

—Double technical for Desmond Mason and Rip in the 4th Q

—Key moment: at the 6:24—mark of the 4th Q both Rip & Desmond Mason drew their 5th fouls

—Then Rip fouled out at the 4:58—mark, he tossed his face mask as he went to the bench and got his 2nd technical and an ejection

—As he left the court Rip was vociferously yelling across the floor at Desmond Mason

—Milwaukee wouldn't miss from the field at all in the 2nd H

—Ben was being held on many rebound attempts

—In the last 3 mins. the Pistons put on a furious rally. It was a 16-3 run to pull within 2: a Lindsey steal and the ensuing bucket by Mike James, plus a deep 3-pter by Rasheed were the highlights

—Damon Jones missing 2 FTs with 9.2 secs left gave the Pistons a great oppty, but…

—The ball slipped out of Rasheed's hands as he rose up to shoot a triple

The Last Play

Tayshaun had the ball at the top and was supposed to make a play, ideally for himself, but to also look for others if the defense converged. Rasheed was deep in the left corner and Lindsey was on the left wing. The play was mis-aligned because Lindsey was supposed to be on the right wing.

As Tayshaun drove, he sensed Lindsey's man coming over to help out, so he dished to Lindsey, who drove, and finding nothing, kicked it back to Rasheed with secs. left.

Tayshaun would later say that he should have taken the shot himself, that he over-anticipated what Lindsey's man was doing.

Notable Stats

*Michael Redd rebounded well from Game 1 with 26 pts

**Bucks had 16 off. rebs to the Pistons 13 (though not a significant difference, the Pistons were +12 in Game 1 and a -3 in this game means a difference of 15 off. rebs and thus 15 possessions that were lost vs. Game 1)

***The Pistons had 10 stls. leading to 18 Buck turnovers

****Rasheed only had 12 shot attempts (this is not going to work when you're behind as much as the Pistons were. Your star players have to be given the opportunity to be stars and rescue the game. Get Rasheed the ball!)

The Pistons shot 24 triples, which is way, way, way too many

As the game went down the stretch, I couldn't believe that Rasheed wasn't seeing the ball in the post. That's exactly what we needed at that point. I thought maybe the coaching staff just wasn't calling the offense for him down low.

But, afterwards, Larry Brown said in his post-game press conference that the players made mistakes by not looking into the post. He said that both Rasheed and even Ben should see the ball inside. And of course he didn't like all the 3-pt attempts.

Another big concern of Coach Brown's was that his team lacked poise down the stretch. You had a player getting ejected, players upset over foul calls, and guys going away from the team concept to try to make up for the deficit with things like triples and a lot of individual play.

GAME 3

PISTONS 95 BUCKS 85

(AWAY, Saturday, April 24th)

—Corn rows for Ben

—1st Q foul trouble: Rip had 2 by the 1:10—mark and Ben had 2 by the 8:42—mark! Both were forced to the bench.

—Memo came in for Ben, and after not playing much in the first 2 games, he played real well with 7 pts in the 1st Q

—Pistons got down 14-6 early as the Bucks shot 7-10 on FGs to start

—Jones was shooting out of his mind early, 3-3 on triples in the 1st Q, including one that was deeeeeeeppppppp

—Milwaukee had 9 fast-break pts in the 1st Q: not good

—Milwaukee led 30-22 after 1 Q

—Jones got his fast-break lay-up blocked by Darvin Ham. What was he thinking?

—Keith Van Horn's 3rd foul came at the 8:12—mark of the 2nd Q

—Tayshaun had the most amazing play in the 2nd Q: after having the ball stripped from him on a break attempt by Toni Kukoc, he hustled back and on the ensuing break, blocked Kukoc's dunk attempt! It was awesome; he got him from behind!

—2 Pistons' fans in attendance, a couple, were "All Detroit": the man had a Wings jersey on and the lady a Tigers jersey and a Pistons' hat

—The Pistons had 12 turnovers at the H, which is way, way, waaaaayyyyyyyyyy too #%&@'n much!

—Bucks led 49-42 at the H

—The Pistons opened up with a big run to start the 3rd Q: in a flurry!

—It was 12-0, 15-2, and 23-4 over the course of the first half of the 3rd Q, featuring several 3-pt plays

—Ben blocked a Van Horn triple try

—It was a double-digit lead, but the Bucks came back a bit by the end of the 3rd Q to make it 74-68 going into the 4th Q

—We saw very little of the Pistons' trap in this game

—Rasheed picked up his 5th foul at the 6:00—mark of the 4th Q, taking him out of the action for a couple of mins. He fouled intentionally to stop a lay-up, which is normally good playoff basketball policy, but in this situation it probably would have been better to have him playing with one less foul.

—Ben was absolutely surreal in the 2nd H! He was capturing, gathering, and sucking up **every** rebound that was available. He finished with 21 rebs. and 3 blocks in just 32 mins. of play, baby!

—Tayshaun blocked a Brevin Knight lay-up down the stretch that was huge

—Rip made some big buckets for us down the stretch

—The Pistons' D' was great in the 2nd H and just locked down on the Bucks in the last several mins. They scored 36 pts the entire 2nd H, baby.

Notable Stats

*Tayshaun had 8 rebs. and 4 blocks!

**Bucks were held to 7 off. rebs.

***Pistons only had 4 stls and Bucks only committed 7 turnovers

****This time the Pistons only attempted 12 triples

*****Bucks were held to 37% on FGs

Now, this is more like it. The superior team taking back control of the series the first chance they get. Rock on boys!

GAME 4

PISTONS 109 BUCKS 92

(AWAY, Monday, April 26th)

—Coach Terry Porter inserted Van Horn into the starting lineup, replacing Brian Skinner

—Van Horn got off to a good start with 3 early buckets, but then not much else later

—The Bucks, as will happen for home teams in must-win situations, got out to a 9-2 start

—The Bucks are doubling Rasheed & Corliss every time they get it in the post

—Pistons were up 28-27 after 1 Q

—This game had a lot of back & forth action in the 1st Q, with shots going in from all over

—Commissioner David Stern and Packers' running back Ahman Green were both in attendance

—Rip was sizzling with 13 pts in the first 16 mins. of the game

—Ben was 5-6 on FTs in the 1st H

—You can hear Rasheed talking on D', even when he's at the scorer's table waiting to check in. In the 2nd Q, his voice could be heard yelling even on TV, "By yourself Lindsey! By yourself!"

—Pistons shot 56% on FGs in the 1st H and had 30 pts in the paint

—Bucks were hot in the 1st H shooting triples at 5-8

—The Pistons were up 52-49 at the H

BLOCK PARTY

In the 1st Q,

—Ben swatted Redd's jumper early
—Rasheed rejected Mason's driving lay-up, then caught it

Then in the 2nd Q,

—Rasheed annihilated Redd underneath (oh yeah, and his shot too) in the 2nd Q
—Memo blocked Smith from behind

During the 3rd Q,

—Ben blocked Redd at the summit
—Chauncey blocked Van Horn from behind!
—Desmond Mason got his flying dunk blocked by Ben

Finally by the 4th Q,

—Ben got another block on Redd
—The Bucks were missing a bunch of shots inside, greatly affected & just intimidated by all the blocks so far in the game

By the time the game was over, the Pistons had 10 blocks! Plus several other forced misses by the mere presence of shot blockers.

—Chauncey had an amazing shot in the 3rd Q, hitting a glasser off one leg while falling down

—Tayshaun is really out & running on the wings in these playoffs!

—He's had a bunch of fast-break dunks

Great Sequence

Jones hits a deeeeeepppppppppp triple with the shot clock running out; then with the crowd going wild, Rasheed gets the ball in the post. He makes several hilarious facial expressions while feeling Smith on his back. Then he spins baseline, scores, and draws

a foul. Next his index finger rises to his lips, telling the crowd to quiet down! That's classic!

—The Pistons were up 74-68 after 3 Q's

—Darvin Ham played a few token mins. at the beginning of the 4th Q

—Staying after it: Lindsey turned it over poorly, then stole it back and scored right away

—Pistons defense was great tonight. They allowed no open looks for Redd at all. He kept trying to drive it inside instead and then the Pistons kept blocking his shots.

—There wasn't much Piston trapping tonight

—At one moment, referee Jim Clark wanted Coach Brown to settle down a little bit and put his hand on Brown's arm as he tried to walk him back towards the bench. Larry did not like that!

—Jones played real well for them: 6-6 on FGs and 3-3 on triples

—Joe Smith had 17 pts and 12 rebs

—Rip finished with 27 pts and Chauncey had 19 pts and 9 assts.

—Meanwhile, Tayshaun did everything as usual

—Pistons were 20-21 on FTs for the game

GAME 5

PISTONS 91 BUCKS 77

(HOME, Thursday, April 29th)

—Van Horn still starting for them

—He got his driving lay-up blocked by Ben early

—Smith had 8 pts in a heartbeat to start the game

—The 'fro is out for Ben

—Mason was 3-3 and 4-6 on jumpers right out of the gate, shooting hot

—Tigers Ivan "Pudge" Rodriguez and Rondell White were in attendance

—Redd got his driving lay-up thrown out of there by Ben

—Darvin got in just before the end of the 1st Q and oddly was shooting jumpers with a lot of freedom. He was 1-3 early.

—He shot the worst air ball I've ever seen in playoff basketball in the 2nd Q

—The Pistons led 24-22 after 1 Q

—Skinner got his driving move blocked by Rasheed

—Very good play by Lindsey: on a 2 on 3 fast-break, he took a charge to break it up in the 2nd Q

—Both teams played a ragged 2nd Q, missing shots and playing kinda sloppy

—Ben swatted Redd on a lay-up, coming out of nowhere

—A 9-0 run opened the lead up for the Pistons in the 2nd Q

—The Pistons led 39-32 at the H

—David Hall, seen on more commercials (for Rock Financial) than George Bush and John Kerry, was even interviewed by George Blaha and Bill Laimbeer on UPN at the H. According to George, Hall is a scratch golfer.

—Meanwhile, on TNT, Craig Sager was seen outside the Chrysler Museum talking about the Motor City and Dodge cars

—The shooting percentages were 34% for the Bucks and 38% for the Pistons at the H; but the Pistons had 10 turnovers at the H

—All of the misses led to a lot of rebounding opportunities. The Pistons had 32 at the H, which is a very high number.

—An 8-0 Pistons run opened up the 3rd Q

—The Pistons seemed to keep trying to make the big play in the 3rd Q, rather than just systematically taking down this team

—Redd, clearly affected by the Pistons' kick-ass defense, shot back to back airballs in the 3rd Q

—By the end of the 3rd Q, the Pistons were up 69-54

—Rasheed was really limited by his plantar fasciitis

—Tayshaun was everywhere tonight, doing everything!

—Tay's stat line went like this: 24 pts, 9 rebs, 8 assts

—27 assts and 21 fast-break pts for the Pistons is very nice

—As Ben went to the bench for the last time, he gave the "Fear the Fro" signal to the crowd and his bench. Rock on Ben!

—Then when Tayshaun went out, he had a big hug for Larry Brown. That's great to see because early in the year, Coach Brown was tough on Tay, and now Coach is saying that he was the MVP of this series.

The Pistons finished off this series just the way you'd like them too. When they won Game 3 in Milwaukee, they weren't satisfied. They went out and approached Game 4 with the same focus and got that one too. Then, back home for this game, they didn't mess around. They just defensively controlled this game from the outset and put away an inferior team.

9

The New Jersey Series 2004 Playoffs Round 2

◆

(The Playoff Diaries: May)

05/06/04—A Game 1 Masterpiece

This series is going to be fun. It's the Nets after all! The same team that ended the Pistons' season last year. So bring your hard hat and grab the lunch pail! It's time to rock!

◆ ◆ ◆

ASK DR. FEVER

Bob: The Doctor is in. Please grab a cold one and relax.

Question: What's up with all these off days in the playoffs? It sucks!

Dr. Fever: It is a bit crazy. What it boils down to is the fact that the NBA wants basketball on TV every night of the week if possible. Originally this series was due to start on Wednesday. Then it would have followed the normal pattern of playing most games every other day.

The way the other series ended up meant that there was no game set for Monday, so they moved the Pistons' series up 2 days.

While this is all well and good to maximize TV revenue and exposure, I am concerned about the quality of the game. With so many days off for many of these series, it can create some rusty, hap-hazard basketball. Just ask the Nets how it felt shooting 27% from the field in Game 1 after having 8 days off.

The Pistons, for their part, had played only 1 game in 6 days prior to the beginning of this series. But, the Nets will have played just 1 game in 12 days until Game 2.

◆ ◆ ◆

SCOUTING THE NETS

After looking at New Jersey from both a statistical and non-statistical standpoint, the following conclusions were drawn:

REGULAR SEASON

Defense

The Nets are a very good defensive team, and they do more than just create turnovers. They rank #4 in pts allowed, #5 in opponents' FG%, and #6 on opponents' assts per game. They are right near the bottom in blocked shots.

Offense

The Nets are a pretty average offensive team overall. They're points per game (ranked 23rd) and FG% (16th) are just above what the Pistons averaged on the year. This team is not particularly deadly on 3-pt shooting.

What they are good at is scoring in transition. They love to fast-break. They also like to score on alley-oop and lob plays out of the half-court set.

It's also important to note that the Nets rank #2 in the league in assts (and Jason Kidd ranks #1 for players) per game, meaning most of their offense comes directly off very good passing and offensive sets where individuals are lined up in positions where they can immediately have an advantage vs. their defender.

Richard Jefferson, Kenyon Martin, and Kidd are "The Big 3" scoring-wise on their roster. After those guys, the Net players' point production falls way off.

KEY CONCLUSION: The Pistons cannot allow this team to run. If the Nets are able to get out on the break, they will be able to get easy scores, jump-start their half-court game, and establish their flow, style, tempo, and tenor of the game. Many times, stopping the initial break might not be enough. They'll have trailers and options that they'll want to explore on the secondary break. Also, the fact remains that just like last year when we last saw this team in the playoffs, they are fairly weak in their half-court offense.

How do the Pistons keep the Nets from running and getting those alley-oops they like? By doing the following:

Key Task #1: Rebound the ball, both offensively and defensively. Offensive rebounds mean more possessions for the Pistons and less for the Nets. It changes the style and tenor of the game away from what the Nets want to do.

Defensive rebounds will keep the Nets from getting second shots, which means less broken floor situations and fewer opportunities for easy scores off of direct passes.

Remember, the Pistons' defense is as good as it gets in the game of basketball. If they keep the Nets from getting the easy stuff, then the Nets are going to have a real hard time scoring out of their half-court offense.

Key Task #2: "Play the right way." Larry Brown says this all the time. In this case it's even more key than normal.

If the Pistons show offensive patience, have good floor balance, work the ball inside, and play unselfishly it will go a long ways towards diffusing the Nets' strengths. Quick shots are usually long shots. One of the oldest rules in basketball is that long shots mean long rebounds; and long rebounds mean fast-break opp-tys for the opposition. This is also why it's important to work the ball inside.

In addition, post-ups and dribble-drive penetration usually mean more trips to the foul line. Getting to the foul line stops the action and allows your defense to get set before the Nets can attack: thus, no advantage and no break.

Proper floor balance means that you have a good proportion of your offensive players on the perimeter vs. the baseline area. If this proportion is out of whack, then you're likely to not have enough people on the perimeter to get back on defense.

Or if too many players are on the perimeter, then you'll have many of the opposition's corresponding players in positions where they're able to leak out. And in the game of basketball, even 2 steps is a tremendous advantage and could mean the difference between scoring a basket on the break or not.

Many times improper floor balance happens because a team is not patient or has guys who are playing selfishly. If a team runs its set plays, then it ends up forcing all 5 defensive players to work on that possession and moves them around. This makes it harder for them to get in rebounding and early break positions.

By the same token, if a guard takes a shot early in the possession, many times the big guys will be spread out (and possibly on the perimeter) as they are trying to set up the offense. If the guard misses the shot, then it's easy for the defense to rebound. Since all the opposition's big players are spread out further on the floor too, they're able to break down the floor faster and get in transition.

Key Task #3: Do not turn the ball over. The Nets are #4 in the league at forcing turnovers and #8 in creating steals. Once again, Jason Kidd is the key reason why. He likes to roam around on defense and wreak havoc.

Obviously, you don't want to turn the ball over against a team like the Nets because they'll turn it into a running oppty. Plus, it puts the style and tenor more into their favor than the Pistons.

Key Task #4: Execute transition defense. The Pistons must be absolutely always conscious of getting back on defense. But, you can't just get back; you've got to match up as well.

When it comes to fast-break basketball, the Nets will take a mile if you give them only an inch. The Pistons need to choke off this propensity that they have to run, as much as possible.

Key Task #5: Do not allow a key bench or role player to come up big for them. This is important simply because if their bench plays well, it can undermine all of the good things that the Pistons do if they accomplish the first four tasks.

Plus, the Pistons are so deep that you don't want to have some of that effectiveness diminished by the Nets' own bench. With Rasheed below capacity due to his sore arch, the Pistons do not necessarily hold a strong advantage over them in terms of offensive & defensive weapons.

Their key bench and role guys are Aaron Williams, Rodney Rodgers, Jason Collins, and Lucious Harris. The Nets bench accomplished very little during the regular season vs. the Pistons.

05/13/04—The Pendulum Swings

Within the last week, we've seen a huge swing of the pendulum in the Pistons—Nets series. At first, it was up high on the Pistons side, with them winning games 1 & 2 by 22 and 15 points respectively. Now, after the Nets won games 3 & 4 by 18 and 15 points, it has swung back hard to the Nets' side.

The last 2 games have been especially bad for the Pistons, as they just got their asses kicked. The team's effort and method of play have come into question. There were very troubling examples of poor play all around in Games 3 & 4.

That is the bad news. The good news is that the series is tied 2-2, and the Pistons have the home-court advantage.

History is also on the Pistons' side. Teams that go up 2-0 in 7-game series go on to win those series 96% of the time.

By the way, did you notice that all 4 playoff series were tied at 2-2? And through those games, the home team won all games, except for the Minnesota—Sacramento series, which is not a typical playoff series anyway.

This Nets vs. Pistons series has been really hard to gauge so far. All 4 games have been blow-outs, and for reasons besides just winning at home.

My guess is that the rest of this series is going to feature much closer, and better, games. Things have a way of evening themselves out over the course of a long playoff series. There are also no more surprises for either of these 2 teams. They both know exactly how the other side is going to play, as well as how they <u>want</u> to play.

These last 2 or 3 games could feature a wild ride of emotions, great defense, and (believe it or not) big-time offensive plays on both sides.

◆ ◆ ◆

ASK DR. FEVER

With everything that's happened within the last week, good, bad, and ugly, we thought we'd try to capture the emotional roller coaster that many of the Pistons' fans are on right now.

It's funny how things work. When the Pistons were winning games 1 & 2, the confidence reverberated around this entire basketball community. After getting hammered in Jersey though, many fans' have felt both frustration and disappointment in their team.

So, shown below are excerpts from some of the conversations that Dr. Fever has had with fans in the days following the last 3 games.

Notice the progression: from feeling like the Nets can't even stay in the series with the Pistons, to frustration and anger after the first loss, and finally, to a dazed feeling of doubt about how good the Pistons really are.

Saturday

Damien, after watching the Pistons simply overwhelm the Nets for the second straight time on Friday night, came in to see Dr. Fever. He had a bounce in his step and couldn't stop smiling when talking with Dr. Fever about Game 2. Two things were clear: he was very proud of his team and he didn't think that they should have any trouble at all finishing off the Nets and this series.

Damien: The Pistons just killed them last night, Doc. Sure we were down at the half, but when the Pistons started playing their way in the second half, there was no way that the Nets could match them. They didn't stand a chance.

And, Jason Kidd can't shoot. This team can't score in the half-court, especially not against the Pistons' D'. I just think the Pistons are so much better than last year and the Nets are about the same.

We're too deep; we have Rasheed; we have Mike James and Lindsey putting extra pressure on Kidd. In fact, I really can't see this series going more than 5 games.

Monday

Jeff came in with a fire in his eyes; all of his movements and body language were fast too. He was furious on this day after watching the Game 3 debacle.

Jeff: Dr. Fever, what the $#%& is wrong with them? That was horrible! We didn't even compete.

Tayshaun did nothing; Rasheed shoots too many three-pointers. And where was Chauncey? When Ben Wallace is your leading scorer, you know it's a bad night.

It's not fun seeing Richard Jefferson dunking and doing whatever he wants to. And Jason Kidd shot the ball very poorly. Imagine what would have happened if he made even half of his shots. We probably would have got beat by 30!

And 64 total points for the Pistons! What the !@#& is that!!??

Wednesday

Chris, a big fan who watches nearly every Pistons game, turned the channel before the end of the third quarter of Game 4. He couldn't stand to watch it any longer. He actually switched back to TNT late that night, only it wasn't for the Pistons; it was to catch some of the Lakers—Spurs game. "At least this is an interesting game to watch," he thought.

Needless to say, he was now very concerned about the Pistons' chances throughout the rest of the series based on their recent play. More mellowed out than Jeff, his confidence in the team began to waver.

Chris: I find myself beginning to doubt the Pistons' ability to win this series. It seems like they are so self-destructive. They throw the ball around in such a careless manner sometimes! Then, the Nets are just off and running and dunking the ball.

Rasheed's injury seems to be really limiting him and now Chauncey strained his back. And only Rip could score! I don't know if it's the Nets' defense or the Pistons' offense, but they can't do anything right on offense anymore. In the first 2 games, they seemed to be really rolling. But now, they couldn't throw the ball in the ocean.

The Pistons played like a much more timid team in New Jersey. This really bothers me because a championship—caliber team is supposed to be able to win on the road. Aren't they?

We keep saying that the Pistons have a great shot, and are maybe even the favorites, to come out of the East. Well, you're not going to get by Indiana if you can't win on the road (the Pacers have the home-court advantage). Heck, you might not even be able to win this series.

See now, I don't know what to think about Game 5. Whereas before the Pistons looked like they were unbeatable at home, it almost doesn't seem to matter right now because the momentum has shifted so much to the Nets. Can we figure out how to score again?

The Pistons are a great home team and The Palace will be jacked up for this game, so I think they'll be okay, or at least I hope so.

I know that George Karl recently said that there's a "karma" and a "spirit" to the Pistons this year and that they easily could be playing for the championship. But now, this series has broken down into just a few games of "must-win" situations.

After talking with many fans this week, Dr. Fever understands how they feel. He had the following comments that he wanted to pass along to the Pistons basketball community:

Dr. Fever: I think it's important, especially in light of the last 2 games, to remember that this is supposed to be fun. Granted, Games 3 & 4 were not in any way fun to watch on TV or listen to on the radio.

But, I think the blowouts are over for this series. We should see some tremendously competitive basketball in each of these last games.

One thing that I've become acutely aware of over the last week is the fact that the high expectations that have been placed on the Pistons to reach the NBA Finals this year, has caused for many fans to have a lack of appreciation for the moment.

It's nice to be as good as the Pistons are, with so much expectation. Now, if they don't get their act together soon and the Nets end up winning the series, then there's no fun in that.

But, based on what's taken place so far, I am anticipating an excitement-filled Game 5, as both teams attempt to take control of this series and establish a consistent level of play. So, whether you're going to The Palace on Friday, or just watching the game on TV, go into it with confidence and energy.

It's okay to be concerned about how they're playing right now, but don't let it affect your overall enjoyment of playoff basketball.

I have a friend who used to make it a point to have a bottle of scotch on hand every spring in the '80s when the Pistons would start their playoff run. The reason? Every year the team would get better and better, but would always get beat and eliminated by the Celtics.

It seemed like the Pistons were always inventing new heartbreaking ways to lose too. Remember when Adrian Dantley threw the inbounds pass into the basket? Or how about the time that a Celtics player, I believe it was Robert Parrish, goal-tended the ball near the end of a key game with no call being made. And then of course, there was the pass by Isiah that Larry Bird stole.

Anyway my friend kept the scotch handy so that he could "drown his sorrows" after difficult losses. These games literally stressed him out that much.

We all work so hard every week and have plenty of stress to deal with all week long. So remember that it's important that stress doesn't permeate the fun things in life too.

05/19/04—"We're Going Back to the D!"

Those were the immortal words yelled by Mike James as Game 6 ended, and the Pistons walked off the floor victors in a contest that many didn't feel they'd have much of a chance of winning.

"New Jersey's great in close-out games". "The Pistons play awful in New Jersey". "The Pistons will be too emotionally and mentally drained to be able to bounce back only 48 hrs. after the Game 5 epic". This was the rationale many used. But the Pistons, ever resilient, gave a tremendous effort that was full of pride. And now, they get a Game 7 with the Nets to decide it all. Right here, in the "D".

◆ ◆ ◆

We have extended coverage of the actual games this week (especially the Game 5 classic) and Dr. Fever wanted to pass along a few quick words of wisdom for everyone who's about to buckle their seatbelt for that wild ride that will be Game 7.

Dr. Fever: Well, here we are ladies and gentlemen! After 6 games and 2 and a half weeks, this series will finally be over.

It has really been one of the most unusual playoff series you'll ever see. Both teams just blew each other out on their home floors in the first 4 games and since have played 2 games that were as tightly contested as you could ever expect.

Game 7 will feature more of the same. It's going to be a battle. Watch out as Jason Kidd plays out of his mind and tries to get a triple-double. Pump your fist as you see a Piston player step up and play big that hasn't in awhile (think Memo, Mike James, Corliss, or Chauncey).

Expect a close game that will feature a ton of defense on both sides. And really for the Pistons to win, there are 2 main areas to watch. They both are tied into keeping Jersey off the break. As has been shown several times in this series, when Jersey is kept from fast-breaking, they can't score. Whereas when they are able to run a lot, they get a feeling of invincibility about them.

The first one is taking care of the ball. Obviously turnovers lead to easy running opptys for them (and usually dunks). The Pistons have, at times in this series, been a little careless with the ball. They can't have situations where they're turning it over on consecutive trips down the floor.

The second big thing is to simply make shots. The Pistons don't even have to shoot that great; they just need to consistently score in the overall sense. This keeps Jersey from grabbing a rebound and going off to the races. It's a lot harder to run when you have to inbound the ball and go up against a defense that's had a chance to set up.

In the 3 games the Pistons have won in this series, they have shot at least 43.6% on FGs. In the 3 losses, they've shot 37.8% or less.

I feel good about Game 7, both as a Doctor and as a fan. In the history of the NBA playoffs, home teams have a record of 71-15 in Game 7s for an 83% winning percentage. Plus, The Palace will be really jacked up for this one!

GAME 1

PISTONS 78 NETS 56

(HOME, Monday, May 3rd)

The opener had a lot of excitement in it on several levels. It was a long time in coming for the Nets, since it has been 8 days since they swept the Knicks. Meanwhile the Pistons have had 4 days off.

This game got started a couple of hours before what would be the Red Wings' last game of the year, getting eliminated in OT and negatively affecting sports fans all over Metro Detroit.

This was also the same night that President Bush was in town. He and country singer Travis Tritt were at a rally in Sterling Heights.

—Props to TNT when they played "Superstition" an old Motown classic by Stevie Wonder in the open

—A new look for Ben in these playoffs: braids!

—Ben rejected Kenyon Martin from behind on his dunk attempt in the 1st Q

—The Pistons had a lot of turnovers early. Many were against the shot-clock and Ben kept ending up with the ball on the perimeter as the clock was about to run out.

—There was clearly a conscious effort by the Pistons to keep the tempo slow and to work the ball inside. The floor balance was great!

—Tayshaun had an incredible alley-oop on a pass from Rip in the 1st Q

—Friendly faces in the house: Joey Harrington (wearing a Tigers' ball cap), Cliff Robinson, and Chucky Atkins!

—The Pistons led 18-14 after 1 Q

—The 1st Q also featured a 14-2 edge in rebs. for the Pistons

—Elden saw a lot of playing time in the 1st H, meaning a lot of rest for Rasheed and Ben

—The Pistons just held the Nets to one shot all night

—One example of the layoff these 2 teams faced was 9 turnovers for Jersey and 11 for the Pistons in the 1st H

—The Pistons were up 37-25 at the H; this score set an NBA record for all-time fewest combined points scored by half-time

—TNT played Kid Rock's "Cocky" (an edited version) when they came back for the 2nd H

—Martin's first 3 fouls were all bad fouls on his part

—Great play by Chauncey and Tayshaun! Chauncey threw a ball down the middle of the court that kind of floated over the defense (a low-liner though) that allowed Tayshaun to run under it, catch it in stride, and then….Tay was grabbed and fouled and still scored, flipping it up from behind his ear, while falling sideways!

—It was a 16-3 run that opened the game up in the 3rd Q

—Elden blocked a Rodney Rogers dunk on the break

—The Pistons were heard to be saying "One jump-shot and that's it!" coming out of every time-out, showing their commitment to getting defensive stops and giving no offensive rebs.

—The Pistons were up 57-39 after 3 Q's

—Then they just kept kickin' ass in the 4th Q!

It was a great victory for the guys. They snapped Jersey's 14 game winning streak vs. the Eastern Conference in the playoffs and did so in style. Defensive style. The 56 total pts the Nets had and the 25 pts that they had by the half were both 2 off of the NBA records for the playoffs. They finished 27% on FGs.

The 5 Keys To Victory

Key Task #1: Rebound the ball, both offensively and defensively.

The Pistons were **excellent** here. NJ only had 7 off. rebs, and the Pistons had 43 defensive rebs, which is just an incredible number.

Key Task #2: "Play the right way." (offensive patience, having good floor balance, working the ball inside, and playing unselfishly)

Very good on task #2. They had 21 assts. on 30 made FGs. This shows tremendous unselfishness. Floor balance was great, and they looked for offense inside early and often.

Key Task #3: Do not turn the ball over.

The Pistons were **okay** on #3. 16 turnovers is just over what teams generally average for TOs in a given game.

Key Task #4: Execute transition defense.

Very good. The Nets actually scored 19 fast-break pts in this game, but it never became the overall theme of the game. In fact, the style, tempo, and tenor of typical Nets basketball was barely felt tonight.

Key Task #5: Do not allow a key bench or role player to come up big for them.

Good. The only player who made an impact for them off the bench was Lucious Harris, who got 9 pts in 26 mins. of action.

GAME 2

PISTONS 95 NETS 80

(HOME, Friday, May 7th)

It was a wild atmosphere at The Palace for this one. The rapper Hush, who sings the Fox Sports' Pistons theme song, was performing outside the atrium before the game.

The 2004 NBA championship trophy was on display inside the atrium during pre-game as well. According to one of the handlers, it is worth $50,000 and is solid gold all the way through. A couple of Pistonsfever.com subscribers were seen checking out the trophy. This was after running into Eric Snow at a local restaurant.

During the player announcements, flames were shooting up from the top of the back-boards and the heat they generated could be felt all the way up into the 2nd level. The Palace was rockin' all night.

At halftime, William Hung of "American Idol" fame performed 2 songs to a rousing chorus of boos. He heard some applause as well, but overall was not happy about the reception he got.

What does he expect? He sucks!

—The Pistons, committing a critical sin against the Nets, took a ton of outside jumpers in the first half. Rather than working the ball into the post, where it belonged, and driving the ball with penetration, they were constantly settling for the first open shot.

—The Nets led 19-18 after 1 Q

—The 2nd Q featured more key errors by the Stones. They gave up way too many offensive rebs. and had several stupid turnovers. As discussed in the last Playoff Diary, these are things that you just cannot allow to happen against the Nets.

—There were very few guys playing well on the offensive end in the 1st H and there was no fluidity

—It was an emotion filled 2nd Q: ref. Joey Crawford teed up Rasheed and then Coach Brown got one, giving the team 2 back to back. Rasheed argued a call vehemently and then went out to half-court. There appeared to be multiple missed calls in that 2nd Q for the Pistons.

—The Pistons were giving up a lot of dunks and points in the paint in the 1st H. The Nets led 24-12 in points in the paint by the end of the H.

—The Pistons were fortunate that the Nets were missing outside jumpers early or their half-time deficit could have been much worse

They were down 46-34 at the H, and to be honest things weren't looking all that good. The Pistons had several problems, not just one or two. They did just a poor job on almost all of the key tasks identified earlier. Victory seemed in doubt, and I found it funny that I thought to myself that the Pistons are going to need to score, and score quite a bit, in the 2nd H in order to give themselves an oppty to win this game. Normally my only concern for this team is defense; the offense can always take care of itself.

Then the second half started!

—The first few possessions of the H went back & forth with each team scoring and turning the ball over

—Then <u>all heck broke loose</u> for the Nets

—The Pistons suddenly were doing all the things that they weren't doing in the 1st H: driving the ball to basket, getting in the post, rebounding, playing under control, giving the Nets no fast-break opptys.

—The offense completely changed, from a jump-shooting focus to a constant focus on working it inside

—Then in the 4th Q, Rasheed drilled 2 triples and Chauncey 1 or 2, I can't remember, but those jumpers just killed the Nets

—Notice how much better the jumpers were, after spending so much time spreading the Nets' defense out and making it work defending the interior

—It's funny, but the whole run started with Ben's offense. He nailed 3 straight shots early in the 3rd Q that got the team going, including jumpers.

—Rip was fabulous tonight, just taking on this huge situation and hitting big shot after big shot. He finished with 28 pts.

The 5 Keys To Victory

Key Task #1: Rebound the ball, both offensively and defensively.

The Pistons were **Very bad in the 1st H; very good in the 2nd H** on this task.

Key Task #2: "Play the right way." (offensive patience, having good floor balance, working the ball inside, and playing unselfishly)

They were **Terrible on #2 in the 1st H; Outstanding in the 2nd H**. The ball was being shared for good shots in the interior.

Key Task #3: Do not turn the ball over.

Good overall. When they settled down in the 2nd H, the turnovers were kept in check. 12 is a good number for this one.

Key Task #4: Execute transition defense.

Bad in the 1st H; good in the 2nd H. There was very little running by the Nets in the 2nd H.

Key Task #5: Do not allow a key bench or role player to come up big for them.

Good. With the exception of Rodney Rogers' 11 pts, they were held in check.

GAME 3

NETS 82 PISTONS 64

(AWAY, Sunday, May 9th)

—NJ adjustment: Kidd guarding Rip (for size) and Kittles on Chauncey

—Rasheed committed 2 fouls in just 2 mins. and had to sit down early in the 1st H

—It was a very fast pace early, completely favoring the Nets; and the Pistons were contributing a lot to it with quick shots

—This fast pace led to 13 fast-break pts in the 1st Q: that is horrible

—Kenyon Martin had 11 pts in only 14 mins. of 1st H action; he had his 2nd foul by the 4:30—mark of the 1st Q

—The Pistons were down 20-5 at one point in the 1st Q

—Ben was the only guy scoring in the 1st Q for the Pistons

—After 1 Q, it was Jersey up 31-13

—The Pistons were down by as much as 21 pts in the 1st H

—Jefferson was throwing in 3's early

—The Nets D' was much stronger tonight

—Rip did a great job of consistently driving the ball to the basket in the 1st H and drawing fouls

—Ben was getting all the rebs. in the 1st H—and some were quite amazing

—Jefferson had 17 pts in the 1st H—way too many

—Ben had 11 pts and 13 rebs in the 1st H

—A 24-12 Pistons' run closed the H

—The Nets had 0 fast-break pts in the 2nd Q

—There were a lot of FTs in that 1st H: 23 for the Pistons and 18 for the Nets

—The Nets led 47-38 at the H

—The 38 pts were a franchise record low for the Pistons in a H

—Notice how Martin feels the need to urge his crowd on; that didn't happen at The Palace by any of the Pistons players because they didn't have to

—Jefferson made everything in the 3rd Q: just unconscious

—He was carrying his team with Martin and Rogers out with foul trouble and Kidd not hitting

—Snoop Dog was in the house

—The Pistons were down 66-52 after 3 Q's

—Lindsey swatted Kidd's jumper early in the 4th Q

—Ben had great passing tonight, especially into the interior

—The Pistons seemed to have a hard time getting the ball into the post all night; a lot of it was based on the angle of the Nets' defender not allowing an entry pass

—This game was long: 2 hours and 50 mins.

—Ben, just amazing and a leader all night, had 24 rebs.

—The Pistons shot 29% on FGs, which was just sick and 64 total pts tied a franchise playoff low

The 5 Keys To Victory

Key Task #1: Rebound the ball, both offensively and defensively.

Good.

Key Task #2: "Play the right way." (offensive patience, having good floor balance, working the ball inside, and playing unselfishly)

Terrible on #2. They couldn't get the ball into the post and did not reverse the basketball. Rasheed took 5 triples, which was half of his FG atts.

Key Task #3: Do not turn the ball over.

Bad. 18 turnovers are too many and quite a few of them were stupid in nature.

Key Task #4: Execute transition defense.

Bad. The Pistons gave up 21 fast-break pts. Although to be honest, the majority of the fast-break opptys for Jersey were created off poor offensive decisions and a lack of shot-making for the Pistons.

Key Task #5: Do not allow a key bench or role player to come up big for them.

Good. No role players really hurt the Pistons. It was all Jefferson with 30 pts.

GAME 4

NETS 94 PISTONS 79

(AWAY, Tuesday, May 11th)

—Pistons were down 10-2 early

—Rip was hot in the 1st Q, shooting 5-6 on FGs; he was taking advantage of his size over Kidd

—Rasheed in foul trouble again: 2 fouls at the 2:50—mark of the 1st Q

—New Jersey had 9 fast-break pts and 12 points in the paint in the 1st Q: <u>that's terrible</u>

—Rip had 10 pts and Jefferson 9 in the 1st Q

—Pistons down 21-18 after 1 Q

—Memo blocked Williams' lay-up early in the 2nd Q

—Memo played well in the 1st H with 8 pts in 10 mins.

—The Pistons were just <u>throwing the ball all over the place</u> in the 2nd Q: that means automatic dunks for Jersey. Corliss was playing like he was asleep out there, throwing it directly to Nets players.

—There were 11 Piston turnovers in the 1st H

—Chauncey hurt his back and is limited tonight and Rasheed tweaked his sore arch

—Way too many off. rebs. for Jersey in the 1st H

—The Pistons were down 47-40 at the H

—Kidd got hot in the 3rd Q

—They want it more than we do

This was just a pitiful performance on every level. The 4th Q was especially hard to sit through. They didn't even compete in that 2nd H.

The 5 Keys To Victory

Basically, the Pistons were either **bad or just plain terrible on all of the keys.**

GAME 5

NETS 127 PISTONS 120 (3 OTS)

(HOME, Friday, May 14th)

This was one for the ages. Everything happened on this night. And that is what made this one basketball game so incredible.

This was like a Shakespeare classic. Only, I think there were more twists in turns in this game than anything that the great writer ever produced.

This game had everything: plots, numerous subplots, heroic performances by star players, heroic performances by non-star players, even several mistakes and tragic plays. And oh, don't forget about the officials! They were there too, in full force, calling enough fouls to allow the game to have a "start and stop" tenor to it.

One of the players making heroic plays, Chauncey, had an interesting day. Both the Detroit News and Detroit Free Press had big stories in Friday's editions talking about how the success of the Pistons in this series was riding on Chauncey's shoulders. That's a lot of pressure!

The Free Press also reported on Saturday that Chauncey had purchased a Bentley earlier in the day on Friday. He hopes to have the license plate read "Big Shot"!

Sure his nickname is "Mr. Big Shot" for all of his clutch plays, but the foreshadowing of this was unbelievable, considering what took place in Game 5.

When I first entered The Palace on this Friday evening, I began to see many things out of the ordinary right away. One of the first things I saw was a life-size Ben Wallace bobble head.

It was quite impressive, standing right in front of the Palace Lockerroom store. Complete with tattoos and everything, this piece of memorabilia came with a hefty price tag. One of the gentlemen assigned to guard it told me it was for sale with a price of $24,000.

Now, I'm still not 100% sure that he wasn't mistaken and meant to say $2,400. But I guess in light of the fact that some of the best Lakers—Spurs Game 6 tickets were going for $15,000 according to TNT, prices at this level of the playoffs are all relative.

Bottom line: if you're rich, you can afford to be "bigger" fans than the rest of us.

Personally, I was just as impressed by the "Detroit Department of Defense" T-shirts being sold inside the store on this night. A new item, it is very sharp and has an edge to it: the way we like it in Detroit.

Upstairs on the concourse level, a few fans were seen grabbing some paper towels to dry off their clothes after getting caught in a downpour that had just begun outside.

The game started earlier than usual. A 7:00 start in Detroit is a rarity, especially on a Friday night. Normally Friday nights during the regular season mean an 8:00 start, which is much more reasonable for people who are getting off work after a long hard week and fighting all the traffic going north on I-75.

When the game began, the stands were somewhere between a half to two-thirds full. It took until the 2nd Q was half over to fill in the rest of the seats.

Why did they have this game start so early you ask? Because the NBA and TNT, who was broadcasting the game, figured they could get this game on and then by about 9:30 or so when it would end, they could show the Minnesota—Sacramento game too. They didn't count on the Pistons' game ending at about 11:15!

—The tempo was too fast early—it favored New Jersey

—The Pistons got down by as much as 12 pts in the 1st Q

—The Pistons were giving up too many drives early

—Bad TOs in the 1st H: 3 by Rip alone

—Actually Jersey had quite a few turnovers as well, mostly in transition

—Brian Scalabrine first got into the game in the 2nd Q. He scored at the 5:27—mark for his first bucket and had 2 more scores for 8 pts in that quarter.

Isiah Sighting

They showed Isiah up on the scoreboard sitting right next to a pretty white lady. I don't know if most people realized that this lady was in fact Chris Laimbeer. With

Bill apparently out of town with the Shock team he coaches, he must have given his ticket to Isiah.

The next day the Detroit Free Press showed a photo (and TNT showed a shot as well) of Isiah smiling and talking with Bill Davidson.

—Towards the end of the 1st H, Jersey shot 2 or 3 air balls near the end of the shot-clock as the Pistons defense was starting to lock them down. They only scored 18 pts in the 2nd Q.

—Tayshaun almost matched them himself with 13 pts in the 2nd Q alone

—The Pistons led 44-43 at the H

—Rasheed smacked Collins' attempt outta there from right under the basket in the 3rd Q

—K-Mart was double-blocked by Wallace & Wallace underneath in the 3rd Q

—Rip was setting up everyone. He had 9 assts through the 3rd Q

—Great block by Tayshaun: swatting Kittles' fast-break lay-up

—Chauncey got it going in the 3rd Q

—Jersey was going through one of their offensive lulls in that 3rd Q, struggling to get anything going

—Despite this fact, the Nets still had the lead by 1 going into the 4th Q

—It was 63-62 after 3 Q's

—The Pistons got into the penalty at the 9:15—mark of the 4th Q; this was very helpful as they shot 13 FTs from that point on in the Q

—A 2-3 zone made an appearance for the Pistons early in that 4th Q

—2 terrible calls went against Ben early in the 4th Q; it was a clean block and a clean knock-away; however, these calls kind of evened out over the course of the rest of regulation

—Ben blocked K-Mart's driving lay-up and it resulted in a jump-ball. The Pistons got the call from the bench—a set play was coming. With Chauncey stationed between Kittles and Collins on the side closest to the Pistons' basket, Ben tapped it way out front, towards Collins' side. This was a great play because Chauncey out-ran the bigger Collins, grabbed the ball, took off down court and got fouled.

—With a couple of mins. to go, Chauncey missed a big driving lay-up on the break (maybe he was thinking of lobbing it up to Ben who was underneath at the time)

—When K-Mart fouled out at the 2:29—mark and the towel went over his head and face, things were looking pretty good

—Rip fouled out on a bad call with 1:40 left in the 4th Q. This was big because the Pistons lost their most consistent scorer and creater tonight.

—The Pistons couldn't hit down the stretch of this 4th Q; they went over 4 mins. without hitting from the field

—Chauncey was struggling to make the big shots that he's become known to do down the stretch. There were 3 key ones that he couldn't convert. In fairness, he usually drills outside bombs in the clutch, and here the Nets were chasing him off those shots, so he had to take shots off the drive.

—He even broke free for a game-tying lay-up near the end, but Jefferson flew in from out of nowhere and blocked it

—At this point, things are just not feeling good and Chauncey's inability to come through is particularly painful

But....

With 2.9 secs. left, the Pistons inbounded the ball off a Nets' FT and were down by 3 pts. Chauncey got it and motored over half-court, and let it fly from about 45 feet. The ball banked in off the glass, and the score was tied! The place erupted and there was a party going on at The Palace!

Overtime.

1st OT

—Martin, Collins, and Rogers all fouled out, which made me happy. That is until I realized that Scalabrine was going into the game in their place. Based on how he played early in the game, shooting like a marksman, I was very concerned. He could be the X-factor that turns this game into their favor.

—Scalabrine played all the mins. of the 3 OTs. It was his first appearance since the 1st H. He immediately drilled a triple.

—Ben fouled out here—a serious blow to the Pistons effort

2nd OT

—Triples by Scalabrine, Kidd, and Jefferson were killers and the Pistons were down 5 pts with 2 mins. left

—One thing to remember for everyone disgusted by Scalabrine killing us on offense is that he did commit several fouls in the OTs

—Something key that I noticed about playing all these OT mins. is that fatigue leads to defensive breakdowns; there were so many times tonight when players on both sides got good shots and scores off of dribble penetration that was not there earlier in the game

—Scalabrine made a huge play to save a possession for them

—Rasheed fouled out, after playing 48 mins.; not bad for a guy playing on 1 leg

—Chauncey missed a big lay-up with a few secs. left; it was short; I don't know if his back was bothering him and he couldn't get lift, or he was tired at this point or what, but that basket would have been huge

—After the Nets missed a jumper with the score tied and the buzzer sounded, signaling a 3rd OT, Larry Brown had a wide grin on his face. He was realizing at that moment how amazing this game really was becoming!

Fandemonium

This is a good point to talk about some of the fantastic people who filled the stands on this night. Needless to say, the fans were taken on an emotional roller coaster throughout this game. One fan even said "I'm going out of my mind!" She was referring mostly to how the Pistons were blowing opportunities to score and win this thing.

For another fan, it was her first game ever at The Palace. Imagine a game like this being your first one! As the game progressed into one series of drama after another, everyone was feeling an increased level of awe by what they were witnessing.

First, a 45-foot shot sends the game into overtime; then several players were fouling out; Jersey would hit huge shots; big plays were happening all over the floor; mistakes were occurring all over the floor too. But after another 10 mins. of overtime action, the score still ended up being tied.

Exclamations like "I've never been a part of anything like this!" were yelled by several fans. And, I think we all discovered a new phrase to describe close, intense games. You've heard of "nail biters." Well this game was a "bladder buster."

Several people were trying to figure out how they could get to the bathroom to relieve themselves, and still not miss any of the game. "Hey it's a timeout…I'm going down right now! Wait a second; it's only a 20-second timeout! I've gotta wait."

This notion of the "bladder buster" became even more serious for fans who had had a couple of beers. And it also affected yours truly.

Though I had no beers on this night (I was on duty working for the people after all) the two waters I had that night were starting to have a serious impact on my internal organs.

When the buzzer sounded after the second overtime, I ran down to the concourse towards the restroom, running more so not to miss the game than anything else.

There was only one problem; several fans had already made it there and others were running to it as well. The line was already going out the door. So I said "Screw it. I'm not going to miss any of this game."

I went back up to my seats, understanding that, hey I can always get a bladder transplant if I need one. But, I would never get this type of playoff moment back.

Fortunately, the transplant was not necessary as I made it to the restroom after the third overtime.

3rd OT

—Tayshaun blocked Kidd's driving lay-up

—Lucious Harris was killer in this session with a traditional 3-pt play and a triple

—And, Jefferson scored a 3-pt play. It was 119-113 for the Nets at this point and things didn't feel good.

—But, the Pistons cut it back to 1 with a minute left

—Then Scalabrine hit a triple as the shot-clock ran out! That sucks!

—With 16.9 secs. left, Jersey was up by 3 and was about to inbound it on the right sideline. After being forced into a time-out before the first inbound attempt, Jersey wanted to inbound the ball to Kidd on the second oppty. The Pistons double-teamed him so he couldn't get it. Then, Lindsey out-worked and out-smarted Scalabrine to steal the ball!

—As Lindsey motored up-court, I was not surprised at all that he stole the ball. In fact, with the way the game had gone up to that point, I had basically expected it to happen just like that.

—Then something bizarre happened: Lindsey quickly drove all the way into the lane, where it looked like he was going to score a lay-up and cut the lead to 1 with like 8 secs. left. But then, he saw Chauncey flash open on the right wing, and passed it out to him for a triple. Chauncey missed and we had to foul.

At the time, I didn't understand what the heck Lindsey was doing. I thought he should have just laid it in; then the Pistons could have fouled and even if the Nets made both FTs, they would have had about 8 secs left for a triple.

The film later though showed that Kittles was back and Lindsey would have had to challenge him. But it seemed like a missed oppty at the time.

As I drove home, I pulled out my cell phone to check my messages. Interested to hear what friends watching on TV thought of this unbelievable game, I dialed up the voicemail number.

Though I did get to hear just what I was hoping for, you can imagine my head shaking when the first message that I listened to was a rather lengthy one from Verizon Wireless informing me that they had just upgraded my voicemail. Good for you Verizon! With many thoughts and emotions running through my body at this point, that was the last thing I wanted to hear about.

Epilogue (to this unbelievable game):

Consider this: 3-pt shots and 3-pt plays killed the Pistons in the 3 OTs. Scalabrine and Jefferson each hit triples in the 1st OT. Scalabrine, Jefferson, and Kidd all each had one in the 2nd OT. Then, Harris, and Jefferson hit 3-pt plays, while Scalabrine and Harris again, hit triples in the 3rd OT. That's nine 3-pt plays in the OT sessions alone and they accounted for 27 pts.

Let's face it: these plays illustrated the difference between the 2 teams. The Nets, with their experience of driving to the NBA Finals for the last 2 years, knew exactly how to react in this type of situation.

Though they made many mistakes just as the Pistons did, they seized the situation by drilling these big shots. Then the Pistons had to make a comeback in all 3 OTs. Instead of being on top and the front-runner, the Pistons had to keep coming back to try to reach their level. This illustrates the point: the Nets are where the Pistons want to be; not where they're at yet.

Kidd even said so afterwards. The Nets were in a position a few years ago that featured Reggie Miller draining a huge shot on them in the playoffs, that really damaged their hopes. He said that having gone through that experience, the Nets were prepared and knew how to react in a situation like tonight's game.

Now that the Pistons have been through something like this as well, they should be better prepared to be the successful team next time.

◆ ◆ ◆

When it was all over, 8 players had fouled out; 5 players had played 50 mins. or more; the Pistons shot 111 FGs; 97 FTs were shot by the 2 teams; it was 11:15 PM; the game was 4 hours and 15 mins. long. TNT's second game that night, Sacramento vs. Minnesota, was already at halftime!

The 5 Keys To Victory

Key Task #1: Rebound the ball, both offensively and defensively.

The Pistons were **Good** on this task. NJ only had 12 off. rebs, which is good for a 48 min. game; let alone a 63 min. one. The only thing that kept them from getting a "great" rating is the fact that they only had 19 off. rebs of their own. When you miss 69 FGs, you would like to get more off. rebs than that.

Key Task #2: "Play the right way." (offensive patience, having good floor balance, working the ball inside, and playing unselfishly)

They were **Good** on #2. If they could have shot better than 38% on FGs, they would have won this game.

Key Task #3: Do not turn the ball over.

Excellent. The Pistons finished with 15 turnovers. That's amazing considering the length of the game and the fatigue that could have made it worse.

Key Task #4: Execute transition defense.

Good. The Nets had 16 fast-break pts. We'll take that, especially when you consider that the Pistons had 15 on the break themselves.

Key Task #5: Do not allow a key bench or role player to come up big for them.

Awful. This was the one task that the Pistons failed to do well and it really cost them. Scalabrine finished with 17 pts and 4-4 on 3-pt shots; Harris had 12 pts. Between the 2 of them, several huge plays killed the Pistons in the overtime sessions.

GAME 6

PISTONS 81 NETS 75

(AWAY, Sunday, May 16th)

—Tayshaun picked up 2 early fouls and had to go to the bench

—The Pistons showed some 2-3 zone to throw a changeup at the Nets offense and keep them out on the perimeter; it seemed to work pretty well

—New Jersey led 13-2 early and was running and gunning

—They had a ton of dunks early

—But then the Pistons went on a 19-10 run to close the Q

—It was a 25-23 lead for Jersey after 1 Q

—The Pistons, especially Ben, were getting off. rebs early, creating several second shot opptys

—BIG LINEUPS: Check this: early in the 2nd Q, the Pistons had a lineup of Chauncey, Rip, Rasheed, Memo, and Ben to match Jersey's big lineup of Kidd, Harris, Williams, Scalabrine, and Martin

—But then, when Collins picked up his 3rd foul at about the 5:30—mark of the 2nd Q, the Nets went to a traditional lineup and the Pistons stayed big. I'm liking that!

—Rasheed swatted Martin's lay-up post move in the 2nd Q

—Memo blocked Kittles' flying dunk attempt in the 2nd Q

—Michael J. Fox and Bruce Willis were in the house

—Rip was sizzling with 16 pts in the 1st H: they were running a ton of screens for him! This is cool, run Kidd through as many picks as possible and wear him down!

—The Nets were out and running early and got 6 dunks when they built the early lead. But, the Pistons' defense tightened so much and they made shots! By shooting 53% in the 1st H, it slows the game down, baby! That's tough for Jersey.

—The score was 50-36 at the H in favor of the Pistons

—Ben had like 13 rebs. in that 1st H

—The Pistons pushed the lead up to 17 early in the 3rd Q

—But then, the Pistons had 3 bad TO's and the offense stalled out with no movement, giving the momentum back to Jersey, and causing them to go on a big-time run

—Tayshaun blocked Kittles' 3-pt shot in the 3rd Q

—The lead was down to 60-57 after 3 Q's

—Rip was rock-solid all night, making plays and scoring throughout

—The Pistons threw a small lineup out there for a little bit in the 4th Q: Rip, Chauncey, Lindsey, Memo, and Ben

—There were some more bad TOs by the Pistons that gave Jersey a chance in the 4th Q

—This game just was tight down the stretch, with the Pistons holding the lead

—The Pistons were more resilient and actually had more energy than the Nets

—With the Pistons up 2, Rip hit a huge shot: he pump-faked, took the bump from Kidd, and drilled the shot to put the Pistons up 4; that was the game

—Scalabrine was scoreless and didn't even attempt a FG

—The Pistons' bench played much better than in Game 5

—Ben, playing like the warrior that he is, got 20 rebs.

—Rip was wearing a jersey that said "Rip City" after the game

The 5 Keys To Victory

Key Task #1: Rebound the ball, both offensively and defensively.

The Pistons were **Very Good** on this task. NJ only had 9 off. rebs. Ben had this many by himself!

Key Task #2: "Play the right way." (offensive patience, having good floor balance, working the ball inside, and playing unselfishly)

They were **Good** on #2.

Key Task #3: Do not turn the ball over.

Bad. This was almost their undoing, as they had a couple of periods of time where they just threw it right to Nets players for instantaneous fast-break opptys.

Key Task #4: Execute transition defense.

Good. The Nets were off & running when the game began, but then the Pistons settled down (and locked-down on the Nets).

Key Task #5: Do not allow a key bench or role player to come up big for them.

Excellent. The Nets only had a total of 8 bench pts, 4 rebs, and 1 asst.

GAME 7

PISTONS 90 NETS 69

(HOME, Thursday, May 20th)

What a great game for Pistons' fans! The best way that I can describe the atmosphere on this night is that it was like going to a rock concert. And part of the reason is that it was such a blowout. That left the issue never really in doubt. Like going to see your favorite band play, it was just fun—pure fun all night.

And there was a lot of partying for a Thursday night! As we pulled into The Palace parking lot to try to find a space before the game, we went right by "tailgate row", where lots of young people where tailgating and rockin' out.

Inside the west atrium, a crowd had gathered behind George Blaha, Rick Mahorn, and Bill Laimbeer doing a TV pre-game show. The crowd was whooping it up and making a ton of noise!

Then I saw the "Isiah on a stick."

Now, I'd like to take a moment to point out that I've seen many things over the years when it comes to Pistons' spirit, but this was truly one of a kind.

A guy had a stick, that was sort of like a paddle, with a game photo of Isiah on it. He told others who were in this mass of people going towards the stairs to the concourse level to, "Give Isiah five! C'mon give him five!" Then, people would slap the paddle with the photo of Isiah on it.

Isiah was represented in other ways tonight too. A couple of his jerseys were walking around, including one of his college Indiana jersey. And, up at the seats, another guy had a Chauncey Colorado jersey on.

As the game was about to begin, the crowd was jacked!

—NJ got out to a lead in the beginning, but then the Pistons took over and never looked back

—Ben has the 'fro out baby!

—The Pistons were up 21-14 after 1 Q and were committing no fouls

—In fact, there weren't a ton of fouls called tonight; a true rarity in this series

—Ben was nailing jump-shots all night! He finished 8-10 on FGs. There's your team's star player stepping up in a big game, must win situation.

—Speaking of jump-shots, NJ was settling for a lot of them

—Famous faces in the crowd: Mayor Kwame Kilpatrick, Steve Mariucci, Dave Lewis, Tom Izzo, Steve Yzerman, and Bob Seger

—The Pistons were up 43-31 at the H

—In the 2nd H, they just overwhelmed the Nets

—Kidd struggled mightily. I didn't realize until someone sitting next to me pointed out that he had 0 pts. This was in the 4th Q, but he finished with this total as well.

—The Pistons' defense was awesome tonight, their offense was awesome, they were just great all over

—Rip was great all night. Did you know he hit 3 triples tonight?

—The big lineup of Memo, Rasheed, and Ben along the frontline made another successful appearance tonight

—Scalabrine scored 0 pts again. Why did Lawrence Frank play him sparingly in Game 6 and for only 5 mins. tonight? If you've got a horse who's hot, you've got to ride him for a bit.

—Tayshaun put the capper on a bad series for him, with a 1-9 shooting night. He has got to play better in the next round.

—After it was over, Ben told the press that the Nets basically didn't play as hard as the Pistons, nor did they want it as much. That's strange.

The rock concert atmosphere continued throughout the night. Beer was flowing. And like many shows I've been to, it was hot in the arena! Earlier in the day the humidity

was listed at 93%. Someone needs to talk to the facilities people at The Palace and tell them to turn on the air!

Waiting in line after the game for Pacers tix was pretty wild. People were yelling as they came down from the concourse level. One guy held up a huge blown up picture (and laminated no less) of Kidd's mug shot from when he was arrested for domestic abuse (or assault, or whatever it was) a few years ago.

Outside in the parking lot, beer bottles and broken glass had to be dodged as we drove out. Lighting was flashing throughout the sky and capped what was truly an electric night at The Palace.

The 5 Keys To Victory

Key Task #1: Rebound the ball, both offensively and defensively.

The Pistons were **Outstanding** on this task. A key way to evaluate rebounding, is to look at the opponents' off. rebs and NJ only had 6 tonight. That is fantastic! Even more so when you consider that they missed 43 shots. Rip and Tayshaun helped out by getting 6 rebs apiece.

Key Task #2: "Play the right way." (offensive patience, having good floor balance, working the ball inside, and playing unselfishly)

They were **Good** on #2. Twenty-one three-pointers were probably too many, and for a blow-out they shot a relatively low 40% on FGs. Otherwise it was good.

Key Task #3: Do not turn the ball over.

Outstanding. To only turn the ball over 8 times, is quite simply tremendous.

Key Task #4: Execute transition defense.

Very Good. The Nets only got 14 fast-break pts and a Game 7 is going to require more than that for a team that relies so much on transition basketball. The Pistons had 12 fast-break pts themselves.

Key Task #5: Do not allow a key bench or role player to come up big for them.

Very good. Rodney Rogers had 13 pts and 7 rebs. The rest of their bench scored a total of 2 pts. Scalabrine had 0 pts.

10

The Indiana Series 2004 Playoffs Round 3

◆

(The Playoff Diaries: May & June)

05/25/04—DEFENSE!

I hope you like defense! Because if you thought last night was some fun, get ready for more! This whole series is going to be like this.

In this entry we break down the Pacers for you. What they do well, and what opptys there are to exploit against them. Then of course, we have the game notes for the first 2 games of the series.

Unfortunately there is no "Ask Dr. Fever" column this week. And you can blame Bob.

Actually, it wasn't his fault. Like so many Metro Detroiters this weekend, his house and the area surrounding it were pounded by the torrential rains we had. As a result, his basement flooded and that meant some serious cleanup. So, Bob didn't have a chance to assemble the questions.

◆ ◆ ◆

SCOUTING THE PACERS

After looking at Indiana from both a statistical and non-statistical standpoint, the following conclusions were drawn:

REGULAR SEASON

Defense

The Pacers are a very good defensive team. They're physical and they're tough. They rank #3 in the NBA in pts allowed, 11th in FG% against, and 3rd in 3-pt % against. These three components demonstrate Indy's ability to lock in on shooters on the perimeter and other scoring threats all over the court.

Knowing Rick Carlisle and Ron Rothstein as I do, this team is very good at taking an opponent's primary strengths on offense and negating them as much as possible. You're not going to be able to run offensive sets the way that you really want to. Scoring is going to be tough to come by at times.

The Pacers also do an excellent job of forcing turnovers (ranked #8) and creating steals (ranked #6).

With Ron Artest wreaking havoc on the perimeter and Jermaine O'Neal blocking and contesting shots on the inside, this team can attack on defense in a variety of ways. Artest is a big and bruising defender who will guard a player just as much before he gets the ball as when he has it. It will be tough for his man to get good position and find his "sweet spots" on the floor against him.

Offense

Here's where you're going to see the biggest difference in this opponent vs. what New Jersey offered in the last round. The Pacers play a completely different style.

If you want to know how they play on offense, just go back to the last 2 years of Pistons basketball when Carlisle was coach and you'll see the exact same style. The only difference is that he now has a great post-up option that he can go to in Jermaine O'Neal.

This is a team that plays a slow style and likes to emphasize certain mis-matches. Role players have very few plays called for them. Carlisle likes to emphasize and feature the players that have the most offensive weapons in their arsenal and hide players' offensive weaknesses.

Obviously with the slow tempo, the Pacers rank pretty low in scoring (20th). They also rank 19th in FG%, but are a healthy 9th in 3-pt %.

Creating turnovers against them won't be easy: they're 9th in least # of turnovers given up and 4th in protecting against steals.

What's interesting is that they get their shots blocked a lot (2nd in the league), illustrating how slow they like the tempo to be. Undoubtedly, this team finds itself up against the shot clock on many occasions and has to put up some shots under duress and heavy defensive pressure. That leads to blocks.

Other Key Variables

The Pacers have a deep bench, and along with the Pistons, are among the deepest and most talented teams around. The Pistons are going to have to watch Al Harrington. A guy who averaged 13 ppg and 46% on FGs during the year, he can be a difference maker. At 6'9" and 250 lbs., he's also a load.

Other than Harrington, they don't have any one player that really stands out on the bench, but rather several that can contribute a little here and there. And that's the point: the Pacers come at you with everybody; some in small ways and some in big ways. They have 5 players who average between 5 and 7 ppg on the bench alone.

They're a true team. That's why guys like O'Neal and Artest could miss time due to injury this year and they still kept right on winning. Their 61 wins were the best in the NBA this season.

THE 5 KEYS TO VICTORY

Key Task #1: Win the battle of the benches. With only 1 day off between every game of this series, the benches of both teams are going to play a vital role. The starters will get a bit tired at times.

With the 2 benches being so evenly matched, the 1 that plays best will probably also be the team that wins that particular game. Also Rasheed's foot will not be able to withstand the constant pounding of playing every other day, at least not to the point that he can play major minutes. Memo, Corliss, and Elden are going to have to produce on both offense and defense.

Key Task #2: Contain their 3-pt shooters. As noted earlier, the Pacers can shoot from outside. If the Pistons can limit their effectiveness on the perimeter, it will not only decrease one of the Pacers' primary ways to produce pts, but it will also serve to help contain O'Neal. He's their only post player. If the Pistons are not forced into chasing hot 3-pt shooters all over the floor, then they can provide some extra help and defensive pressure on O'Neal.

Key Task #3: Don't allow it to become a Ron Artest-type of series. If Artest is able to do a lot of what he likes in this series, it'll turn him into a star. It will also do in the Pistons.

Artest has a very unique style. His shot doesn't look pretty, but it goes in quite often. He'll miss lay-ups, but then hit triples. He likes to drive. Artest will block your shot, he'll knock it away, and he'll steal it. He also likes to bruise people on both defense *and offense*. Sometimes watching him play is like watching a bull in a china shop.

If Artest is able to get into a comfort zone playing successfully in the way outlined above, then the Pistons' oppty to win is diminished.

Key Task #4: Use athleticism to provide periodic advantages. The Pistons are a very athletic team, with several horses. The Pacers have guys who are bigger and thus a bit slower than the Pistons.

The Pistons should use this to their advantage to do things like create some fast-break opptys, defend all over the floor to the Pacers' primary scorers, and create steals.

Key Task #5: Use experience and smarts to keep a better focus and edge than the Pacers. The Pacers are so young, it's unbelievable. They have 3 players on their roster who came straight out of high school to play in the NBA within the last handful of years. Only a couple of their players are over age 30.

Other than Reggie Miller (and little-used Kenny Anderson and Anthony Johnson), no one on their team has ever been this far in the playoffs. The Pistons, meanwhile, have been to the Conference Finals before and just came off a tough series vs. the two-time defending Eastern champion. They grew a lot from that 7-game experience. The Pistons have more veteran players and leadership as well.

The Pistons should be able to out-wit the Pacers a couple of times in this series. Also, if they don't get frazzled by things like officiating (which they have been known to do in the past) then they stand a good chance of prevailing.

06/05/04—OH YEAH!

The Pistons are back in the NBA Finals! And they did it by beating the Pacers in what was a classic Conference Finals battle.

The scene after Game 6 was electric! Confetti was flying from the rafters, some fans pushed their way onto the court, and smiles were everywhere. As the guys took turns holding the Eastern Conference championship trophy, I could see Rasheed was grooving.

And he kept grooving even while being interviewed on ESPN. As Joe D, Rasheed and the others were interviewed, the mics were hooked into the Palace sound system, but it didn't matter. The fans were cheering so loud (and chanting "Beat LA") that you couldn't hear what any of the guys were saying.

At one point, during a timeout in the 4th Q, Kid Rock went onto the court and started waving the Pistons' flag around to stir the people into even more of a frenzy than they already were at that point. Then when Rasheed came out onto the floor, he slapped five with him.

The Kid made his way into the Pistons' locker room after the game as well and was congratulating the guys.

When we went out into the parking lot after the game, horns were honking and people were having so much fun!

Now, in the words of Kid Rock, the Pistons are "Packing up my gang and (heading) out West"—from the song "Cowboy"

GAME 1

PACERS 78 PISTONS 74

(AWAY, Saturday, May 22nd)

—For the 3rd straight game, Larry Brown went with a no-tie look. He's being superstitious since the Pistons won the last 2 games of the Jersey series with that look.

—At the beginning, Chauncey went over to say hello to Rick Carlisle and Ben gave him a little hug

—Ben blocked Jeff Foster from right under the rim

—The Pistons showed a real focus on getting their guards involved early. Jamaal Tinsley can't guard Chauncey and Rip's too fast for their shooting guards.

—Tayshaun was having a lot of trouble staying with Ron Artest. Artest kept getting by him and going to the rack.

—The Pistons were up by as many as 9 in the 1st Q and it looked like they were poised to take this game

—The Pistons led 26-22 after 1 Q

—The Pistons had a ton of 1st H turnovers: 11; that's not going to work

—The Pacers were getting it done in the paint in the 1st H. They kept isolating 1 on 1 and beating the Pistons to the basket. They were also getting off. rebs.

—Corliss cannot score and Elden looks terrible

—There was a lot of over-officiating in the 1st H

—Both teams threw some zone at each other, trying to disrupt and surprise the other team

—The Pacers led by as many as 9 in the 2nd Q, just taking control of the game right back from the Pistons

—Al Harrington had 14 pts in the 1st H and Jermaine O'Neal had 13 pts in the 1st H

—Chauncey had 17 pts in the 1st H

—The Pacers led 48-41 at the H

—They fronted Rasheed all game and the Pistons settled and didn't look for other ways to get him the ball

—This is terrible, because the entire Piston offense revolved around guards shooting jump-shots (or in the case of the 1st H, Corliss missing inside)

—Somehow, don't ask me how, the Pistons were only down 61-58 going into the 4th Q

—Chauncey was great in the 1st H, but got only 1 pt in the 2nd H; he was trying to get the rest of the off. involved and flowing early in that H, but then made some bad decisions and played badly towards the end (in one case he air-balled a triple with under 2 mins. to go)

—Tayshaun hit a big triple with under 2 mins. to go

—But, Miller did the same and it was his only basket of the game

—Ben finished with 22 rebs. (19 defensively) and 5 blocks

—This was just a bad playoff game all around for both teams: the Pistons threw the ball around like it was poison, they made poor decisions on offense, and gave up a bunch of 2nd H off. rebs. The Pacers missed a lot of make-able shots all night and shot 34% on FGs.

The 5 Keys To Victory

Key Task #1: Win the battle of the benches.

The Pistons were **Terrible** on #1. The Pacers bench outscored the Pistons 19-9. Corliss and Elden played horridly.

Key Task #2: Contain their 3-pt shooters.

Good. They were 4-15 on triples.

Key Task #3: Don't allow it to become a Ron Artest-type of series.

Good. Artest was 6-23 on FGs and missed a lot of shots on drives.

Key Task #4: Use athleticism to provide periodic advantages.

Okay, but they got too many off. rebs.

Key Task #5: Use experience and smarts to keep a better focus and edge than the Pacers.

Very poor. Turnovers and bad decisions kept the Pistons from taking what was an excellent oppty to steal a road game.

GAME 2

PISTONS 72 PACERS 67

(AWAY, Monday, May 24th)

It was Joe D's birthday and Rasheed had guaranteed victory.

"I'm guaranteeing Game 2. That's the bottom line. That's all I'm saying. They will not win Game 2. You heard that from me. Ya'll can print whatever you want. Put it on the front page, back page, middle of the page. They will not win Game 2."

—2 quick fouls on Ben: they were both **terrible** calls

—As a result, Ben only played 5 mins. in the 1st H

—Chauncey blocked the much bigger Bender from behind, right under the rim

—Rasheed, pressing to try to back up his statements, was 0-6 in the 1st Q

—The Pistons could not put the ball in the basket in the 1st Q

—The Pacers led 17-12 after 1 Q

—Boy, the Pacers take a lot of bad shots

—There was a bunch of knock-aways and steals by the Pistons in the 1st H: just playing good defense

—Memo played real well in the 1st H, helping out a lot while Ben was out; he had 9 pts and 4 rebs

—The Pistons had 8 blocks in the 1st H

—The Pacers led 43-37 at H

—O'Neal had 16 pts and Miller 15 pts in the 1st H

—You can just feel how intense (and tense) this game is

—The Pistons had 21 bench pts in the 1st H

—Serious 3rd Q defense: Tayshaun blocked Artest right at the basket; Rasheed blocked O'Neal's post shot; Rasheed then blocked Artest at the rim; then Tayshaun got Artest again on a drive; Ben threw Al Harrington's shot into about row 5

—Rasheed got it going in the 3rd Q, after a really bad 1st H

—The Stones were up 55-54 going into the 4th Q

—Ben swatted O'Neal's shot into the TV cameras from down low in the 4th Q

—The Pistons have set a team playoff record in blocks with 19!

—It is amazing to watch Rip & Miller go at it

—Rip scored a couple of big-time baskets and FTs to give the Pistons the lead in the last couple of mins.

—After 4 Miller FTs cut it to a 2-pt lead with less than a minute left, the Pacers were on the break and threw it up to Miller for a sure lay-up. Then Tayshaun ran down the play and blocked it at the last possible moment!

—Consider this about Tayshaun's play: he was behind the half-court line when the pass was already in the air and he closed all that ground in about 1 second. When he blocked the shot, his elbow was level with the bottom of the backboard! He was soaring! Then he fell into the cameras and the first few rows of people. It took him awhile to get up from there. But his teammates had rushed in to help their comrade.

This is by far one of my favorite Pistons games of the last several years. It featured so much incredible defense and was just a war. It was so much fun (and tense!) to watch and see these guys just go at each other and not give any offensive players any daylight ever!

To illustrate what kind of night it was, there was one play where a Pacer (I believe it was O'Neal) got blocked by first Ben & then Rasheed (or was it the other way around? Who cares!) on the same play!

Great job by the guys tonight.

The 5 Keys To Victory

Key Task #1: Win the battle of the benches.

The Pistons were **Good** on #1. The Pacers bench did more than double up the Pistons' on rebs. and blocks, but the Pistons doubled them up on pts. Those 23 pts (21 in the 1st H) helped hold the team in the game when they most needed it and when Ben was in foul trouble.

Key Task #2: Contain their 3-pt shooters.

Outstanding. They were 3-20 on triples.

Key Task #3: Don't allow it to become a Ron Artest-type of series.

Outstanding. Artest was 5-21 on FGs and 0-4 on triples. He wasn't overly imposing on defense and he couldn't figure out how to score on Tayshaun when he drove.

Key Task #4: Use athleticism to provide periodic advantages.

Very good. The Pistons had 10 stls and defended all over the floor.

Key Task #5: Use experience and smarts to keep a better focus and edge than the Pacers.

Good. The Pacers seemed a little fazed (especially Artest) by what was happening in this game. Rasheed's guarantee may have even played into this ***edge.***

GAME 3

PISTONS 85 PACERS 78

(HOME, Wednesday, May 26th)

—Rasheed showed up at the arena with a Lions' Dre Bly jersey on

—Artest opened up guarding Rip

—Rasheed scored a 3-pt play off a 1-handed alley-oop that didn't really slam down, but just found its way in

—There were a lot of good signs early in this game: the Rasheed oop, Ben getting 3 scores right at the rim, Corliss throwing passes on the money for hoops (including a behind the back pass for a dunk!)

—The Pistons got a lot of 1st Q dunks

—The Pacers defense seems to be breaking down early

—The Pistons were up 27-14 after 1 Q

—To open up the 2nd Q, the Pistons went 8 mins. with no FGs (they were scoreless in the first 6 mins.); they scored only 9 pts in the Q

—Pistons led 36-30 at the H

—Rasheed looks real good; he's playing with a lot of energy; the injury doesn't seem to be bothering him as much as it was

—The Pistons were up 56-45 going into the 4th Q

—The Rasheed Effect: understanding his protégé, Jermaine O'Neal, he drew an offensive foul on him, and then forced a travel. He then hit a triple and blocked Harrington's 3-pt attempt (all in the 4th Q).

—Then Ben also knocked it away from O'Neal

—Carlisle got a tech. by going all the way out to half-court in between Q's for no reason other than to fire up his team

—ESPN's broadcast crew kept saying how close the Pacers were in score, despite how poorly they were playing. Do they like the Pacers better than the Pistons?

—The Pacers showed some zone—that's odd for a Rick Carlisle team

—There were 3 bad fouls in a row called on Rasheed in that 4th Q

—Rip and Rasheed finished with 20 pts and Ben had 17 pts, 16 rebs, and 3 blks

—The Pistons shot 44% on FGs—that's good for this series

—As the buzzer sounded, a frustrated Miller kicked the ball into the stands

The 5 Keys To Victory

Key Task #1: Win the battle of the benches.

The Pistons were **Bad** on #1. The Pacers' bench outscored the Pistons 26-9, out-boarded them 15-5 and created 5 stls.

Key Task #2: Contain their 3-pt shooters.

Excellent. They were 5-19 on triples.

Key Task #3: Don't allow it to become a Ron Artest-type of series.

Very Good. Artest was 4-13 on FGs and is still perplexed by Tayshaun's defense on his drives.

Key Task #4: Use athleticism to provide periodic advantages.

Okay. The defense was great in the 2nd Q, to help hold off the Pacers and keep it close when the offense was struggling. However, the Pacers had 10 stls.

Key Task #5: Use experience and smarts to keep a better focus and edge than the Pacers.

Good. When you shoot 1-10 on triples and only score 9 pts in a Q (the 2nd), there's a good chance you're going to lose. But, I felt a confidence all night that the Pistons were going to pull it out. They did the things necessary to win this type of game.

GAME 4

PACERS 83 PISTONS 68

(HOME, Friday, May 28th)

Earlier in the day, I had eaten lunch at Spargo's Coney Island in Auburn Hills, and all the waitresses were wearing basketball necklaces (think of like Hawaiian leis or Mardi Gras beads). I asked one of them about it and she said that David Hall of Rock Financial comes in to eat there all the time and left these necklaces for them.

The Palace staff was also passing these out at the west atrium before the game. They were quite a popular item, as people kept asking where to find them at.

It was a beautiful spring night and the sun was shining as I arrived at The Palace. Unfortunately, this game was a mess on every level.

—In the 1st Q, Artest finally broke through and scored 12 pts. He looked very confident.

—The Pacers sprung a little surprise on the Pistons and started Croshere in place of Foster. The Pistons had probs. with this all night, because his defender, be it Rasheed or Ben, was pulled away from the basket, opening things up on the inside and eliminating a shot-blocking presence. There were also several occasions where Croshere found himself wide open and drilled 3-pters.

—He finished 3-4 on triples

—The Pacers were rolling early and had a 29-17 lead going into the 2nd Q

—For the first time in this series, the Pacers' offense is flowing and looks like a real offense. There's flow, execution, and fast-break buckets.

—Down 49-39 at the H, I mentioned to some friends that the Pistons are lucky they're not down by a lot more. <u>They were not passing the ball side to side or being patient enough on offense. Turnovers were undermining the whole effort (and they were completely unforced). The Pacers held a 24-12 edge in pts in the paint</u>.

—It only got worse from there. Throughout the 2nd H, the Pistons weren't shooting it to score; they were shooting it just for the chance of getting it up on the rim.

—The Pistons were down by over 20 pts in the 2nd H and some boos came from the crowd

—The Pistons gave up a lot of lay-ups, with no help-side

—With all the bad, unforced turnovers, and poor shot selection, the Indiana defense only gets stronger. This put the Pistons stuck in a bad cycle.

—The Pistons had 2 assts. in the 2nd H

This was just a poor, terrible effort on the Pistons' part. What were they thinking? A lot of people were let down by this performance.

Think of all the fans who had delayed their Memorial weekend plans so that they could attend the game. I also personally know of some big sacrifices that were made by some fans to attend the game.

One had to find a baby-sitter for the evening (figure about $30 for that plus the $60 for the tix). Another group of fans, many of whom are Pistonsfever.com subscribers, had to employ creative driving strategies in order to make it in time to the game right after work.

The 5 Keys To Victory

Of the 5 keys, the Pistons were **bad** on #1 (bench scoring) and just **completely horrible** on all the rest.

GAME 5

PISTONS 83 PACERS 65

(AWAY, Sunday, May 30th)

It was a wild day in Indianapolis. The Indy 500 was today and a tornado hit very near Conseco Fieldhouse. And Pistons fans were in the house! About 500 made the trip down for the game.

—Pacer injuries: O'Neal is playing with a leg brace after hurting his knee in the last game; Tinsley's leg is hurt in 3 places and received treatment throughout the game; he rode a stationary bike when not on the floor

—A rarity for this series: there was hot shooting early for both teams

—Ben blocked Foster's dunk in the 1st Q; the Pistons were intimidating all night and had 13 total blocked shots

—A 12-4 run to end the 1st Q meant a 25-17 Pistons lead

—Weird sight: a Pacers fan right under the basket was waving an inflatable pink flamingo around. What the $#%& is that?

—The Pistons were 1-10 on FGs to start the 2nd Q

—Rip was sizzling and scored 19 pts in the 1st H

—The Stones held a 41-36 lead at the H

—As Rip continued to shoot lights out, the Pistons pushed up to a 62-53 lead going into the 4th Q

—Freddie Jones was hot for them as well. He was 3-4 on triples and finished with 13 pts.

—A 14-5 run by Indiana, coincided with a big Piston FG drought at the beginning of the 4th Q. As they've done at different times in this series, the Pacers went to a small lineup and had success during this run.

—As the Pistons took control of this game for good, a fun moment happened when Rasheed got the ball in the post. He was on the left side with a small guy on him (I think it was Miller). As he saw the double-team come from the top, he had a big grin on his face. When the second defender got closer, he spun baseline away from the defender and drained a sweet, high-arching rainbow. It was classic. His smile continued as he ran back on defense.

—As the game wore on, I thought we needed another guy other than Rip to step up and score. A second guy was going to have to emerge. That guy was Rasheed. He pumped in 22 pts and the Pistons knocked out the Pacers.

—The Pacers, just like every game but Game 4, struggled mightily to score against the Pistons D'.

—Rip was sensational and finished with a career playoff high 33 pts

—The Pistons just controlled this game all night; the Pacers never led once

—Carlisle said afterward that his team didn't understand how hard and unselfish you have to play in this type of situation. To win this game, it was going to require an even greater effort in those 2 areas than they displayed in the Game 4 victory.

—Croshere was 0-7 on FGs

—The broadcast of the game featured a commercial that had Pistons fans buzzing; it was Rasheed explaining his tattoos that featured all the members of his family; the artwork looks like Egyptian hieroglyphics. That commercial was great.

—Ben had 5 blocks tonight

—The Pacers were held to 33% on FGs

The 5 Keys To Victory

Key Task #1: Win the battle of the benches.

The Pistons were **Bad** on #1. The Pacers' bench outscored the Pistons 26-11; Harrington and Jones had 22 by themselves.

Key Task #2: Contain their 3-pt shooters.

Outstanding. They were 4-21 on triples. The Pistons' D' shut down the interior, leaving the Pacers with no choice but to hoist up shots that were deep and poor.

Key Task #3: Don't allow it to become a Ron Artest-type of series.

Very Good. Artest was 4-15 on FGs. He did finish with 11 rebs. but was not a difference-maker out there.

Key Task #4: Use athleticism to provide periodic advantages.

Good. The Pistons' athleticism, coupled with Indy's hobbled players, allowed them to D' the heck out of the Pacers' offense. Plus no one could catch Rip as he ran around on offense.

Key Task #5: Use experience and smarts to keep a better focus and edge than the Pacers.

Very Good. The Pistons came in with an excellent focus and purpose. They got a big road win in a key situation. The Pacers, as Carlisle had pointed out afterwards, did not approach this game in the right way. Also, both Miller and O'Neal got technicals, while the Pistons got none.

GAME 6

PISTONS 69 PACERS 65

(HOME, Tuesday, June 1st)

This was the game that pushed the Pistons into the NBA Finals, and as a result, pushed them into the NBA's upper echelon; most likely for years to come.

—Ben had the 'fro out for this big game

—Uncle Kracker sang the national anthem, wearing a Pistons jersey. There were so many celebrities here tonight; it is hard to remember them all. Chuck Daly, Kid Rock, Tom Izzo, Steve Mariucci, Joey Harrington, and even Rick Sund (?) were all there.

—This game got off to a horrible start. The Pistons were down 11-4 out of the gate and 23-9, leading to a 23-11 deficit after 1 Q.

—The Pacers <u>are playing so loose and are shooting the ball confidently</u>

—Looking for an edge, Carlisle started Al Harrington

—Artest was guarding Rip

—At one point in the 1st H, things were so bad that a friend pointed out that the Pistons <u>were shooting something like 14% from the field</u>

—A few boos came down from the stands. There was a lot of tension all night, because we all just wanted the team to seize this moment, win on their home floor where their fans can appreciate them, and party. The time is <u>now</u> for this team to go to the NBA Finals.

—I hate to point this out, but this game in the 1st H, was eerily reminiscent of the Game 4 debacle

—Part of the problem was that <u>Indiana was owning the paint</u>. They were blocking shots, and the Pistons had no confidence to make these shots. Ben was doing a lot of twisting and turning inside instead of just powering it up.

—The Pistons were down 33-27 at the H! This means that they held Indiana to 10 pts in the 2nd Q, but could only score 16 pts of their own. I'm not sure if the guys were just nervous and tight or what, but they missed nearly every shot they took. Maybe the magnitude of this moment got to them, since they've never been in this position before.

—The Pistons were 10-42 on FGs in the 1st H

—Big plays in short minute time spans often decide these types of games. Just prior to the H, Artest hit a triple, and then Rasheed answered with a triple of his own. But then Croshere hit another triple to end the H. That was sort of deflating. The Pacers looked like a team ready to take on this situation and get it done.

—One thing's for sure, I felt strongly that if the Pistons could just make a few baskets in a row, and pull close, then this crowd would erupt and carry this team to the victory.

—The 3rd Q went back & forth and the Pistons only trailed by 4 pts going into the final Q. With the offense still struggling, the team just seemed to have a hard time getting over the hump. Pulling even and getting the lead was going to be tough. It would require several big plays to be made in the 4th Q.

THE DIFFERENCE MAKERS

There were 4 big plays that did indeed turn this game into a Pistons victory:

—Chauncey hit 2 triples to pull the Pistons even twice. Both came around the mid-way point of the 4th Q. This finally got them even.

—Tayshaun, in what was truly a spectacular play, blocked Harrington's dunk right at the summit. This was a huge momentum swing play because it was on the break and had Harrington thrown that one down with authority, the Pacers would have been surging with confidence. Instead, the Pistons could now smell the oppty to win this thing.

—Tayshaun also rose up and buried a deep shot (it was either a 3 or his foot was on the line, it was hard to tell from where we were sitting). That was huge. The play was for Rip, but he was overplayed on the left-side, so Chauncey threw it to Tay on the right and when he rose up to shoot it, I knew it was in. I knew it despite the fact that he had missed shots all night (he finished 3-12 on FGs).

There's something about this kid playing big in big moments. There was just also something about that situation, where you could just feel the Pistons positioning themselves to win this game.

—Then, Ron Artest hit Rip in the face for a flagrant foul. Seeing him laying on the ground holding his face, all I could think is that Artest was going for his nose. Rip's already broke the nose twice this year. The Pacers said they had to get more physical with Rip before this game. Plus Artest is known for these types of incidents.

Here was the problem for Artest: it was the turning point in the game and finally gave the Pistons the lead (for the first time all night). It was a lead they would never relinquish.

Rip hit both FTs, and then as Chauncey missed a jumper, Rasheed soared in and dunked in the stick-back. The Pistons now had a 4-pt lead and that was basically the game.

The 5 Keys To Victory

Key Task #1: Win the battle of the benches.

The Pistons were **Terrible** on #1. Croshere scored 12 pts himself.

Key Task #2: Contain their 3-pt shooters.

Good. They were 6-21 on triples.

Key Task #3: Don't allow it to become a Ron Artest-type of series.

Excellent. Artest did have 10 rebs, but was only 4-13 on FGs and committed the error that gave the Pistons the lead for good.

Key Task #4: Use athleticism to provide periodic advantages.

Good. The Pistons got 15 off. rebs, Tayshaun's block was huge, and Rip's speed and quickness wore Artest down over the course of the game.

Key Task #5: Use experience and smarts to keep a better focus and edge than the Pacers.

> **Good.** The Pistons took care of the ball. In this type of situation, where the pressure is great and the shots keep missing, there's a real possibility of throwing the ball away multiple times. The Pistons didn't do this.

Also, the Artest play showed the difference in the 2 teams. That was a bonehead play at a bad time for the Pacers. The Pistons, meanwhile, didn't get caught up in it and let Artest get in their head. In fact, Rip was more determined to score over him than he was before. The pull-up Rip made on the baseline after the incident was also just a huge play.

11

The Lakers Series 2004 Playoffs Round 4—The NBA Finals

◆

(The Playoff Diaries: June)

06/06/04—<u>THE 2004 NBA FINALS!</u>

Though few are giving the Pistons much of a chance to win this series, it can be done. If the Lakers have proven one thing in these NBA playoffs, it's that they're not invincible.

So, here it is: the game plan for how to <u>"Beat LA!"</u>

<u>SCOUTING THE LAKERS</u>

After looking at L.A. from both a statistical and non-statistical standpoint, the following conclusions were drawn:

<u>REGULAR SEASON</u>

Defense

The Lakers are an average defensive team. They rank #16 in the league in both ppg allowed and FG% allowed. They do however, defend the 3-pt shot well and rank #7 in that area.

One thing that the Laker defense does do particularly well is in the area of creating steals and turnovers. They rank #10 and #11 in those areas respectively. Also, they're in the top half of the league in assts allowed per game. Taking all this together, suggests that they do a good job of playing passing lanes and denying ball entry to key scoring points on the floor.

Interestingly, only Shaq blocks shots for them. No one else challenges opponents on the interior.

Kobe is by far their best defender. He's athletic and can cover a lot of ground. Consider though, that Shaq is relatively slow on defense and Karl Malone and Gary Payton are old.

When San Antonio beat the Lakers twice in the second round, Tony Parker went off, using his quickness to exploit Payton.

CONCLUSION: The Pistons offense will need to move the ball well, featuring side to side action and from inside to one block, over to the opposite side on the perimeter. This will force their older players to have to cover a lot of ground, hopefully wearing them down, but most importantly creating open spots for shots that the Lakers just can't get to in coverage.

Offense

This is the strength of the Lakers' team. They rank #3 in scoring and #4 in FG%. It should be no surprise then that they are #4 in assts and #1 in drawing fouls. Obviously Shaq has a lot to do with creating fouls.

The Pistons probably won't be blocking as many shots as we've come accustomed to in the last round. The Lakers rank #2 in not getting their shots blocked. This probably has to do with how the triangle offense spreads out the floor and has defenders placed in positions away from the paint.

The Lakers also do not turn the ball over, so the Pistons are going to have to score a lot out of their own offense and not rely on turnovers leading to fast-break or easy baskets.

The Lakers are only #25 in 3-pt %. This means that the Pistons should be able to swarm and provide a fair amount of help-side defense on the interior to help contain Shaq on the block and Kobe's drives without too much fear that the Lakers will make the Pistons pay with 3-pt shots.

CONCLUSION: The Pistons need to get to the FT line, get off. rebs, and give the Lakers no off. rebs. By doing these 3 things, they can keep the ball away from LA's offense as much as possible and not allow them to get a real rhythm and flow going. It will also help the Pistons to be able to force the style and tenor of the game to be more in their favor than the Lakers.

Other Key Variables

The Lakers have no bench. I pointed this out to someone when the Pistons rocked them at The Palace in November. Their starting lineup is fantastic, but their bench is weak and fairly "un-dynamic."

The Pistons will need to beat them with their entire team attacking the Lakers and their "Fabulous Four". With athleticism, the bench and starters can find advantages, even against Shaq. You want to try to beat them down the floor and "beat them to the spot", both offensively and defensively.

Speaking of Shaq, look for the Pistons to involve him in a lot of pick & rolls and use Rasheed and/or Memo to pull him away from the basket. The more that he's out on the perimeter trying to defend, the more the inside is opened up for the Pistons.

If the Pistons take away transition baskets (can be accomplished partially by getting to the foul line), then the Lakers will be forced into playing half-court basketball against possibly the best defense in the league. The more this happens, the more the Pistons D' can figure out the L.A. offensive attack and lock in on it.

This, once again, will also help the Pistons to establish the tempo, tenor, and style of the game into their favor.

During the regular season, the Lakers averaged over 12 ppg less in their losses vs. their wins. They also shot 5.5% less on FGs. These are significant drop-offs and show the type of lulls that the Laker offense can experience.

The Lakers also have 3 games in which they've scored no more than 74 pts in these playoffs.

PLAYOFFS

Speaking of the playoffs, the Lakers are 12-5 in the NBA's second season. They've had their periods of domination: Five of their wins are by 11-24 pts. Four are by 6-10 pts and three are by 5 pts or less, which includes two by 1 pt.

Interestingly, when they lose, they tend to lose big. Three of their losses are by 10 or 11 pts and one is by 18 pts! They also have a 2-pt loss in there.

What does all this mean? Among other things, that the Lakers are not invincible. They can be beaten.

There are a few themes that were common throughout their playoff losses this year. One was FTs. Teams that beat them always shot a lot of FTs. They also always shot well from the field.

When opposing guards are able to score against the Lakers, it leads to success, probably because it forces Kobe to have to expend a lot of energy on defense and the opposing point guard is able to exploit Payton's lack of quickness.

HOW THE PISTONS CAN BEAT THE LAKERS

Key Task #1: Clear the glass, both offensively and defensively. As mentioned earlier, if the Pistons can give the Lakers little in the way of second shots, then the Lakers are forced to constantly go up against a stifling Pistons half-court defense. A defense that only gets stronger the more it faces an opposing team's sets.

In addition, if they can get some offensive rebounds, the Pistons will be able to not only help themselves with more scoring chances, but they will also keep the ball away from the Lakers and their vaunted offense.

Key Task #2: Get to the foul line. A lot of FTs has been a recipe for success for every playoff opponent who's won games against the Lakers this year. And, it allows the Pistons D' an opportunity to set up.

The Pistons will need to get to the line by being in constant attack mode. This means Chauncey & Rip, but also Tayshaun and Rasheed on the move. Depending on the match-ups, Rasheed might not have as many post-up opportunities against the Lakers as he has had in the past. This would particularly be the case if Shaq is guarding him or coming over to help double on him. In these scenarios,

Rasheed and some of our other frontcourt players would be better off both catching the ball and initiating their attack with movement.

Key Task #3: Move the ball. When the ball goes side to side and inside-out, the older Lakers will have to cover a lot of ground on defense. The Pistons can also make Shaq have to move around and try to defend people (which he's not particularly good at).

If the Pistons use a lot of activity, from both people and ball, and use their tremendous depth to come at the Lakers in waves, then they can win.

All of these things also just make it easier to score.

Key Task #4: Use athleticism to provide advantages. Just attack them with speed, run Kobe through a ton of screens, and involve Shaq as much as possible on defense. Rasheed and/or Ben ought to be able to beat the Lakers down the floor (and to the ball) in various situations.

Key Task #5: Limit their transition opportunities. It's a simple philosophy, but if you keep a high-scoring team from getting easy opportunities to score, your chances of winning go up tremendously.

Key Task #6: Guards must score well. If the Pistons' guards are grooving and getting it done on offense, particularly Chauncey & Rip, then it will open things up for everyone else on offense.

This is particularly important when you consider that every team that has beaten the Lakers in these playoffs has shot a good % from the field. The Pistons will need to do the same.

GO PISTONS!

06/15/04—WORLD CHAMPIONS!

I've been around this team a long time; this is one of the proudest moments I have of them—ever!

GAME 1

PISTONS 87 LAKERS 75

(AWAY, Sunday, June 6th)

—Mr. D made the trip

—Good start for the Pistons

—Rasheed hit a triple right out of the gate

—Everyone except Ben scored early

—The Pistons do not appear to be nervous as this game unfolds, other than Ben on offense (he missed a lay-up and shot an air ball jumper)

—Rasheed got 2 quick fouls and had to come out

—Shaq got a bunch of off. rebs in the 1st Q

—The Pistons got a lot of steals and blocks early, establishing their style of play

—The Pistons made enough little mistakes in the 1st Q to keep LA close

—The Pistons led 22-19 after 1 Q

—Shaq had 11 pts in the 1st Q; Chauncey had 8

—Chauncey, while saving a ball in the 2nd Q, went flying over the first row, tumbling and landing on his back. He seems to be okay though.

—The Lakers took a lot of quick and perimeter-type shots in the 1st H

—The Pistons missed a lot of lay-ups in the 1st H. And FTs (they were 14-22)!

—Elden looks good against Shaq

—The Pistons were down 41-40 at the H

—Shaq had 20 pts in the 1st; Kobe had 12; the rest of their team only had 9

—The Pistons had 10 turnovers in the 1st H and the Lakers had 8

—5 fouls on Payton at the 3:30—mark of the 3rd Q

—8 pt lead at one point in the 3rd Q for the Pistons

—Ben blocked Kobe's jumper just before the end of the 3rd Q

—The Pistons were up 64-58 after 3 Qs

—An 11-2 run by the Pistons early in the 4th Q gave them a 13 pt lead

—Corliss was guarding Shaq for a little bit in the 4th Q

—LA missed a lot of triples

—LA's first FT attempt of the 2nd H came at the 4:37—mark of the 4th Q

—Rasheed was dead-solid perfect on his shots all night

The 6 Keys To Victory

Key Task #1: Clear the glass, both offensively and defensively.

Good. The Pistons only gave up 13 off. rebs. They had 9 of their own, which is about average given the high percentage they shot on FGs.

Key Task #2: Get to the foul line.

Very good. The Pistons had 30 FT atts, which is a bunch. They only had 8 after halftime, however. All these atts kept the Lakers from running, and gave the Pistons' defense the oppty to get set up.

Key Task #3: Move the ball.

Not bad. You know, the Pistons didn't really have to move the ball that much tonight since they got plenty of good opptys off of dribble-drive penetration. Also, the plays the Pistons were running led immediately to a shot on the first option. They did not need to reverse the ball. LA played poor half-court defense.

Key Task #4: Use athleticism to provide advantages.

Very good. The Pistons got 9 steals and outscored LA on the break 10-4.

Key Task #5: Limit their transition opportunities.

Outstanding. The Lakers only had 4 fast-break pts and were unable to get a run going to help them come back.

Key Task #6: Guards must score well.

Very good. Rip & Chauncey scored a combined 34 pts and Lindsey hit for 5 pts. Rip missed a lot of shots tonight, but he drew so much attention from the Laker defense that it opened up opptys for other Piston players all over the floor.

GAME 2

LAKERS 99 PISTONS 91 (OT)

(AWAY, Tuesday, June 8th)

—Rasheed destroyed Malone's driving lay-up in the 1st Q

—Kobe was initiating the offense in the 1st Q

—At the 3:07—mark of the 1st Q, Rasheed picked up his 2nd foul and had to sit down

—Quite a few Laker turnovers early

—Luke Walton made his first appearance of the series at about the 4-min. mark of the 1st Q

—Kobe got inside and the Piston defense closed so quickly that he had options 2 and 3 gone in a fraction of a second on the pass, and thus had to just toss it to no one. The ball just sat there in the lane until a Piston scooped it up.

—The Pistons missed a lot of easy and good shots in the 1st Q

—The Pistons were down 18-16 going into the 2nd Q, but the game was being played at their tempo and style

—After a steal, Chauncey got a 2-handed dunk on the break

—Not a good sign: Luke Walton was playing like a star in the 2nd Q. He had 7 pts, 5 assts, and 3 rebs in the 1st H.

—The Pistons are giving up a lot of lay-ups

—Malone aggravated his sore knee by banging it on another Laker player and is in serious pain

—After falling down on a shot attempt inside, Malone got the ball back after the Pistons missed and was looking to score on the break. But Tayshaun swarmed in and blocked his lay-up.

—The Pistons just played terrible in the 2nd Q

—The Laker D' is tougher, but I mean come on! The Pistons should still be able to score on good looks and not turn the ball over.

—Pistons down 44-36 at the H

—The Stones have had a lot of shots go in and out tonight

—Why is Shaq making his FTs in this series?

—Rasheed was dominating Malone in the 3rd Q—scoring over him every which way

—Payton looks like a shadow of his former self

—Pistons really weren't playing that well through 3 Q's and the Lakers were making big plays, but the Stones had pulled to within 2 pts going into the 4th Q. You've got to feel good about that!

—The score was Lakers up 68-66 at the end of 3 Q's

—Chauncey had 16 pts in the 3rd Q

—The Lakers went pretty small in the 4th Q for awhile

—Ben blocked Shaq on the weak-side in the 4th Q

—Shaq got his 5th foul at the 6:12—mark of the 4th Q and had to sit down

—Tayshaun blocked Kobe's jumper late in the 4th Q

—Shaq came back in at the 3:05—mark of the 4th Q

—The Pistons, especially Tayshaun (who got 3), were getting a bunch of off. rebs in the 4th Q

—A deep triple by Kobe, way behind the 3-pt line, tied it up with 2.1 secs. left

—Ball went through Rasheed's hands and out of bounds on the ensuing possession: overtime.

—In the overtime, the Lakers were real aggressive and Shaq and Kobe were really grooving. The Pistons, meanwhile, became tentative and lost their attacking edge. They only scored 2 pts in the OT.

—Luke Walton was still everywhere in the OT, making it all happen

—Rasheed blocked Kobe on his drive near the end

—Kobe was very pumped up afterwards. Hey congratulations, Kobe! You just barely escaped with a single victory in 2 home games.

The 6 Keys To Victory

Key Task #1: Clear the glass, both offensively and defensively.

Outstanding. The Pistons got 19 off. rebs! They held the Lakers to only 9 off. rebs.

Key Task #2: Get to the foul line.

Excellent. The Pistons shot 31 FTs; Chauncey was 13-14 himself. However, you would like to see his teammates make more of these free atts; the team finished 21-31.

Key Task #3: Move the ball.

Not good enough. The Lakers' defense was out pressuring the ball and extending out to the perimeter in a way that was very different than their effort in Game 1. When the Pistons didn't move the ball side to side or inside to out, it kept the older Lakers from having to move around. That just allowed their D' to become stronger. This is a big reason why the Pistons only shot 39.5% on FGs.

Key Task #4: Use athleticism to provide advantages.

Kinda good, but not really good enough. Chauncey killed Gary Payton and Rip had many scores. The 2 combined for 53 pts, but the bench didn't do enough and instead of taking advantage of Luke Walton, he out-quicked the Piston defense. Meanwhile, an injured and hurting Malone should have been taken advantage of and was not.

Key Task #5: Limit their transition opportunities.

Not bad, until overtime. The Lakers had 13 fast-break pts, which is just a little too much in this type of series. The OT is where the majority of the fast-break buckets were for them.

Key Task #6: Guards must score well.

Good. Rip & Chauncey paced the team in scoring, but Rip was only 10-25 from the field.

GAME 3

PISTONS 88 LAKERS 68

(HOME, Thursday, June 10th)

It was a rainy night outside the arena as we pulled into the parking lot. There were several scenes that were new for me at an NBA game and that are unique to the Finals. These included bomb sniffing dogs and media personnel located all the way up into an entire upper level section of the arena.

The bomb sniffing dogs are a result of the current climate we live in and the fact that this is a championship round. The media included people from all over the world. There were 1500 credentials issued for this game.

—Ben had the 'fro out!

—The Bad Boys: Isiah, Vinnie, Joe, and John Salley were on the floor for the ceremonial jump ball

—Rasheed got 2 fouls early again! Limited 1st H playing time again!

—The Pistons were up 24-16 after 1 Q

—The scoreboard said that the crowd was part of an NBA record 21 million fans that have attended NBA games this year

—Faces in the crowd: Barry Sanders, Vince Neil, Tom Izzo, Steve Mariucci, Alan Trammell, Kirk Gibson, Eminem, Renee Zellweger, and Steve Yzerman

—Luke Walton had 3 fouls early and did nothing

—It was hot inside The Palace!

—One sign had a picture of some huge purple underwear and it said "Shaq's Thong"

—The Laker D' was not as tough tonight as it was in Game 2; in fact, not at all

—The Pistons were up 39-32 at the H, which is great. However, they could have been up by a lot more. They missed some easy shots and made some bad decisions.

—Kobe had 1 pt at the H!

—The Pistons only had 5 assts at the H; LA was 2-13 on triples in the 1st H; the Pistons only had 4 turnovers

—FT advantages: the Pistons shot 12-18 while the Lakers were 2-3 in the 1st H

—Shaq got 4 fouls at the 6-min mark of the 3rd Q

—Chauncey had a great series of 3-pt barrages in the 3rd Q: he hit 2 triples and had a traditional 3-pt play for 9 big pts

—The Pistons are getting every loose ball!

—They want it more!

—The Pistons' hard traps and aggressive D' are affecting LA and putting them in uncomfortable positions on the floor

—The Pistons were up 63-51 after 3 Qs

—Lindsey destroyed Fisher's jumper early in the 3rd Q

—The Pistons poured it on in the 4th Q

—The Lakers were held to 37% on FGs for the game; Kobe finished with 11 and Shaq with 14! This is fantabulous!

—The Pistons won by 20, but it quite honestly could have been much worse

The 6 Keys To Victory

Key Task #1: Clear the glass, both offensively and defensively.

> **Outstanding.** The Pistons got 15 off. rebs and the Lakers only had 7. That's how you keep a team's offense down.

Key Task #2: Get to the foul line.

Excellent. The Pistons got 30 FTs and finished 21-30. This allowed the D' to just set up and stop the Lakers.

Key Task #3: Move the ball.

Very good in the 2nd H; not so much in the 1st H. The Pistons had 12 assts in the 2nd H and just shredded the Lakers, by attacking them from all angles. The 5 assts in the 1st H are not enough.

Key Task #4: Use athleticism to provide advantages.

Outstanding. This is where the Pistons killed them tonight. They were first to every loose ball. Obviously the older Lakers were getting beat with speed by the younger Pistons. But consider the fact that Elden out-ran (by the majority of the court) Shaq and got a break-away dunk!

Key Task #5: Limit their transition opportunities.

Good. The Lakers 13 fast-break pts that they had were insignificant to the overall Laker attack.

Key Task #6: Guards must score well.

Excellent. Rip & Chauncey combined for 50 pts and were at the forefront of the Pistons' attack.

GAME 4

PISTONS 88 LAKERS 80

(HOME, Sunday, June 13th)

As we rolled into the parking lot, we noticed a huge scaffolding with a sign that read, "Hard Work Pays Off". That's awesome!

This scaffolding was erected so that all the broadcast media could run their lines of wires to their trucks without having to expose them to all the cars that were pulling in. It was over the driveway that leads in from Lapeer Rd near the loading docks. There were so many media trucks and satellite dishes, it was unreal.

And boy, were the fans pulling in. We arrived 2 hours early and the lot was already significantly filled. Several people were tailgating.

A storm was brewing overhead with lightning flashing through the sky. The Stanley Cup (courtesy of Bill Davidson's Tampa Bay Lightning) the Shock's 2003 WNBA championship trophy, and this year's NBA championship trophy were all on display outside the atrium in a tent for fans to take pictures of.

—The Pistons were down 22-21 after 1 Q

—In that 1st Q, Chauncey was scoring at will, but the team only had 2 total assts, while the Lakers had 9.

—Shaq was just dunking the entire 1st Q

—LA had 14 points in the paint

—It was clear that the Lakers were doing different stuff on their offense and on defense of the Pistons' pick & roll

—Shaq had 10 pts in the 1st Q and Chauncey had 9 pts

—After 2 Q's the Pistons were up 41-39

—In that Q, Malone had a real weak attempt going inside against the 2 Wallaces. His shot was demolished.

—Kobe then got blocked by Rasheed on a break-away lay-up

—Rasheed just controlled the paint for the last segment of the 2nd Q: knocking the ball away, knocking passes away, blocking shots

—Mike James had a couple of breakaway lay-ups near the end of the H when Chauncey sat down with 2 fouls

—The Lakers had 13 assts to the Pistons' 5 at the H

—However, FTs favored the Pistons, who were 17-23, while the Lakers were 4-8

—In the 1st H, there was no real flow for the Pistons' offense; part of it was all of the LA fouls stopping the action

—The Laker D' is better than the last game

—The Pistons led in fast-break pts, 15-3 at the H

—LA still led in points in the paint, 22-16

—Ref Dick Bavetta was jogging in place, stretching it out, and dancing to the music before the 2nd H started. It was hilarious!

—After 3 Q's the score was tied 56-56

—In that Q, Kobe made his third incredible shot of the night under duress. The D' on him is giving him nothing!

—In the 4th Q, there was a stoppage of play for a "30-second infectious disease time-out". What!!??

—Kobe got a tech. and had to be held back by an official before he got his second one

—Hey Kobe, it's not the officiating. You're just getting beat by a superior team, with the best defense in the league!

—The Pistons pulled away in the 4th Q the way that champions do. They made a few plays, shut the LA offense down, and Rasheed scored everything.

—The Lakers were worn down by the end of this one

The 6 Keys To Victory

Key Task #1: Clear the glass, both offensively and defensively.

Good. Each team only had 9 off. rebs. That's a good job of keeping LA from getting extra opptys.

Key Task #2: Get to the foul line.

Absolutely Outstanding. The Pistons got 41 FT atts. That's awesome! Making more than 68% would be nice though.

Key Task #3: Move the ball.

Much better in the 2nd H than the 1st. Eleven 2nd H assts, 3-pt bombs by Chauncey, and smooth play by Rasheed paced the Pistons' offense into the lead.

Key Task #4: Use athleticism to provide advantages.

Very good. The Pistons outscored them 21-5 in fast-break pts and their speed wore the Lakers down in the end.

Key Task #5: Limit their transition opportunities.

Excellent. The Lakers only had 5 fast-break pts.

Key Task #6: Guards must score well.

Excellent. Rip & Chauncey combined for 48 pts and James and Hunter each scored 4 pts.

GAME 5

PISTONS 100 LAKERS 87

(HOME, Tuesday, June 15th)

This game wasn't even as close as the final score shows! The Pistons killed them! They were up by as much as 28 pts in the 4th Q!

Kobe guaranteed the win. You should know Kobe, only Rasheed can make good on guarantees!

—Kid Rock brought his buddy, Hank Williams Jr. to the game; Jack Nicholson was also there

—For those of you who were sick of the Laker love-fest going on during this series, courtesy of ABC, it was a welcome sight to see some former Piston Bad Boys being interviewed in the pre-game. In the first game, there was like 4 Lakers from their glory days being interviewed. Tonight it was Chuck Daly, Rick Mahorn, and Bill Laimbeer. Billy looked great with his "'89–'90 Back to Back Champions" hat on.

—Karl Malone, probably most Pistons' fans least favorite Laker, did not play. His knee injury finally took its' toll on him. Slava Medvedenko started in his place.

—Slava hit 3 quick jumpers early; then he did virtually nothing the rest of the game

—Shaq sat down at the 6-min mark of the 2nd Q with 2 fouls

—Kobe opened up defending on Chauncey and Payton was on Rip. That's not good for either defender.

—Big play: Ben got a steal and breakaway dunk in the 1st Q

—The Pistons were up 25-24 after 1 Q

—Rip had a great steal from Kobe on his drive in the 2nd Q

—Rasheed had 2 quick fouls by the beginning of the 2nd Q again

—For awhile in that 2nd Q, the Pistons were scoring every time down

—Kobe was cold early and Shaq got his 3rd foul at the 3:30—mark of the 2nd Q

—Slava had 10 pts at the H, making him the first Laker to reach double figures, other than Kobe or Shaq, in this entire series. Fisher also finished with 10 tonight.

—It was a big 2nd Q for the Pistons, especially Memo who had a 6-pt barrage of his own. He filled in nicely for Rasheed and his foul troubles.

—Big Ben, who had a talk with Dr. J before the game, scored 11 pts in the 1st H

—The Pistons led 55-45 at the H

—The Temptations, in true Motown style, performed at halftime

—Rasheed got his 4th foul at the 7:05—mark of the 3rd Q; the Lakers went to a small lineup. Things could have gone the wrong way at this point in the game.

—But the Pistons went on a 10-2 run that became a 22-6 run!

—Ben had 10+ rebs himself in the 3rd Q

—After 3 Q's the lead was 82-59 for the Pistons!

—At one point, the lead swelled to 28 pts!

—Ben was everywhere, doing it all throughout. He finished with 18 pts and 22 rebs

—In the 4th Q, the Lakers gave up and the Pistons kept playing hard. In fact they were playing just as hard on defense in the 4th Q as they did when the game was still in doubt.

—It was sheer bedlam at The Palace when the buzzer sounded. But the tape showed that ABC showed just as many shots of frustrated Laker players and staff as they did of Pistons players celebrating.

The 6 Keys To Victory

Key Task #1: Clear the glass, both offensively and defensively.

Great, just Great! The Pistons had 20 off. rebs! That's just being more aggressive. The Lakers had 14 of their own.

Key Task #2: Get to the foul line.

Outstanding. The Pistons had 39 FT atts. Chauncey and Rip combined for 19 atts. You'll never lose if you go to the line that many times.

Key Task #3: Move the ball.

Good. It really only took a couple of passes to crack the Laker defense. They were so easily exposed that multiple passes were not absolutely necessary.

Key Task #4: Use athleticism to provide advantages.

Really great. The Pistons were not just one, but two, three, and sometimes four steps ahead of the Lakers all night. They beat them to all the loose balls and when Chauncey & Rip weren't beating them off the dribble to draw fouls, then Tayshaun and Big Ben were soaring above, through, and around them. Tay finished with 17 pts and 10 rebs!

Key Task #5: Limit their transition opportunities.

Good. The Lakers had 15 fast-break pts, but it never became a positive momentum shift for them or their offense.

Key Task #6: Guards must score well.

Good. Rip & Chauncey scored a combined 35 pts. In the words of Rip, "Yes sir!"

PART II

12

"Heaven Must Be Like This!"

"It feels like heaven! Like the Ohio Players said, 'Heaven Must Be Like This'. Heaven must be like this!"

Isiah Thomas shouted these words immediately after the Pistons won their first ever NBA title in 1989. He was surrounded by media and other people as he was literally floating into the locker room.

In the days that followed Game 5 of the 2004 NBA Finals, many fans got to experience first-hand what this feeling is like. There was such an outpouring of positive emotion all over Metro Detroit. Sheer euphoria was gripping the area.

Really, the two and a half weeks that encompassed the end of the Pacers series, continuing on into the Finals, through those days after the last game ended, were filled with excitement and memorable moments.

The first order of business was to figure out how to get tickets to the Finals. If there was any way possible to get into the arena, my friends and I had to figure it out.

Not long after the Pacers series was over, The Palace announced that tickets for the three games at home were going on sale one memorable weekday morning. The big question was, how is it going to work? They only had 2,000 tickets available for each game. That's not many when you consider that it's the Finals and everyone comes out of the woodwork to buy tickets. It wouldn't just be the true die-hard fans that you had to compete with. It would be anybody and everybody.

Adding to the intense intrigue surrounding the availability of tickets was the fact that 1,000 seats for each game were going to be set aside for internet sales only, leaving the other 1,000 for purchase at The Palace box office. Since the online tickets would sell out practically instantaneously (someone said later that they heard that those tickets were gone 30 seconds after they went on sale) it meant that the best shot was to actually go over to the box office and compete in the lottery.

That's right: a lottery would determine whether or not myself and many other die-hards would be able to attend a Finals game. When I arrived about an hour before the actual drawing, the line had already begun to circle around a good portion of the building.

As I stepped into line, I was hopeful. After all, I had a plan. Some friends were going to be on the internet right at 10:00 AM trying to get through. At the same time, I would be trying to win the lottery at The Palace. We figured that if we hedged our odds this way, it would increase our chances.

As the line proceeded forward and fans grabbed their lottery tickets, I noted how unique the atmosphere was at The Palace. There was excitement in the air! The Pistons were in the Finals playing on basketball's greatest stage.

There was also some nervous tension that only increased as we neared the 9:30 drawing. Looking around we all knew that with so many people there (some estimates held that 2,000 people showed up) and the knowledge that each person could purchase a maximum of six total tickets for the three games, it meant that many were going to go home empty-handed. *Please God don't let it be me!*

The media were also assembled to capture the "fandemonium" on TV. A friend later told me that she spotted me in line on Fox 2's news broadcast.

As it got close to 9:30 and we approached our date with destiny, everyone started to gather in the drive right outside The Palace atrium on the west side of the building. A man who appeared to be part of crowd control for The Palace addressed us with a bull horn. He said that very soon the drawing would take place to determine which lottery numbers would be part of the first group to go inside and buy tickets.

Then we saw Palace President Tom Wilson and Vice President for Public Relations Matt Dobek work their way through the crowd to the center. As the moment of truth neared, someone near me said this experience is "more intense than the games."

Tom started out by joking that they had some wonderful concert tickets available for sale today. Once he drew the ticket that indicated who the winners would be, there were exactly three different types of reactions experienced by people.

One was yelling out "Yes!" and sprinting towards the building entrance. These were people who obviously had won. Others walked away frustrated or dejected. They were going to have to watch the games on TV. The last group walked around confused because it wasn't totally clear who all had won. I fit this last category.

Eventually another announcement was made via bull horn that cleared up the confusion and I felt a surge of energy flow through my body. I did indeed hold a winning lottery number! I was going to be one of the first 100 people to go through the doors and get tickets.

At the doors, the scene was chaotic. There were several winning lottery ticket holders lined up outside the door, surrounded by others who were hoping more numbers would be drawn so that they could get in. It was crowded in that small area and there was some light pushing and impatience grew.

Once those of us that had winning lottery numbers were finally allowed in, a great sense of relief swept over us. We're going to the NBA Finals! Then I heard someone say that he just witnessed someone pay $1,000 for one of the winning lottery tickets. This is crazy!

When I got to the ticket window, I purchased the maximum six tickets and was overjoyed. My friends and I were going to be sitting at the top of the arena, but who cared?! We were going to the Finals, baby!

When it came time for those three games to be played at The Palace, the Lakers were in town for about a week. This is because the NBA Finals always feature the 2-3-2 format and the middle three games would be played in Detroit.

The Lakers' cover was truly blown when a local radio station announced that they were staying at the Townsend Hotel in Birmingham. Apparently encouraged by the station, some fans assembled at the parking ramp across the street from the hotel during one of the first nights of the Lakers' stay and began making a bunch of racket so as to keep the players from getting any amount of good sleep.

The police came by to break it up, but this whole incident created an interesting side story to the NBA Finals: seeing the Lakers hanging out around town. A friend, Kirk Baldwin, and I decided to stop by the hotel on the day before Game 4.

Since it was a Saturday, a lot of people were out and about. Some were just kind of walking by the hotel keeping their eyes open for a glimpse of Laker players. Then when we saw the team bus pull up, several people gathered.

While we waited for the Lakers to come out and board the bus to go to practice, we had some fun conversations with other fans and residents of Birmingham. "We saw Kobe walking to dinner last night" or "Some of the players were at the movies the other night" were some of the stories that we heard.

Being that it was Birmingham, there were also many people walking their dogs. Most of them were little ones, so between the dogs, the upscale environment that is Birmingham and the Townsend, and the fact that the Lakers were in town, gave it the feel of being like we were in a mini L.A.

On this day no one was harassing the Lakers, it was more just a case of the spectacle created when a team this famous comes to town. Some in attendance were big Shaq or Kobe fans. At one point, Michele Tafoya and Stuart Scott who were reporting for ABC walked by, perhaps also heading to the Laker practice.

When the team appeared and began to board the bus, the crowd cheered for Kobe, who in turn, barely acknowledged them. It was interesting though that the loudest cheers went up for Shaq. Even though Jerry Buss and Mitch Kupchak prefer Kobe, it is clear that the people love Shaq.

A few nights later, after the Pistons polished off the Lakers in a series that the people around here won't forget for a long time, a friend, Joe Conrad, and I drove into Royal Oak and there was a party going on! Earlier Joe had dumped a bottle of champagne on my head. The people in Royal Oak that night were having a great time themselves.

The police closed down Main Street to traffic and pedestrians, so basically everybody just flooded the sidewalks. Many had just watched the game on TV in one of the city's bars. Horns were honking and happiness abounded. All three of the main local newspapers, the Detroit News, Detroit Free Press, and Oakland Press had people out selling "special editions" of their papers announcing the Detroit Pistons as the new NBA champs.

The next day, the goal was to find some brand new "NBA Champions" T-shirts and hats. The Palace had announced that a tent was set up in the parking lot that was filled with shirts. At about noon, the tent was packed and a long wait ensued for anyone hoping to get their hands on some great merchandise.

Over the course of the next several days, I made numerous trips to the tent as they were adding new items all the time. Some would sell out and then be replenished again either later in the day or the following day.

These items, particularly the shirts and hats, were so popular that they started a new mini fashion statement in Metro Detroit. They were seen all over during the summer of 2004. I can remember that during one trip to the grocery store while wearing an "NBA Champions" T-shirt, another guy noticed mine and immediately looked down at his own, which was different, to compare the two. Then there was the time that I saw the golden retriever wearing a championship T-shirt.

This was two days after the final game, waiting outside in the line to get into the rally that was at The Palace. The parade was earlier in the day downtown and then the Pistons received a police escort the 30 miles or so that it takes to get to The Palace.

The parade was overwhelmingly fun for everyone involved. And did the people come out! Over 1 million fans filled downtown Detroit for the parade and the gathering of the players at Hart Plaza.

The parade took longer than expected since many fans had gone past the sidewalks into the road and surrounded the players and the cars that they were riding in. They were just trying to get as close to their team as possible.

Wives and children of the players rode with them. Some players had camcorders to capture the moment. Rasheed looked great wearing his Gordie Howe Red Wings jersey. Larry Brown was wearing an Ivan "Pudge" Rodriguez Tigers jersey and cap.

When they finally made their way up to the stage at Hart Plaza, there were several memorable moments. The sun was glistening off the river behind the stage and Joe Dumars had a cigar in his mouth throughout (though it was unlit). The entire Pistons' staff, including scouts and members from the front office were assembled. Also there were Mayor Kwame Kilpatrick and Governor Jennifer Granholm.

Pistons broadcaster, George Blaha, was the first speaker. He said, "Detroit is the City of Champions again!" This was a great reference to Detroit's old nickname from earlier in the century when its' sports teams seemed to win all the time.

Kilpatrick compared the city to its' team, saying that the team displayed the values of hard work, dedication, and commitment in the same way the city's residents do.

Owner Bill Davidson was next and he had a lot to say! He began like this: "Over the past couple of weeks there's been a lot of bullshit going on in this country." This got the fans fired up.

He then referred to the 8-1 odds that had been placed on the Pistons' chances to win the series against the Lakers and said, "Bullshit!" Next: "Actually they (the Lakers) were lucky to win one game."

Mr. D went on to praise the Pistons' fans, saying that they were much more passionate about their team than the Lakers' fans were. Though not naming Jimmy Kimmel or anyone else, the next pointed observation referred to his dissing of Detroit and the residents' behavior: "Once again a lot of bullshit going on as to how you were going to respond to the victory."

Mr. D doesn't say much, but when he does, it's always worth listening to! In his 80's, he's one of the most successful businessmen in the country. On this day he said what many of us were already thinking.

Though not as colorful in his speech, Pistons President Joe Dumars had words that carried equal significance. He thanked the coaching staff and Larry Brown, saying that they performed under a lot of scrutiny. He said about them, "This is by far the best staff that I've ever been around." Being that Joe D had played in the NBA for 14 years, this says a lot. He also said, "Mayor Kilpatrick is right. These players represent Detroit as well as any team has ever represented a city."

When the players spoke, many of them thanked Joe for bringing them to the team. Tayshaun also thanked the 22 teams who passed on him in the draft, and though he's often credited with being the guy who put the team over the top, Rasheed said that the Pistons were already a great team before he arrived and that he "just brought a little bit extra."

Ben thanked Larry Brown for allowing him to shoot and be a part of the offense—something past coaching administrations did not. "I'm not just a defensive specialist. I'm a basketball player." Chauncey proclaimed that the "Bad Boys are back!"

The crowd was chanting various players' names throughout and there were multiple references by some of the speakers to keeping free agent-to-be Rasheed in Detroit. Even the crowd got into it, "We want 'Sheed! We want 'Sheed!"

The rally was great! Pistons fans filled The Palace to show support and let their heroes know how proud they were of them. The number of different championship T-shirts on display was quite impressive. There must have been at least a dozen different styles being worn by fans on this day. Young and old were in attendance, including quite a few families.

When the players came out, it was absolute bedlam at The Palace! As each player spoke, it was just about impossible to make out anything that they were saying because the crowd was cheering so loud. One of the few things that you could make out for sure was Rip yelling over and over again, "Yes sir! Yes sir! Yes sir!" He said it a total of 14 times!

When Chauncey took the microphone, everyone in the arena was chanting, "M.V.P.! M.V.P.! M.V.P.!" Chauncey then encouraged the crowd to "give it up for Darko" (who was not in attendance at either the parade or the rally due to surgery on his broken hand) and then saying, "Carmelo who? Who?"

Palace President, Tom Wilson, said that in 15 years at The Palace, the team has "never, ever, ever seen fans like you!" He also said that the media that was in town from all over the world for coverage of the Finals claimed that the Pistons fans were the loudest and most passionate of all.

Larry Brown kept his Tigers hat on from the parade but changed his jersey to a Detroit Lions Charles Rogers jersey. Memo was very soft-spoken and Corliss was barking!

When George Blaha introduced Ben as the last speaker, he said that Ben "fits this city like a hand in a glove." After Ben said a few words, he did his best, "Detroiiiitttttttt Basketbaaaaallllllllllllll!" and then dropped the microphone so that it fell to the stage while he spread his arms out like a baseball umpire making a "safe" signal.

After it was over, many fans were still partying in the parking lot. Some were trying to get on TV. Others had actually surrounded the players' cars as they pulled out. Much like how they surrounded their floats and cars during the parade, this was one last outpouring of gratitude to the players for raising up the spirits and hopes of a city and metro area that embodies the very spirit that the team plays with.

These stories all describe the great response that followed the Pistons' championship win in Metro Detroit. But the full effect of the victory could be felt outside of Detroit and outside of Michigan too. There were the stories that trickled in: a friend who works for a large company in Chicago saw a co-worker wearing a Darko Milicic jersey the day after the championship was won; and several sports fans across the country were pulling for the Pistons to beat the Lakers as a positive strike for the underdog. This was only intensified by the fact that whereas the Pistons just seemed to be like regular guys, the Lakers were all Hollywood: star players, selfish play, internal bickering, and Kobe's indiscretions.

While traveling this summer I encountered some people with interesting view points on what had just taken place. At an Arby's somewhere south of Toledo, Ohio, an employee—who had a striking resemblance to Bill Clinton—spotted my Pistons T-shirt from far away and yelled out "Detroit Pistons—they're the team that destroyed the Lakers, both literally and figuratively."

When talking with him for a few minutes, he revealed that a good portion of Ohio were Pistons' fans. Toledo has always had a connection to Detroit sports teams, but he was saying that it extended far beyond that city for the Pistons. Apparently people there are just very pleased with how they play.

Later on that same trip, a hotel lobby in Petersburg, Virginia was buzzing about the Finals. Some were just very impressed with the Pistons' play; others couldn't believe that the Lakers were about to trade Shaq. I remember very distinctly seeing a lot of head shaking over that one.

13

"Beat L.A."

The 2004 NBA Finals showcased two franchises going in opposite directions. The moves that took place following the series also show a different philosophy in how the teams are run.

When the Lakers entered the series, they had been in the Finals for four of the last five seasons. They also had won three NBA titles in that span and were considered NBA royalty. The Pistons on the other hand, hadn't even played in the Finals since 1990.

This also means that the Pistons are young and should be primed for their own extended run at multiple championships. For the Pistons, the 2004 season is believed to be the beginning of something rather than the end of it. With the youth of this team, combined with the fact that the likes of Chauncey Billups, Richard Hamilton, Ben Wallace, and Tayshaun Prince are getting better as players every year, it is easy to see why optimism is currently running so high within the Detroit basketball community. Each of these four players are continually adding dimensions to their game, making them even harder to defend and prepare for as an opponent.

The veteran play of Rasheed Wallace, Antonio McDyess, and Lindsey Hunter will keep the team playing at a high level and able to contend while the likes of Carlos Delfino and Darko Milicic grow and develop their games to a high level. This team is planned out well for future success. It is clear that Joe Dumars' one singular goal as team president is to have the team compete for and win the NBA championship.

As such, he has brought in players that play with that same mindset of winning being the number one priority above all else. They play with an edge. Most were doubted throughout their careers and pushed aside to make room for other players on their respective teams. For this reason, they will always be underdogs and thus will always play with something to prove.

From a business perspective, the team has good salary cap flexibility, which means that Joe is free to make changes as he sees fit in order to keep the team competitive.

The Lakers, on the other hand, appear to be going in the opposite direction. When the season ended, two of their key players, Karl Malone and Gary Payton, had reached the twilight of their careers and two others, Kobe Bryant and Shaquille O'Neal, couldn't stand the sight of each other anymore.

While those of us that live and work in the value-laden Midwest chuckle at the idea that two men could let ego and selfishness ruin a tremendous opportunity to compete for multiple additional championships, the Laker players involved and the management around them didn't hesitate to allow it to happen.

When you first hear that Shaq is going to demand a trade from the team, you think to yourself, *That'll never happen,* because normally these types of things work themselves out. Even if the two men hate each other, you generally assume that sensibility will eventually take over.

That's why it was surprising how easily everyone involved accepted what was about to happen. Lakers' General Manager Mitch Kupchak worked very quickly to make the deal happen as soon as the season had ended. Moving Shaq was key to keeping Kobe happy. Really, most of what the Lakers did during the summer of 2004 was to keep Kobe satisfied.

The team now looks so different from the group that was partying in Hawaii in October. They traded away the man Kobe couldn't stand, gave him a contract reportedly worth $136 million, and pursued heavily the man he would really like to see coaching the Lakers: Mike Krzyzewski. In fact, many familiar with the situation in L.A. believe that Phil Jackson, a man who has won nine NBA championships as a head coach (tied for the most ever), was forced out because Kobe had no use for him anymore.

This shows a clear difference in how the two franchises are run. While the Lakers would do anything to keep their star "franchise" player happy, the Pistons, when last faced with the possibility that their superstar would leave (Grant Hill in 2000) were unwilling to do anything more to appease him than offer a large contract.

Heck, the same was true of the most important figure in Pistons' history. Isiah Thomas was not given a much-rumored deal to become the team's general manager when he retired. Whereas in LA, one man is bigger than the rest, in Detroit no one is bigger than the franchise or its' vision of winning at the highest level.

It was interesting to watch the coverage of how the two teams handled their off-season personnel moves. While the Pistons went largely under the radar, re-signing key component Rasheed Wallace, and strengthening the bench with the additions of Antonio McDyess and Carlos Delfino, the Lakers had massive national media coverage. While this is somewhat tantalizing to watch and hear about: the dismantling of a champion, with a lot of money thrown around, and a soap opera-like atmosphere categorizing the relationship between the key figures, it seems out of place to give the Lakers so much coverage.

The Shaq to Miami trade was discussed for multiple days on end in both the broadcast and the print media. This is somewhat understandable being that he is one of the most dominant forces to ever play the game and anything involving him is interesting. But, I can remember one morning having "Sportscenter" on in the background while doing other things. Literally, every time I turned around over the course of the next hour, the show had some new piece on the "Coach K to the Lakers saga."

As all the speculation subsided though, the story seemed very simple. The Lakers went after Coach K to satisfy Kobe, who was a free agent and considering leaving the Lakers for another team. Kobe was recruited heavily by Coach K when he was young and likes his coaching style. Coach K was torn by the thought of leaving Duke University, probably the most important thing in life to him (next to his family), and accepting a huge payday with the Lakers. In the end he couldn't do it. Kobe, satisfied both that the Lakers made the effort to go after Coach K and because they got rid of the two men he disliked most, Shaq and Phil Jackson, re-signed.

With recent history showing us time after time that college coaches don't make good NBA coaches, the Lakers are undoubtedly better off with the man that they ended up hiring as head coach, Rudy Tomjanovich, who's already guided two Houston Rockets teams to championships. Rudy grew up in Hamtramck, MI, right in the city of Detroit.

So that means that the Lakers will be relying on a native Detroiter to help get them back to the level that the current team from Detroit is already at.

14

Misperceptions and "We're Still Garbage!"

During the month of June, there were many misperceptions floating around as the basketball world turned its focus to Detroit and its basketball team. The media was at the epicenter of these misperceptions, which unfortunately can influence fans and their viewpoint.

There was misperception regarding the city of Detroit and its citizens, how "great" the Lakers were supposed to be, and how prepared the Pistons were to perform in the NBA Finals.

When the Finals first opened, it was not surprising that a Lakers bias existed, in both the print and television media. However, the amount of "pro-Lakers" coverage that was prevalent throughout the ABC broadcasts, particularly in the first couple of games, was quite astonishing.

As the series progressed and the Pistons proved that they were the better team, the coverage started to even out somewhat, but the final game featured just as many shots of dejected Lakers walking to their locker room as it did of the Pistons celebrating their first championship in 14 years.

That was ridiculous and even though it had several fans throughout Metro Detroit yelling at their TV screens as it was happening (as well as many who simply muted their TVs and turned on local radio to hear George Blaha's call of the game on WDFN and the affiliated radio stations instead of ABC's), it paled in comparison to the frustration experienced by many at the shots that were lobbed at the city by "comedian" Jimmy Kimmel.

During Game 2 in LA, Kimmel was interviewed at halftime in a fairly transparent attempt to promote his TV show on ABC. During the interview, he said something to the effect that the Lakers better win the championship, because if the Pistons did, then the citizens of Detroit would "burn the city of Detroit down."

This was an out of line comment by Kimmel, but the rumored monologue that he had taped later in the week for his talk show was especially crass. The monologue was so bad that ABC pulled it so that it would not air. He apparently just went on and on, ripping Detroit left and right: just being a complete ass.

Though not as heavily publicized, another incident involving negative comments about the city occurred during the Pacers series when Doc Rivers, doing color analysis for ESPN, made reference to people running around the city in masks. He inferred that the city didn't need more of that than it already had. It was a poor attempt at a joke involving Rip Hamilton's face mask potentially becoming a fashion statement in the Detroit area.

These are all cheap-shots delivered to the city because of its notoriety for mayhem. Some idiots burned a cop car after the Tigers won the World Series, a race riot ravaged the city, and it has been known as the crime capital of the nation. What's interesting is that none of these incidents is even remotely recent: for example, the Tigers won the World Series 20 years ago and the race riot happened in 1967.

Is there crime and murder in the city today? You bet. But, Detroit seems to be forced to be covered by that shroud of a negative image much more so than the other big American cities that face the same problems. This negative label gets thrown around so haphazardly by individuals in the national media and other people, that you have to laugh. Most of these people know nothing about Metro Detroit or its residents.

It might interest Jimmy Kimmel to know that nothing burned on the night that the Pistons won the championship. In fact nothing of significance featuring crime happened at all. I live in the Metro area and never once felt the compulsion to strike a match.

In the days following the last game, I did not encounter one person who said, "You know what? The Pistons just won the championship—let's go burn something or rob someone!"

That sounds silly, but the way Kimmel put it, you would have thought that we're all savages here and are unable to control ourselves. We've gotta destroy something!

So what is Detroit really? It is a metropolitan area full of many different kinds of people from many walks of life. A far more accurate description or label to give it than the ones that the national media clings to, is that of genuine, real, hard-working, and good people.

I have met several people who have moved here from other parts of the country and when I ask them what they think of living here, the response is almost always the same: "The people here are so nice. Much nicer than where we lived before."

The people of Metro Detroit are also hard-working individuals. There is a blue-collar mentality that is pervasive throughout every sector of the working people here. In fact, Palace Sports & Entertainment President Tom Wilson is fond of saying that even the white-collar executives in the area believe that they're blue collar.

In Detroit, someone's worth is not measured by anything fake: personalities included. Their worth is judged by their work ethic. If you were to take a snapshot of an image that represents this area the best, it would not be that of a gun or a raging fire; it would be of workers putting in a full day on the line making cars for the rest of the nation to get around in. Or it could be something just a little different.

One day during the playoffs, I was driving around town and passed a scene that embodies the spirit of this blue-collar town. There was a group of construction guys working right by the roadside. A Cat dirt scooper was in the background. One of the guys had a cowboy hat on. There was a dog tied up in the foreground. This whole scene was classic and I thought to myself, *This is what this city and its team are all about.*

Speaking of the team, a common theme throughout the Finals and in the ensuing celebrations, was that of how closely the Pistons resemble their city. This is a team committed to hard work. It values success over individual glory. The Pistons are not a pretty team; they don't float through the games with amazing offensive grace. But they really wouldn't want to be pretty. And in 2004, they outworked, outhustled, and outfought everyone on their way to winning it all.

But, they certainly had their doubters coming into the Finals. An overwhelming majority of media had picked the Lakers to defeat them. Several had said that it wouldn't be close: they'd be lucky to win a game or two. This was part of another big misperception floating around the basketball world at the time.

When it was all over with and the Pistons had completed the "5 game sweep", people finally started to realize that the Pistons not only should have been mentioned as able to compete with the Lakers, but that they should have actually been favored to win it when the series started. Looking at it from a true basketball perspective, this seemed like an accurate point of view. Unfortunately, the media let other things cloud their judgment.

The biggest problem was the over-saturation of the Lakers into the media and the basketball psyche of the casual fan. The Lakers are constantly talked about. *Shaq said this today at practice, Kobe scored this many points while not passing to his teammates, Gary Payton doesn't like Phil Jackson, the triangle offense creates open jump-shots, Derek Fisher is a clutch player,* and on and on.

The stories about Payton and Karl Malone accepting less money to come to L.A. to try to win a title before they retire as well as Kobe's sexual assault case (which has received an enormous amount of coverage) only further served to cause the Lakers to be a conversation piece all year long. By the time they got to the Finals, the Lakers' brilliance during the 2004 season had been largely over-estimated.

Most media (and fans for that matter) just assumed that the mere presence of Kobe and Shaq would be enough to carry their team to the championship. After all, the Pistons had no stars; how could they compete with a team that featured two of the best ever to play. Oh yeah, and the Lakers also had two other future Hall of Famers in Payton and Malone.

The problem with that last one is that Payton and Malone are old and could not keep up with the younger, more explosive Pistons. Also unable to keep up with the more explosive Pistons was the Lakers' bench. It was fairly obvious to the astute basketball eye that the Pistons had the better bench.

But there were some major media personnel that still claimed that the Lakers had the better bench before the series began. Their supporting evidence? That Derek Fisher and Kareem Rush are deadly outside shooters. Rush hitting six triples during a Western Conference Finals game against Minnesota really stuck in the minds of those that cover the league.

The problem with this point of view is that while it is true that both Fisher and Rush can certainly stick the three, it is also true that they can't do anything else. And, while a guy like Rush can have a good time spotting up against a Minnesota defense that allows him to keep shooting it even while on a roll, he would not have that luxury against a Pistons defense that was better and would take that away. The Pistons didn't allow Fisher and Rush to get open outside at all, taking away their strengths. Since neither player can create offense off the dribble, they were effectively eliminated as offensive threats.

The fact that the Pistons had no true superstar was also being used as a reason that they would lose in the Finals. That's understandable since the last time a team won the whole thing without a clear cut, hands-down superstar was 14 years ago. The name of that team? The Detroit Pistons.

The 2004 Pistons were a lot like the 1989 and 1990 versions of the team that also won championships, in the sense that each of these teams was so deep. They did not rely too heavily on one or two players to provide the majority of the scoring. All three teams had several players that when working together could overwhelm their opponent.

Perhaps the point that is the most solid when making a case against the Pistons beating the Lakers, was the Pistons' lack of experience at playing in a championship series. This was a concern that I had, because there's usually nothing like experience in these situations. Amazingly though, the Pistons showed no signs of nervousness and played in the Finals like they were destined to win it.

It was already mentioned earlier how much of a Laker bias ABC showed during the series. There was also a strong Laker bias on the part of their players. When the Pistons were rising up to meet the challenge in the first two games, the Lakers still only talked about themselves in post-game interviews. It wasn't what the Pistons were doing that was leading to their own success; it was what the Lakers weren't doing. Now that it's over, it's quite clear that the Lakers were delusional.

So, all this misperception and disrespect shown to the team and its city were way off base from the beginning. But as the Pistons kept winning, they were still slow to win over believers. All of this only served to fuel the Pistons' fires.

When they would come out of a huddle during a timeout, the Pistons would be heard to say often, "We're still garbage!" They were kicking the Lakers' asses all over the floor, winning four games by a combined total of 53 points and yet they still weren't a good team. It's just that the Lakers weren't playing up to their potential.

15

Ask Dr. Fever

You may have noticed that the last few entries of the "Playoff Diaries" featured no "Ask Dr. Fever" section. Dr. Fever would like to apologize for his lack of contributions there at the end of the season.

To make up for it this chapter was submitted, commenting on the season that was. Re-printed here is the transcript of an interview that Bob did with Dr. Fever towards the end of the summer. He answered some questions in summing up the great season of 2004 and to speak on where the team goes from here.

Bob: How has the summer been treating you Dr. Fever?

Dr. Fever: Well, I tell ya, it's been crazy! There have been so many people that have been so fired up with excitement about this team, that it's been real enjoyable.

Bob: In your mind, what were the most memorable moments of the season?

Dr. Fever: Well, certainly Tayshaun's block in the Indiana series was huge. That will go down as one of the greatest plays in Pistons history. You know, when the Pistons destroyed the Lakers in Game 3, it was the moment when you sort of knew that they now had turned the corner and were going to—barring a successful cloning experiment of Kobe and Shaq—pull this thing off.

During the regular season, I think the 13-game winning streak (which was a franchise record) was very memorable, along with the stretch after they acquired Rasheed in which they held, everyone it seemed, under 70 points.

Bob: Joe Dumars said that the win vs. New Jersey in Game 6, after the devastating triple-overtime loss in the prior game, was the moment when he felt that the team had a real shot to win it all. Did you sense the same thing?

Dr. Fever: Yeah, you know they had a couple of moments like that during the playoff run. Normally what makes a team a champion is that unique ability to persevere when setbacks or even chaos is happening to them. It's the ability to put it behind you and stay focused on the victory ahead.

As Game 5 was experiencing a tremendous ebb & flow, the Nets kept setting the pace that the Pistons had to follow. The Nets seemed to have that extra ingredient that the Pistons were lacking and that is necessary to advance to the championship level. When they bounced back and beat the Nets in Game 6 on the road and shredded them in Game 7, it showed that the Pistons were actually in the process of developing that extra ingredient.

So, Game 6 against Jersey was indeed huge. Also, Game 2 and Game 5 vs. Indiana were both games that indicated that something special was about to happen. Here that extra ingredient was really developing. All three games followed tough losses and the Game 5 win was after a very poor performance by the Pistons; a crushing loss at home in which they were embarrassed.

When you can bounce back like that, stare failure straight in the eye, and come back to win, particularly on the road, then you know that you have the three key intangibles that make up the necessary extra ingredient: the heart of a champion, mental toughness, and a killer instinct.

Bob: Speaking of the killer instinct, the Game 2 against Indiana featured an interesting subplot in which Rasheed guaranteed victory beforehand. After Tayshaun's block and the Pistons had won the game, it seemed to give Rasheed and the Pistons a swagger and confidence that really they could do whatever they wanted to. In a way it was like Rasheed and the Pistons were laughing at their opponent, like, "We're here to beat you and take this series and there's nothing you can do to stop it!"

Do you think that the guarantee and the ability of the Pistons to back it up, gave the Pistons an edge that they were able to carry with them throughout the rest of the playoffs?

Dr. Fever: Oh, I definitely think that it put their confidence on a higher plane and did give them a bit of an air of invincibility. Winning under those circumstances on the road in Game 2 also put them in a great frame of mind to be able to win Game 5 later in the series.

One more thing about Tayshaun's block—it was a clear example that the Pistons were ready to win the title now, whereas the Pacers were too young and not quite ready to do it yet. After the game was over, I think it was Jermaine O'Neal who said something like, "It was a great play. He almost killed himself to do it."

The way he said it, made it sound like, "That was amazing; if Tayshaun is going to make a play like that, then more power to him."

In other words, Tayshaun was willing to "kill himself" to win the game, whereas Pacer players were not willing to do that. Now, that's what you can truly call a killer instinct.

Bob: That Pacers series also featured one of the worst performances by the team in the 2004 playoffs—the 83-68 loss in Game 4. Especially for a home game, this seemed like such a bad effort on every level for the team. When that game ended and Pistons fans took into account the many descriptions of how good the Pacers were from both national and local media, there was a lot of doubt that crept into many fans' minds. Maybe the Pistons weren't really ready to take the next step and get to the Finals during this season. Can you comment on that?

Dr. Fever: Well, that game was frustrating, and even embarrassing on many levels. The natural inclination is to think that the team would be in serious trouble at that point, particularly since it was now tied 2-2 with two of the last three games of the series scheduled to be played in Indiana.

But, when you look at history, it is not necessarily surprising that they were able to get destroyed in a game like that and then bounce back and win the series, and eventually the NBA title. Back in 1988, the Pistons found themselves in a similar position against the Celtics in the Conference Finals.

The Pistons, just like this year, were up 2-1 in the series with Game 4 at home. They would then go out and have one of the worst shooting performances that you could imagine in an NBA playoff game. Though they only lost by 1 point, 79-78, it was an ugly game, particularly given the situation. And, a home team in the 80's should be able to score more than 79 points! Now the series was tied and just like this year, the Pistons' opponent had the home-court advantage.

The Pistons then went into Boston, got a big road win, and came home to close it out in a close Game 6, 95-90. What followed was an epic seven-game NBA Finals with the Lakers.

Bob: Speaking of '88, I know you and I have talked about this on a couple of different occasions—this year felt like 1988 all over again. There were many similarities: the Pistons were playing in the Finals for the first time; it was against a team that had a ton of experience at that level; that team was the Lakers; and virtually no one picked them to win against the Lakers. What was the difference this year vs. '88 in how they were able to beat the Lakers?

Dr. Fever: And don't forget—to beat them soundly! The most obvious difference was in the area of player injuries. Back in '88, Rick Mahorn was hobbled with back problems and couldn't even hardly play by the end of that series, and Isiah Thomas had so many numerous problems that it caused the Pistons to have to defeat two enemies: the Lakers and their own limitations caused by injured bodies. If memory serves, Isiah had wrenched his back, endured several scrapes and cuts on his face and head, and sprained his ankle. By the time Game 7 rolled around, his ankle was the size of a grapefruit and he couldn't compete.

The other big difference is in how the two teams matched up with each other. In '88, it was more evenly matched across the board between the Laker players and the Piston players. This time around, the Pistons were by far the deeper and more dynamic team. And a lot younger.

The player match-ups, with the exception of Kobe and Shaq, favored the Pistons at each and every position. Gary Payton couldn't stay with Chauncey and Karl Malone couldn't handle Rasheed. And the bench match-ups were overwhelmingly in the Pistons' favor. Also, other than Shaq, the Lakers had no size, and they were going up against one of the biggest and most effective frontlines in the league.

Bob: Plus Karl Malone was injured and…

Dr. Fever: Doesn't matter. Even if he were 100% healthy, he wouldn't be able to match-up favorably with Rasheed. Malone as a 41 year-old was trying to handle the athleticism and power of the 29 year-old 'Sheed. The only real shot Malone would have had would be if he started flailing those infamous elbows around and knocked out 'Sheed and several other Pistons players.

Bob: Though it seems minor now, a lot of fans were upset during the Indiana series when they saw what the Pacers had set up for pre-game introductions. The scoreboard flashed blue-collar work images like welding, jack hammers, etc. Plus, a factory whistle sounded. The whole presentation was comparing the Pacers' play to a blue-collar work ethic and telling the Pacers' fans, "Sixth man, it's time to go to work!" It appears that they just copied the Pistons' mantra and marketing theme of the past few seasons. Was Rick Carlisle behind this?

Dr. Fever: Not that I'm aware of, but who knows? While you could make a case that the Pacers are the second most blue-collar team in the league, it would have been nice if they could have come up with something original. I'm a big fan of originality.

Bob: Regarding Carlisle, how were the Pistons better-equipped to win the title this year vs. how they were last year? Obviously the team was stronger—Rasheed Wallace will do that for you; but it seemed to many that Coach Brown had the team just more ready for this moment. Do you agree?

Dr. Fever: Yeah, I think so. That's not to take anything away from Carlisle, who obviously is a fantastic coach—he got his team to the best regular season record in the NBA and to within two games of the Finals.

But the Pistons just seemed to be in a lot better position to adjust to changing conditions. You notice that when Ron Artest and Jermaine O'Neal got limited by the Pistons' defense, the Pacers didn't have an answer. That's always been the knock on Carlisle: he's too slow to make adjustments.

You know the Free Press had a very good assessment of how the Pistons are different now under Coach Brown, on the day that the Eastern Conference Finals were set to begin (Saturday, May 22nd, 2004). I just happen to have a copy right here...yeah here it is. Perry Farrell, Michael Rosenberg, and Drew Sharp all gave their take on Carlisle.

Both Farrell and Rosenberg pointed out how the offense is much more dynamic under Coach Brown. Farrell had a quote by Joe Dumars illustrating how hard it was to score when playing offense as three on five or four on five. This was a direct reference to how some players, especially Michael Curry and Ben Wallace, were not allowed to shoot under Carlisle and were not involved in the offense. Rosenberg pointed out that the Pistons run more, get offensive boards, have everyone involved in the offense, and use more creativity on offense now than they did under Carlisle.

The most obvious example of how the two coaches differ in philosophy is the following quote by Rosenberg: "Think of Carlisle as the architect of a skyscraper, designing every piece in the most efficient, orderly and functional way, down to the last ashtray. Think of Brown as the designer of a botanical garden, planting flowers here and bushes there and trees over there, watching how they interact, understanding that the whole scheme is always changing."

Bob: Well this is good stuff, Doc. Are these all the reasons that Carlisle was replaced as head coach?

Dr. Fever: Yes, they were part of the reasons for the move. Others had to do with the problems that Carlisle had in his relationships with the players. Once again, to reference the article, Sharp said that his "inflexibility in game management and generally poor communicative skills created an environment ripe for team dissension." He also went on to say that Carlisle's lack of trust in his players and a poor relationship with his star player, Ben Wallace, were key problems as well.

I'm asked all the time about the Carlisle decision, and the points made by these three writers give the best interpretation that I've seen so far of what really happened with the coaching change.

Bob: Last question for you Dr. Fever. The Pistons made a fairly significant move during the summer when they traded key reserve Corliss Williamson for Derrick Coleman and Amal McCaskill. The reason for the move is obvious—it clears a good amount of salary cap space, which will help the team when it comes time to sign Tayshaun Prince and Ben Wallace to new contracts.

But Corliss will be missed. His productivity has gone down, but he never complained about his role and always seemed to be focused on helping the team win. Could you comment on Corliss briefly?

Dr. Fever: Well Corliss is a class act. He's a wonderful guy and was always genuine and nice to everyone who's ever met him. But, it's like we always say, "This is a business." The move was really solid from the standpoint that his game has deteriorated quite a bit from when he won the "Sixth Man of the Year" award two years ago and that it did clear up quite a bit in the way of salary cap space.

You know it's funny: in the summer of '89, the Pistons were devastated by the loss of Rick Mahorn in the expansion draft, following the first championship. But this year they were actually hoping to lose someone like Corliss in the expansion draft in order to clear out a contract. When that didn't happen, they ended up trading him.

It shows you how much the league has changed. The name of the game now really is salary cap flexibility. Without it you can't add key pieces to your team and run a real risk of losing some of your big impact players by being outbid by other teams.

Bob: Well thank you Dr. Fever! Have a good rest of your summer.

Dr. Fever: You're welcome. It was a pleasure to be here today, and as one of my patients likes to say, "Remember to ice the pick & roll."

16

The Future: 2005 and Beyond

The Detroit Pistons came a long way in a short period of time. When Joe Dumars first became team president in the summer of 2000, things seemed very bleak for this franchise. Grant Hill, easily one of the best players in the league at the time (and probably the most naturally-talented Piston ever) decided to leave for Orlando that summer.

I can remember thinking that the Pistons were now going to be several years away from being a major player in the regular season—let alone the playoffs. But, this decision to abandon Detroit by Hill actually turned out to be one of the most key player transactions that Joe executed in building the Pistons into champions.

He got Ben Wallace as part of that sign-and-trade deal, setting the stage for a Pistons team to be built on defense, hard work, and guts. Ben is obviously the centerpiece around which the whole rest of the team is built and is the most important member of the 2004 championship team.

Another player transaction executed that summer was the drafting of Mateen Cleaves. Coming off a National Championship that same year, in which Cleaves led his Michigan State Spartans both on and off the floor, he seemed like a good addition for the Pistons at the time.

Cleaves didn't fare too well in his first year in the NBA and has been a bust ever since. But remarkably, even though the move of drafting Cleaves was a mistake, Joe turned it into another opportunity to pick up key pieces to the championship puzzle.

He traded Mateen to Sacramento as part of a package that brought Jon Barry to the Pistons. Barry, though he wasn't part of the 2004 championship team, played a key role in helping to propel the Pistons towards the top of the NBA heap.

His fiery play and lethal three-point shot were strong characteristics of a bench brigade (aided by Chucky Atkins and Corliss Williamson: other acquisitions by Joe) that helped to spark a sometimes lackadaisical Pistons' offense during the 2002 and 2003 seasons. But, the team could only get so far with someone like Barry playing a key role.

His lack of defensive ability, propensity to sometimes make bad decisions on the floor, and his age all led to the decision to let him go as a free agent. He was replaced by Bob Sura, a player who could defend, made better decisions, and was younger. It looked like a good move...

But Sura lost his jump-shot and didn't end up playing a key role. So, he was included as part of the trade that brought in Rasheed Wallace in February of 2004. Obviously this was a great move as Rasheed put the Pistons over the top, as the final piece to the championship puzzle.

In between the pickup of Ben and the trade for Rasheed, Joe signed, traded for, or drafted the likes of Chauncey Billups, Richard "Rip" Hamilton, Tayshaun Prince, Mehmet Okur, and Corliss Williamson: all key components to the championship team.

Each move was brilliant—and gutsy. Many fans and some media couldn't understand trading Jerry Stackhouse, the star and face of the team at the time, for Rip. But Joe knew what he was doing throughout. The entire four years he was shaping this team, sanding off its rough edges, and strengthening it to be the best in the NBA.

Former Pistons coach Doug Collins once said that there are three kinds of NBA players: winners, losers, and champions. There is a difference between being a winner and being a champion.

Being a champion requires something more; something different than what every other player does. There are a lot of guys in the league who can score a bunch of points, but there is a far smaller number who are willing to work hard enough and make the sacrifices necessary to win it all. All of the core Piston players embody this spirit.

So, having players that are willing to sacrifice and work harder than their opponents is one key element in winning a championship. Another is of course talent.

Chauncey, Rip, Ben, and Rasheed are all among the most talented players in the league at their respective positions. The rest of the roster is made up of role players that provide a dynamic and varied attack on offense and defense.

This leads into the last key element which is fit. The players have to fit together properly—like pieces in a puzzle. This includes the well-used sports terms, "chemistry" and "synergy" both indicating that a team has players that get along well and play at a very high level together. The collective will and energy of the players make the team successful and is in many cases, more important than sheer, raw talent.

The Pistons obviously have great chemistry and synergy. The players seem to genuinely like each other and play together so well. It's very rare that you see a group of players assembled and each one doesn't really mind who scores, just that they win.

Another aspect of having the proper fit is a little more abstract, but is key in building teams into winners. Certain players need to provide certain things at key times to help push the team over the top.

For much of the 2004 NBA season, Joe had to hear several people in the national media criticize the drafting of Darko Milicic over Carmelo Anthony in the prior summer's draft. Interestingly though, many fans that you talk to in Metro Detroit both then and today like the move. They seemed to have a better understanding of Joe's vision from the beginning: it's not about finding star players; it's about finding players that have the right "fit" to make up a championship team.

Though very offensively-talented, Anthony's lack of defense, penchant for pouting, and selfish play on offense wouldn't play well here in Detroit. Not from teammates, not from fans, and certainly not from Coach Brown.

During the 2004 Summer Olympics in Greece, Coach Brown and Anthony were not on the same page. According to Larry, Anthony was not "buying into" what the coaching staff was trying to establish for the team's game plan and approach to winning. Then Anthony had to be asked to join his teammates for the end-of-game huddle and shaking of hands with the opposition following one of the early games.

Whether Darko turns into a player with the proper work ethic, enough talent, or fit so that he can be a key contributor on a championship team remains to be seen. He's so young and raw that it will be quite awhile until the verdict is in on him as a player.

If he doesn't pan out, then certainly almost everyone is going to say that drafting him over Anthony was a mistake. "Despite his flaws" they would say, "at least Carmelo has talent and could provide scoring."

While this may be true, one of the greatest mis-calculations that people tended to make when criticizing the draft decision this past season, is assuming that because Tayshaun Prince doesn't score at as high a level as Anthony at the small forward position, the Pistons are somehow screwed.

Tayshaun had his ups and downs all year. Sometimes he would make poor decisions with the ball and other times he went through long stretches with little offensive production.

But, ask Reggie Miller how it feels to have his breakaway lay-up blocked at the end of a big playoff game. When Tayshaun ran Miller down (who at the time had a full quarter of the court lead on him) running about 50 feet in one second, he not only saved a two-point lead in that game, but he probably saved the Pistons' season. Once the Pistons took Game 2 in the Conference Finals, they suddenly had the momentum and were well on their way to winning the championship.

A play like this will live in infamy for Pistons' fans for years. There are a handful of these types of plays for each championship team every season. They are the ones that become the difference between being a champion or being just a winner. Rasheed playing fearlessly on sheer guts (and one leg) in the New Jersey series featured another of these key moments and how Rip played and the team rallied around him after Ron Artest gave him the cheap shot hit in Game 6 was another.

And to finish the thought on Tayshaun, his defense on Kobe Bryant in the Finals was nothing short of extraordinary. Granted, the whole team gave him great defensive help. But it was Tayshaun's ability to keep Kobe in front of him (and thus from penetrating the lane where he is so dangerous) and to get up and challenge all of Kobe's jump-shots, that were most important in bringing one of the greatest players in the history of the game down to a level that was manageable (and thus, beatable).

So, Joe's vision of how to build his team into a champion was right on target, built with all the right pieces. Now he has a new vision of how to keep the Pistons competitive to give them opportunities to win additional championships in the near future.

The summer of 2004 saw the Pistons lose the likes of Mehmet Okur, Corliss Williamson, and Mike James. Meanwhile, players such as Antonio McDyess and Carlos Delfino joined the team. The trading of Corliss was big since it cleared his three-year, $18 million contract off the books. This gives Joe salary cap flexibility for the future so that he can keep his core group of players in tact.

The signings of Antonio and Carlos were big, but the most important player transaction of the summer was the re-signing of Rasheed Wallace. The Pistons were a very good team before Joe traded for Rasheed, but they were still lacking something. They were not going to be able to win the title the way that they were currently constructed.

But when Rasheed came in with all his confidence, energy, and aggression, it put the Pistons over the top. Oh yeah, and he is an excellent scorer, rebounder, and defender too.

With Rasheed's ability to score inside and out, the Pistons' offense has become so much more potent. Plus, he's tremendously unselfish. He shares the ball, and that makes everyone's game improve.

But an even greater benefit that he provides to the team is his defense. With both he and Ben inside, opponents are stymied anytime they try to score underneath. Some shots are contested; many are blocked; several are just plain destroyed by one of the Wallaces defending his territory: the paint. No offensive rebounds are available against the Pistons anymore with these guys gobbling up every missed shot.

The Pistons were pretty amazing during the 2004 season after they acquired Rasheed, going 20-6 during the regular campaign and winning the NBA title. The exciting thing for Pistons fans to consider is that he wasn't even fully-acclimated into the team last year. The coaching staff had to integrate him in on the fly (particularly on offense).

Now, with a full training camp with the team and the opportunity to be completely integrated and play with the same group of players for the entire season, Rasheed and the team, will be an even more formidable combination for opponents to face.

Two of Rasheed's teammates, Carlos Delfino and Antonio McDyess are new, but will only serve to bolster the team's already dominating defense. According to those that have seen him play overseas (Carlos is an Argentinean who played in Italy) he is a tough defender on the perimeter. This could make him a potentially great backup choice for Rip and Tayshaun.

Meanwhile, Antonio's ability to defend all over the floor will be a nice addition to the bench. For that matter, he's far more rangy and athletic than Mehmet Okur. Since Coach Brown loves using pressure and a lot of activity on defense, Antonio should fit in real well. Plus, he's another dynamic scorer that gives opposing defenses another weapon to have to contend with.

With Rasheed being part of the team for the entire year now, and Carlos and Antonio becoming part of the mix, many feel that the Pistons will be even stronger than they were in 2004. The fact that the core group of Chauncey, Rip, Ben, Rasheed, and Tayshaun are all 30 or younger, means many years of excellence ahead for this team. Of the five, only Rasheed has already reached his potential. The other four continually get better every year, adding new dynamics to their game and weapons to their offensive arsenal. Now, if Carlos and Darko round into form as key contributors, the Pistons could win multiple championships in the upcoming years.

In addition to Joe Dumars, two other key Pistons made big decisions during the summer of 2004 that positively impact the team going forward. Both Rip and Ben turned down invitations to play for Team USA in the summer Olympics.

When they were first invited, I remember thinking, *Oh no; they'll probably accept the invitations.* This was of great concern at the time, because had they gone they would have been opening up some opportunities for the Pistons to be depleted and vulnerable going into the 2005 season.

One of the biggest problems for NBA players who also play in the Olympics, is the sheer wear and tear on the body. The NBA season is extremely demanding. Even non-playoff teams play 90 games of exhibition and regular season contests. The Pistons then also played 23 playoff and Finals games, meaning 113 games over nine months. These nine months also featured numerous practices, shoot-arounds, and training camp. The body can only take so much.

Most NBA players like to use the summer to do two things with the body: rest and train. The initial rest period helps the body to rejuvenate itself after a long season and also helps to heal up all the nagging injuries that accumulate over the season and only get better with rest.

When they train, they are getting their body in condition and ready for the next season. Many add strength or flexibility. Some will do numerous repetitions of select basketball drills in order to improve their skill-set. This could be something as simple as becoming better at dribbling with the left hand, adding a new post move, or adding the three-point shot to a player's repertoire.

All of these little things really add up over the course of the NBA season. After the Pistons' first ever championship in 1989, Isiah Thomas worked on his three-point shot all summer long. The very next season, he unleashed this shot in full fury against the Portland Trail Blazers in the Finals. The Blazers couldn't stop Isiah and he ended up winning the Finals MVP award, averaging over 27 ppg while the Pistons won their second straight championship.

For all these reasons, it benefits the Pistons that Rip and Ben elected not to go to Athens to compete in the Olympic Games. Another is the simple fact that quite a few players who compete for Team USA during the summer end up with strange injuries at some point during the following regular season.

Their team doctors and trainers can find no other cause for the injuries other than the gradual break down of the body due to the wear and tear of playing basketball basically year-round. This is something that the Pistons don't want; particularly since as the reigning NBA champions, they will have a target on their backs the size of the Pacific Ocean. Everyone will want to beat them and they'll get each team's absolute best effort for every game that they play. This is why repeating as champions will be a new challenge that is unique and quite different from that of winning the first one.

Taking all of the factors mentioned in this chapter into consideration, the Pistons have done all the right things during the initial aftermath of their championship run of 2004 in order to be able to compete for additional championships throughout the next handful of seasons. The personnel moves and the decisions that were made were sound ones.

Obviously you never can tell if the hunger will be the same for these players to win it again after they've already accomplished it once. And, they'll have to be cognizant of what former Lakers championship Head Coach Pat Riley used to refer to as "The Disease of Me."

He used to maintain that after a team won the championship, there is a certain amount of selfishness that creeps in. Whereas before, each player was willing to sacrifice and do whatever it took to win, now they start thinking in terms of *What can I accomplish as an individual? How can I become more involved in the offense so that my scoring average goes up? How many All-Star teams can I make? How can I start and play more minutes now that I've paid my dues on the bench for all these years?* And of course, *How can I make more money?*

The last one is always tough for franchises that try to stay competitive after winning a championship. Everyone wants to be compensated more for their contribution towards achieving the sport's ultimate goal. As you raise everybody's salary though, it means less money that you can afford under the salary cap for adding new players to keep the mix of the team strong.

How the Pistons handle these issues remain to be seen, but right now the future looks bright here in the "D".

Epilogue

It was a great year, memorable in every way. It was a season filled with ups and downs, player changes, and a big coaching change.

The team itself was an enjoyable group of players to root for and follow all year long.

My friend Jay Wise always says that what impresses him the most about the Detroit Pistons is that it's not a team made up of jerks or prima donnas. He's right.

And what a great group of guys:

Ben Wallace: The foundation on which this whole team is built and quite simply the best defensive player that I've ever seen.

Rasheed Wallace: Energy, confidence, and the most multi-talented player on the roster.

Tayshaun Prince: Never complains and though he's had his ups and downs, seems to come through when it counts most.

Richard "Rip" Hamilton: The best mid-range jump-shooter in the game.

Chauncey Billups: The Finals MVP who can score, run a team, and play excellent defense at the point.

Mehmet Okur: Multi-talented and emotional, Memo wants to be the best.

Elden Campbell: Looked like a young man playing against Shaq in the Finals.

Corliss Williamson: The leading scorer for the Pistons' bench and just a great guy.

Lindsey Hunter: The second time around was sweet for Lindsey; plays great on-the-ball defense.

Mike James: Provided energy for the Pistons' full-court trap and his shot looks like Tim Hardaway's.

Darvin Ham: Born and raised in nearby Saginaw, his dunks are unforgettable.

Darko Milicic: Shows his age often; I'll never forget the image of him with bandages on his ears after they got infected when he pierced them right in the middle of the playoffs.

When the season had ended, many lauded the Pistons for their play. This blue-collar, hard work approach coupled with the ability and desire to play as a team, was thought to represent the future of the league. Sports Illustrated writer Phil Taylor even suggested that the Pistons "saved the NBA" with their play. Many others said that teams would follow a similar model of building with players that are unselfish and know how to play roles. There would be less of an emphasis on having superstars to lead the way to championships.

After Team USA finished a disappointing third in the 2004 Summer Olympics with a team filled with young, star players who lacked a knack for playing defense or playing unselfishly, NBA Commissioner David Stern said that the Pistons are an example of how the game of basketball should be played.

Though all these positive comments are wonderful and fitting for a team of the Pistons quality, it is still very unclear if their run at the 2004 NBA title will change the focus of how teams are built and how individuals develop their games.

The Pistons still have plenty of doubters. None other than Shaquille O'Neal had this to say immediately after joining the Miami Heat: "Rip Hamilton was the only talented guy on that team. Let's face it. They beat us because they played together. Everybody did their part."

The second part of his comment is right on; the first part is completely useless. Obviously the Pistons have several talented players. It sounds like he's trying to say that if the Lakers had played together as a team, then the Finals would have had a different outcome. Shaq is living in a fantasy land.

Meanwhile, Jermaine O'Neal and Dallas Mavericks owner Mark Cuban have gone on record as saying that the Pistons benefited from injuries to key players in each round of the playoffs (Jason Kidd, O'Neal, and Karl Malone). These are very weak statements by two men who don't get it.

First of all, if you're going to point out injuries, then you have to talk about Rasheed's foot problem. He could hardly walk in the New Jersey series. He was blocking shots while standing flat-footed. Chauncey also was battling some ankle and back problems and had a much worse injury in the prior year when the Nets beat the Pistons to go to the Finals.

Secondly, suggesting that a healthy 41 year-old Karl Malone would have made a difference in an NBA Finals in which the Pistons clearly dominated, is laughable at best.

So, it's unclear if anything will actually change in how the rest of the league's teams and players play this great game. Though not as prominent as before the Finals began, disrespect for this team and what it has accomplished still remains. Much like that of the national view on Metro Detroit.

But, you know what? I don't think the team or metro residents give a #$%&!

Sources and Acknowledgements

The objective information presented in this book comes from a variety of sources including my own experiences and conversations with other fans, from the print and broadcast media, and from the internet.

The Detroit News and Detroit Free Press coverage of the Pistons on a daily basis was most useful, along with NBA.com and Pistons.com. The latter two were particularly helpful to verify statistical information.

It is also appropriate at this time to acknowledge specific individuals within each of these forms of media for the contributions that they make every year. Chris McCosky of the News, Perry A. Farrell of the Free Press, and Dana Gauruder of the Oakland Press have covered the Pistons for many years, providing fans with a wealth of information on the team every day of the season. It gives many fans something to look forward to when they pick up the paper each day and provides a welcome alternative to depressing "regular" news stories. Each of these three men has always provided a unique perspective of the team with the highest level of quality and professionalism.

The national networks of ABC, ESPN, and TNT provide great opportunities to see some of the best NBA games every year. Also, I think I speak for Pistons fans everywhere when I say that the coverage of the team provided by local broadcasters over the years has been memorable and provides for very entertaining viewing and listening experiences. Fred Mcleod and Greg Kelser of Fox Sports Detroit know the team so well that watching a game and listening to their commentary lets you feel like you are right there courtside seeing it happen.

The Pistons Television Network carried by UPN Detroit for years, (and beginning with the 2005 season, will now be carried by WB Channel 20 and WDIV Channel 4) has been producing first-rate broadcasts for as long as I can remember. George Blaha and Bill Laimbeer describe the action in a very enthusiastic and unique way. I'm not sure if George realizes that he's as well-known and appreciated by fans as most of the players. He has a real flair for his delivery and though I know that Dr. Rock is producer, Pete Skorich, I'm still not sure what exactly the name "Dr. Rock" means. Maybe one day Dr. Fever will meet Dr. Rock and I'll be able to find out.

George of course also handles radio broadcasts on the flagship station WDFN, AM 1130, as does Mark Champion. Also contributing is "Rockin'" Rick Mahorn. It's not always easy to help an audience understand what's going on when they can't see it. These three help the fan to visualize what's happening, exactly as it happens.

And to all the local media: keep making it fun for all of us fans who look forward to each and every game, and along with it your perspectives.

Index

Symbols

A

B

C

D

E

F

G

H

Y

Z

0-595-66948-4

Printed in the United States
25024LVS00002B/31